Writing Baseball

THE SOUTHERN ILLINOIS UNIVERSITY PRESS SERIES

Other Books in the Writing Baseball Series

Man on Spikes
ELIOT ASINOF
Foreword by Marvin Miller

Off-Season
ELIOT ASINOF

My Baseball Diary
JAMES T. FARRELL
Foreword by Joseph Durso

The Best Seat in Baseball, But You Have to Stand!
The Game as Umpires See It
LEE GUTKIND
Foreword by Eric Rolfe Greenberg

Full Count: Inside Cuban Baseball
MILTON H. JAMAIL
Foreword by Larry Dierker

Owning a Piece of the Minors
JERRY KLINKOWITZ
Foreword by Mike Veeck

The St. Louis Cardinals: The Story of a Great Baseball Club
FREDERICK G. LIEB
Foreword by Bob Broeg

The National Game
ALFRED H. SPINK
Foreword by Steven P. Gietschier

THE CHICAGO CUBS

Series Editor's Note

In 1943, G. P. Putnam's Sons began a series of major league team histories with the publication of Frank Graham's history of the New York Yankees. From 1943 to 1954, Putnam published histories for fifteen of the sixteen major league teams. The Philadelphia Athletics ball club was the only one not included in the series, though Putnam did publish a biography of Connie Mack in 1945. Of the fifteen team histories, only one, the St. Louis Cardinals history, originally published in 1944, was expanded for a later edition.

Thirteen of the fifteen team histories in the Putnam series were contributed by sportswriters who were eventually honored by the Hall of Fame with the J. G. Taylor Spink Award "for meritorious contributions to baseball writing." Three Spink recipients actually wrote eleven of the team histories for the series. The famed New York columnist Frank Graham, after launching the series with the Yankees history, added team histories for the Brooklyn Dodgers and the New York Giants. Chicago sports editor and journalist Warren Brown, once dubbed the Mencken of the sports page, wrote both the Chicago Cubs and the White Sox team histories. Legendary Fred Lieb, who, at the time of his death in 1980 at the age of ninety-two, held the lowest numbered membership card in the Baseball Writers Association, contributed six team histories to the Putnam series. He also wrote the Connie Mack biography for Putnam.

For our reprints of the Putnam series, we add a foreword for each team history by one of today's most renowned baseball writers. The bibliography committee of the Society for American Baseball Research has also provided an index for each team history. Other than these additions and a few minor alterations, we have preserved the original state of the books, including any possible historical inaccuracies.

The Putnam team histories have been described as the "Cadillacs" of the team history genre. With their colorful prose and their delightful narratives of baseball history as the game moved into its postwar golden age, the Putnam books have also become among the most prized collectibles for baseball historians.

Richard Peterson

THE CHICAGO
CUBS

WARREN BROWN

With a New Foreword by Jerome Holtzman

Southern Illinois University Press
Carbondale and Edwardsville

First published 1946 by G. P. Putnam's Sons. Copyright © 1946 Warren Brown
Writing Baseball series edition published 2001 by Southern Illinois University
    Press. Reprinted by arrangement with G. P. Putnam's Sons, a member of
    Penguin Putnam, Inc.
Series editor's note and foreword copyright © 2001 by the Board of Trustees,
    Southern Illinois University
Printed in the United States of America
04 03 02 01   4 3 2 1

Library of Congress Cataloging-in-Publication Data
Brown, Warren, b. 1894.
    The Chicago Cubs / Warren Brown ; with a new foreword by Jerome Holtzman.
        p. cm. — (Writing baseball)
    Originally published: New York : G. P. Putnam's sons, 1946.
    Includes index.
        1. Chicago Cubs (Baseball team) I. Title. II. Series.

GV875.C6 B76 2001
796.357'64'0977311—dc21
ISBN 0-8093-2368-0 (paper : alk. paper)   00-061261

The paper used in this publication meets the minimum requirements of
American National Standard for Information Sciences—Permanence of Paper
for Printed Library Materials, ANSI Z39.48-1992. ∞

CONTENTS

ILLUSTRATIONS

FOREWORD

WARREN WILLIAM BROWN WAS THE MENCKEN OF THE SPORTS page. Unlike many of his colleagues, he was an independent thinker, a sophisticated loner who often wrote with a blistering pen, sparing neither friend nor foe. Baseball was his principal turf, but he was knowledgeable in all the major sports and for more than a half century had a front row seat at all of the big events.

He was among the most prolific sportswriters of his time and the fastest. James Kearns, his teammate on the *Chicago Sun* who wrote the secondary column, challenged Brown in a contest to determine who was the quicker writer. Brown won. He completed his column in twenty minutes.

"That must have been one of his slower days," observed Bill Gleason, who later worked with Brown on the *Chicago American*. Gleason recalled that after an afternoon at the racetrack, Brown stopped at the office to write his column before journeying to Comiskey Park for a night game.

"All of us stood around and watched," Gleason recalled. "We clocked him. It took him twelve minutes."

I have no confirmation, but I remember someone saying he wrote this book about the Cubs in four or five weeks, during spring training, between his regular chores. It wouldn't surprise me. When he sat down at the typewriter, he was not indecisive. He let it fly. I doubt he ever rewrote a paragraph. He knew what he wanted to say and usually said it with wry amusement.

Most of today's big-name columnists who deliver only two or three times a week would collapse under Brown's workload. When

I traveled with him, and long before, he wrote six columns a week in addition to his daily baseball coverage. He had a Jesuit education and was versed in Latin but never paraded as a scholar. His prose was clean and elegant and easily understood.

I worked with him for ten baseball seasons, when he was covering the White Sox, and soon discovered he had an obsession about being first. He was always the first on the team bus, the first to claim his seat in the press box, and the first to leave.

One day in Boston, on a getaway Sunday doubleheader, I checked out of the Kenmore Hotel early but didn't get to Fenway Park until the second inning of the first game. Almost immediately, Warren was at my side, asking where I had been. I told him I had a leisurely breakfast and had been strolling through the Boston Commons.

"Your bag was in the lobby before mine," he said. I could see he was upset. It was as if I had broken his string.

He was an intimidating presence, especially to the younger writers. "I had fought in World War II and was a father," Gleason said. "But I never called him Warren. It was always Mr. Brown. And he never said, 'Bill, you can call me Warren.'"

No one tangled with Mr. Brown. There was a day at Connie Mack Stadium, White Sox versus the A's, when he received a wire from the office. It was a Kentucky Derby Saturday. An editor advised him the section would be tight and asked that he keep his story short.

After the game, Mr. Brown rolled a sheet of paper into his typewriter and wrote "The White Sox won 5–2."

Dan Daniel of New York, known as the "Arnold Toynbee of Baseball," was the only one I saw take liberties with him. Daniel, who was his elder, approached him from behind in the Yankee Stadium press box and tousled his hair. I was curious to see the response. There was no objection. They were old comrades.

During the games there were times he didn't seem to be paying attention. He was either working crossword puzzles or reading a paperback. But I never heard him ask how a play went. I am convinced that because of his experience as a ballplayer he knew more inside baseball than any baseball writer in the country, probably enough to manage a big league club.

Born in San Francisco, then an incubator for baseball talent, Mr. Brown was a gangling, hard-hitting first baseman and once hit two bases-loaded triples in the same inning. He played with Sacramento of the Pacific Coast League in 1914 for three months during summer vacation between his junior and senior year at St. Ignatius College, now the University of San Francisco.

He competed with and against dozens of players who graduated to the big leagues, among them Harry Heilmann, a future Hall of Famer and a .400 hitter with the Detroit Tigers. In a city high school championship game against Sacred Heart, Mr. Brown led off with a home run over the right field fence. Heilmann also homered, but his was to left field, thirty to forty feet shorter.

Mr. Brown often told about a spring exhibition game against the White Sox, who were training on the West Coast. Dutch Ruether, later a pitching star with Cincinnati but then a teammate at St. Ignatius, had held the White Sox to three hits and was in such command that Brown, playing first, had nineteen putouts. St. Ignatius was ahead two to one going into the ninth, but Ruether lost the lead when Buck Weaver hit a two-run, inside-the-park home run to put the Sox ahead three to two.

"Our side still had a chance," Brown recalled in his 1947 biography, *Win, Lose or Draw*. He led off the ninth with a smash over third base. The third baseman recovered the ball but overthrew first base. In his haste to reach second Brown tripped and failed to touch first base. He was tagged out by second baseman Morris Rath.

"Of all things, I was out for failing to tag first base! I raved. I ranted. Nor did it help things when Rath spoke softly in my ear and said, 'There are only three of 'em out here. You ought to be able to touch 'em all.'"

Typically, in his clever style, Mr. Brown got even. One day when Rath was playing in the Coast League he missed a base. "You may be sure," Mr. Brown recalled, "that I had ready for publication a soft answer that turned away Rath."

Mr. Brown may have had the potential to reach the big leagues but decided he had a better opportunity as a sportswriter. He had been a stringer for several San Francisco papers and broke into the newspaper business full-time in 1916, with the *Call-Post*.

After a brief apprenticeship, he jumped to the *San Francisco Bulletin* where he began his career as a baseball writer. He then moved east and in his early twenties was named the sports editor and columnist of the *New York Evening Mail*. This was in the so-called golden age of sports writing. Among his contemporaries were such luminaries as Grantland Rice, Bill Corum, Westbrook Pegler, Hugh Fullerton, Hype Igo, Bugs Baer, Heywood Broun, and Damon Runyon.

When Brown met Runyon for the first time, Runyon said, "I've heard of you. You're that fellow from San Francisco, is that right?"

Warren said that was correct and asked the great Runyon, "What is your name?"

"And from then on we were big buddies."

It was during his New York stay that Mr. Brown began gaining a national reputation as an after-dinner speaker. He was the master of ceremonies at the annual New York baseball writers' dinner. Babe Ruth was at the head table. The Babe's age was repeatedly mentioned. Was he thirty-two or thirty-three? When the banquet went into extra innings, Mr. Brown observed, "I don't know how old he is, but he's a year older now than when this dinner began."

He was in great demand as a toastmaster and presided at hundreds of such dinners. The Boston writers continually asked him to return, and once he arrived in Chicago he was an annual fixture at the Chicago dinner. More often than not, he was the star of the show.

His most memorable introduction was in Buffalo where Yankee manager Joe McCarthy was the honored guest. Dr. Daniel Dafoe, who had recently delivered the Dionne quintuplets was on the dais. "And now," said Mr. Brown, "the man with the greatest delivery in the history of the national pastime."

His last move was to Chicago, in the early 1920s, where he reigned for more than five decades. He was the sports editor and lead columnist for the *Chicago Herald Examiner* and its successor, Chicago's *American*. He had two hitches with the *American* and between them was the first sports editor and columnist for the *Chicago Sun*, which began publishing in 1941.

He was elected to the writers' wing of the Hall of Fame in 1974 and died four years later at the age of eighty-four.

JEROME HOLTZMAN
April 2000

Charlie Grimm

THE CHICAGO CUBS

⊖ I ⊖

BATTING PRACTICE

IN MOST HISTORICAL NARRATIVES OF THE ORIGIN AND GROWTH of baseball, it is related that Abner Doubleday, puttering around his experimental gardens at Cooperstown, New York, evolved in 1839 the creation which has since flowered on any soil trod by an American.

It is not revealed whether any ancestor of the organization now known as the Chicago Cubs was around Cooperstown at the time to lend Abner a helping hand with rake or hoe. If there were none, then this was about the only occasion of note in all baseball's life and times that a Cub or a forerunner of a Cub wasn't around and about. And in most cases, the life of the party.

Cubs, and those from whom they descended in baseball's evolution, have been involved chiefly in the National League. As a matter of fact, but for them there might have been no National League. They have crossed the border into the American League frequently since its foundation.

Going or coming, they have been in and out of all the other leagues, great and small, organized and unorganized. Their influence has been felt, heard, or glimpsed wherever professional baseball as such has been exploited. If their traces cannot be found as far back as Abner Doubleday, they have been discernible since the day when it was first discovered that some men could play baseball for money, and for everyone who could, there were myriads of others willing and eager to pay for the privilege of witnessing the performance.

The story of this organization falls naturally into three chronological sequences—the Spalding-Anson, the Chance, and the Wrigley eras. It will be patent that the last state of the club is no more diverting than the first. Or vice versa.

In each era there has been the same marked tendency of the existent principals to get in their own hair, or in the hair of everyone else who played professional baseball for a living, or sponsored the efforts of those who did play. And no especial thought is given here to the fact that at one stage of baseball's existence, no self-respecting performer was considered in full dress unless he wore a beard, or at least a set of handle-bar mustachios.

Whether the organization be known as White Stockings, Colts, Orphans, or at long last and longer lasting, Cubs, its story is one of repeating history. It is one of coming events casting shadows before, of incredible jinxes, of contradictions, of tremendous surges upward to baseball's heights, of dull, sickening thuds accompanying a plunge to baseball's depths.

Year after year, since baseball became a paying proposition, Cubs or their predecessors have either been setting enduring records, or having enduring records set against them. These records have been made on the playing field, in the counting room, and in the marts of barter and exchange.

Throughout the club's existence, its players, individually and collectively, have been thrown in conflict, for better or for worse, with practically all the other storied teams and players at one time or another.

Since baseball's party lines, National League and American League, became well defined at the outset of the present century, Cubs have figured in most of the records, artistically, financially, and politically.

There have been times when their contemporaries found it difficult to get along with them, but there has never been a time when professional baseball could get along without them.

> Well, here come the umpires.
> The game's about to begin.
> It may go extra innings.

⊖ II ⊖

THE GAME BEGINS

IF YOU ARE AT ALL FAMILIAR WITH ACTIVITY IN THE NATIONAL League of Professional Baseball Clubs, you will know that no game is legal unless it is played with a ball carrying the trademark of A. G. Spalding. Now even if Spalding hadn't gone into the manufacture and sale of sports equipment, it is no more than right that his name should be on the National League's official baseball. Without him it is possible that there would have been no National League. Without him there would have been no need to begin this story of the Chicago Cubs and their predecessors.

He came into baseball's records as a pitcher for the Forest City team of Rockford, Illinois, in 1866. Before he retired in the early 1900's to a quiet life in California, Spalding had seen his beloved game firmly established in this country and known the world over. His counsel and advice, his influence and intense fervor where baseball generally, and the National League particularly, were concerned not only kept the game advancing but may well have saved it from a decline and fall among the lesser sports.

After five seasons with Rockford, Spalding moved on to Boston, where he joined the strong local National Association nine in time to pitch it into the first of a string of four successive championships.

While all this was going on, out in Chicago William A. Hulbert was doing the best he could with a franchise in the Association.

Until now the Chicago team's chief claim to fame had been

successful participation in baseball's first 1–0 game, in which St. Louis had been defeated during the 1875 season. This created as much a sensation at the time as did the news that one Charles C. Waite had deigned to protect one of his gnarled hands with a glove, in a profession where all others were wont to tackle baseball with their bare hands. The first 1–0 victory served to counterbalance the doubtful distinction of having been beaten 9–0 in a game with the New York Mutuals in 1870, thereby becoming baseball's first shutout victim.

In midseason of 1875, Hulbert had the urge to acquire some better material before another campaign began. Perhaps he was moved to immediate action when Joe Borden, of the Philadelphia Athletics, chose July 28 of that year to pitch baseball's first no-hit, no-run game, beating Chicago 4–0. It is interesting to note that baseball slang in the early days had a word for shutting out a team. The word was "Chicagoing" them—but whether that was because Chicago teams were accustomed to blank the enemy or vice versa, deponent saith not.

At Boston Spalding was then in the process of winning fifty-six games, while losing but four. Others on the club, notably Ross Barnes, a remarkable hitter, Cal McVey, and Jim White, as well as Spalding, were coveted by Hulbert. He decided upon a raid. His persuasive eloquence was not lost upon Spalding. In turn A. G. put the convincer on his distinguished teammates, who were perfectly willing to join him in the exodus to Chicago.

Playing with Philadelphia in the Association was Adrian C. Anson, a native of Marshalltown, Iowa, who had been discovered by Spalding a few years before and staked to a job at Rockford. Anson also yielded to the Hulbert-Spalding sales talk, which doubtless contained some suggestions that the place for a ball-player of the west was in the west, and thus Chicago seemed assured of some grade A material for its 1876 campaigning.

All these negotiations were supposed to be hush-hush. But word got around then, even without the aid of see-all, know-all, tell-all columnists. The good people of Boston were very indignant at the raid upon their heroes. They recalled—and so did

6

Hulbert and Spalding—that there was such a thing as the black list for players who signed to join one team while still under contract to another.

To anyone else but Hulbert and Spalding, this must have been an impasse. They, however, had not yet used up all their ideas. "Let us start a league of our own," they said, in effect. And it was so decided. A preliminary meeting at Louisville got things started, and on February 2, 1876, interested parties from hither and yon gathered in New York and founded the National League.

Charter members were Chicago, Boston, St. Louis, Cincinnati, Louisville, and Hartford. From New York the famous Mutuals joined up. And from Philadelphia came the Athletics, whose baseball descendants were one day to inflict upon the Chicago Cubs the most horrendous inning in world series history.

Hartford's club president, Morgan G. Bulkeley, was chosen as the League's chief executive. A year later he was succeeded by Hulbert, who held office until the time of his death in 1882.

Hulbert's first year of office was notable for his casting into outer darkness some reprehensible characters of the Louisville club, whose machinations were definitely not to be classified as "for the good of baseball."

In Baseball's Hall of Fame at Cooperstown, New York, the plaques of Spalding and Anson are among the original selections. But Hulbert has been overlooked, though not Bulkeley. The reason for this is as much a mystery as the continued absence of one honoring William A. (Bill) Lange. That player, an outfielder with the Chicago White Stockings of Anson's time, produced a record that stamped him as one of the most remarkable all-round performers of all time.

However, such things have been happening to the Chicago Cubs and their predecessors, on the playing fields and in the council chambers, down through baseball's ages.

But enough of this; A. G. Spalding is out there preparing to pitch. He is operating in a box six feet square, some forty-five feet from the batsman. In delivering the ball, he is required to use the bowling style in vogue in the English game of cricket.

7

But whatever his limitations or his advantages by 1876 standards, Spalding is about to pitch this first Chicago National League club (of which he was also manager, captain, and secretary) to the first of its sixteen championships.

⊖ III ⊖

SPALDING DELIVERS

A CHAMPIONSHIP CAME TO CHICAGO IN THE FIRST YEAR OF the National League's existence. To give a general idea of what sort of a club these title-winning ancestors of the Cubs really were, here are scores of four consecutive midseason games in that first National League season: July 20—Chicago, 18, Louisville, o; July 22—Chicago, 30, Louisville, 7; July 25—Chicago, 23, Cincinnati, 3; July 27—Chicago, 17, Cincinnati, 3. Eighty-eight runs in four consecutive games!

Less than half as many games were played in that inaugural as constitute a complete season's schedule now. The sixty-six which were played resulted in fifty-two Chicago victories for a .788 percentage. This was noteworthy enough by the standards of any day, but the team's winning record was less astonishing than A. G. Spalding's own personal contribution.

He pitched sixty of those sixty-six games, winning forty-seven and losing thirteen. In the half dozen in which he did not pitch, he appeared in the outfield, exchanging places with Cal McVey, one of the four players President William A. Hulbert had lured from Boston.

In that pioneer Chicago National League club, Ross Barnes, the second baseman, gained the batting championship with a .403 mark. In a game on July 27 of that memorable season, Barnes came through with six hits in as many times at bat. Such a performance has been recorded many times since, but this was the first.

It wasn't as remarkable, perhaps, as Barnes's feat of leading

9

the National League's hitters in a Chicago uniform. In doing that, he joined what is yet a very small and very select company. For starting with the first season of the league's existence and moving down to the last notation in an official scorebook of 1945, there have been just six National League leading batsmen who have done their successful slugging for Chicago. Adrian Anson qualified three times. George Gore and Mike Kelly of Anson's era also joined the party. Then there was a long wait until Heinie Zimmerman made it in 1912 for Frank Chance's Cubs. Thereafter came an even longer pause until Phil Cavarretta checked in during the 1945 season.

Barnes, however, was the first. Inasmuch as Cavarretta also turned up in a season in which the Cubs won the league championship, therein lies the lengthiest of all the parallels with which Chicago National League baseball history abounds.

If Spalding and Barnes seem to have gained most of the places of prominence in those records of 1876, it should not be thought that the others were to be lightly regarded. They were not. They were a very handy group. All of them. Ballplayers had to be in those days, for though the dawn of 1876 found a rule passed which permitted substitution before the fourth inning, the roster of Chicago's first championship club fails to disclose more than one man who might have to sit it out while his teammates did battle on the field.

Such substitutions as took place then consisted mainly of a player already in the game exchanging positions with someone else. There wasn't very much traffic from bull pen to pitcher's box, or from bench to bat, for the good and sufficient reason that there were few, if any, idle players on the bench or in the bull pen.

While of considerable help to Spalding in gaining that first of all the National League championships for Chicago, Anson was not yet grown to the full stature that was to be his for a stretch of more than twenty years on the playing fields, and forever in the annals of the game.

Roaming the Chicago outfield was Robert Addy, who ten

10

years before had electrified all Rockford, if not all baseball, by sliding into a base by design, not accident.

Beside Addy, patrolling center field, was Paul Hines. He was a talented artist, but it was not until two years later, when Hines had transferred his outfielding from Chicago to Providence, that he came up with an individual fielding exploit which will keep his name fresh in the record books as long as they are kept.

Playing against Boston on May 8, 1878, Hines executed baseball's first triple play unassisted. The Chicago National League club, which had Hines and let him get away, had to wait forty-nine years before it was able to boast that one of its very own was capable of such a trick—James Cooney, who snuffed out three Pittsburgh Pirates, one by one, in a continuous play on May 30, 1927.

While this story is concerned chiefly with Spalding's activity against a Chicago background, most of his brilliant competitive history was made elsewhere. His 1876 season, which brought a championship to Chicago, was his last as a pitcher. The following year he divided his time between first base and second base, but in between games he found time to organize the sporting-goods house which still bears his name. He turned the management of the club over to Anson at the end of the 1878 season, one year after his retirement as an active player from the game which he, as much as any other man, helped mold into America's National pastime.

For the record, A. G. Spalding left behind a seven year total of 396 major-league games pitched, of which he won 252, while losing but 68. Small wonder then, that the National League's official baseball bears his mark to this day!

☙ IV ❧

ANSON COMES TO BAT

IF A. G. SPALDING SUCCEEDED IN GETTING NATIONAL LEAGUE baseball started in Chicago in the grand manner, it was Adrian C. Anson, his protégé, who kept it going on the field with a bang.

Anson was born in Marshalltown, Iowa. His formal education took place at Notre Dame, though it is to be doubted if very many alumni of that football-minded institution ever wake up the echoes cheering his name, as well they might. For few of all Notre Dame's long line of athletic heroes have ever gained the lasting fame that is "Pop" Anson's.

Anson's baseball career began in his home town, and within a year he was scouted by Spalding, then doing a spot of pitching for Rockford's Forest City team. Anson joined up at Rockford as a third baseman. The Forest Citys of Rockford, with whom Spalding had gained his own early fame, paid Anson $66.66 a month, which made him neither the highest priced nor the lowest on the club, since salaries ranged from $50 per month to $100.

This was a high scoring unit, and it reached its peak in a game at Ogdensburg, N. Y. At the end of five innings, the Forest Citys had sixty runs, the home team none. Anson and his mates were weary from running around the bases, and the Ogdensburgs were wearier from chasing drives hither and yon. So it was agreed to call the game at the end of the fifth, lest all participants collapse from sheer exhaustion.

It was performances such as these which caused Philadelphia to reach out for Anson, and he was going strong at the time when

Hulbert and Spalding were plotting the foundation of a new and stronger Chicago club.

It was while he was still a member of the Athletics that Anson became a part of baseball's first international expedition. He was one of a selected group which visited England in 1874, to demonstrate the game to as many of the king's subjects as cared to look on.

Perhaps there was nothing unusual about that. But there certainly was something news-worthy in the fact that Anson and his accomplices, surcharged with the spirit of international amity, temporarily abandoned their own game, about which they knew all there was to know, and took up cricket, a game about which they knew nothing.

There was extant at the time in England the Marylebone eleven, masters of all they surveyed in cricket. This was the All English Eleven, as famous in its way as any All American Eleven that might crop up—with this difference—the Marylebone team actually got into action. It was no figment of anyone's imagination, restricted to a dash of printer's ink and a sprinkling of the photoengraver's art.

Well, the best was none too good for Anson and Company. They didn't know much about cricket, but they did know there was a bat to be swung and a ball to be hit. They understood something about that. So well did they understand it that when the weirdest challenge match in all cricket history was over, the All Americans had 107, the All English 105.

Anson, the player and terrific batsman, retained his post as player-manager through 1897. It took him just one season to get his managerial bearings, and in 1880 his team won the first of five championships that were to be his legacy, as well as a goal for any subsequent Chicago National managers to reach. So far none has. Frank Chance, the Peerless Leader, gave it a good try through the early 1900's, but fell one championship short before he gave up. Charlie Grimm was two away from the goal at the end of the 1945 season, and going strong. But Anson's five are in the book.

13

Nor was this the only record Anson's managerial genius acquired for his White Stockings. His first championship, that of 1880, came his way through the medium of 67 victories and 17 defeats, for .798. That is the highest winning percentage in all baseball history. Though it came out of a season in which there were played but a few more than.half as many games as are now standard, the feat stands as much apart in its own class as does Chance's record of 116 victories and 36 defeats, when he gained his first championship for the Cubs in 1906. Thus in pre-1900 baseball or post-1900 baseball, the Chicago Nationals possess each of the winningest seasons.

Of Anson's personal record as a player an entire page of statistical matter might be appended. He played through twenty-seven years of professional baseball. Twenty-two of them were in the National League and with his beloved White Stockings. In just two of those twenty-two seasons did his batting average fall below .300, and then not by much. Twice it soared above .400, reaching .407 in 1879, his first year as manager. In 1887 he lifted his average to .421. He led his league in these two seasons and did it again in 1888 with a comparatively modest .343.

Though most players of his time were Jacks-of-all-trades, Anson was primarily a first baseman, and anything but a fancy Dan. But when he advanced to the plate, bat in hand, Pop Anson was really working at his trade.

There was at all times a fine understanding between Anson and his discoverer, A. G. Spalding, now identified as owner of the club. This accounted for the amazing collection of baseball stars of the eighties and after, who fought under the banner of Anson.

Pop, it so happens, is the only one of all that gallant company who has accompanied Spalding to Baseball's Hall of Fame, but before this story takes a turn into 1900 and the interleague clashes with a rival major league, you will be permitted to judge for yourself whether or not Anson was the lone highly accomplished artisan of Chicago National League baseball in his time.

William A. Hulbert   © Sporting News   A. G. Spalding   © Sporting News

Bill Lange

Adrian "Pop" Anson

☉ V ☉

"POP" AND HIS BOYS

THERE IS ONE GHASTLY INCIDENT IN THE CHICAGO CUB HIS-tory—the matter of a certain seventh inning in a 1929 world series game with the Philadelphia Athletics. In it ten runs were scored against the Cubs. Cub fans would like to forget it, if they could.

Perhaps an incident in Anson's time will be useful for subject-changing the next time the Athletic avalanche of runs and hits is brought up. On September 6, 1883, Anson's boys met up with Detroit and everything was going along peaceably enough until the seventh inning was reached. Then things started. Before the inning was over, twenty-three men had gone to bat for the White Stockings. Eighteen of them made hits. Eighteen of them made runs.

Tom Burns, Ed Pfeffer, Fred Goldsmith, Ed Williamson and Billy Sunday each batted three times. There were two doubles and a homer for Burns, two doubles and a single for Pfeffer, three singles for Williamson. Burns and Williamson each scored three runs in the inning. In all its history, baseball has never known a display of batting power such as that.

What mattered it if in those days a base on balls did count as a hit? It also counted as a time at bat. However, the catcher now had to catch the ball on the fly, and not on the bounce, to retire a man on the third strike.

Nearest approach any Cub team, at least, ever made to that 1883 batting orgy took place on August 25, 1922, when Bill Killefer's team racked up a 26–23 victory over the Phillies.

However, the similarity of this to the episode of 1883 was entirely coincidental. True, Marty Callahan of those latter-day Cubs did get to bat three times in the fourth inning when the Cubs scored fourteen of their runs. But all told, just nineteen men batted in that inning before the Phillies got the situation under control. Anson's boys were just getting warmed up when the nineteenth man batted in their inning against Detroit.

It could be that it was the memory of this awful carnage which eventually caused Billy Sunday to hit the sawdust trail and become an evangelist.

This Detroit interlude of Anson's time might also be useful as a counterirritant for latter-day Cub fans, called upon to explain how it was that championship clubs of the Grimm regime just couldn't seem to beat Detroit, while those of Chance couldn't seem to beat anyone else in postseason play.

The stand of Anson in Chicago was productive of one record-establishing performance after another by his boys.

Five times an Anson pitcher led the National League. Four times his pitchers were able to produce those rarities of the hurling art known as no-hit, no-run games.

Larry Corcoran, who led the pitchers in 1880 and again in 1881, was not content with one no-hitter in his Chicago career. He turned in three.

The first was against Boston in 1880, this being the first year in which a base runner was ruled out if struck by a batted ball. Eight balls entitled a batsman to a pass that season.

The next was against Worcester in 1883, the year in which the National League decided to pay its umpires fixed salaries.

The third no-hitter by Corcoran was against Providence in 1884. A batter could now get to first on six balls.

Providence was also shut out without a hit by John Clarkson in 1885, during his league-leading season. Clarkson turned in such feats as making eight put-outs in a game on July 1, that year. On September 30, the previous year, he fanned seven of the New York club in a row. Forty years later the Cubs were to experience that same treatment at the pitching hand of Dazzy Vance of Brooklyn.

At the risk of being regarded as sissies, the catchers were employing chest protectors for the first time in 1885.

Nor were these all the individual exploits which Anson's boys produced for the edification of those early Chicago National League team followers.

In the 1886 season, from May 5 to July 1, James McCormick pitched sixteen straight victories.

In 1890, from August 6 to October 3, John Luby pitched seventeen straight victories. He was working under a much changed code of relations between pitcher and batsman, however. Calling for low or high balls by the batsman was abolished. Five balls entitled him to a pass. He was allowed four strikes this season, but that concession was taken away hurriedly. For the first time the batsman wasn't charged with a time at bat when he drew a pass, and he was also allowed to take first when hit with a pitched ball.

It must be noted that in the case of both McCormick and Luby, some historians place the figures at twenty-four straight, but the chances are it was two other fellows who were meant.

Returning to the attacking prowess of Anson's boys, there is something to be said of George Gore's production. In a game on July 9, 1885, he contributed three doubles and two triples, which seemed a fair day's work for a fair day's pay. In a game against Providence (why were Anson's boys always picking on Providence?) in 1881, Gore stole seven bases. Maybe the fact that the pitching distance was now fifty feet had something to do with it.

Against Cleveland on July 24, 1882, Abner Dalrymple and Mike Kelly each got to bat eight times in a game, and in an 1891 game Walter Wilmot drew six bases on balls. The modern four-ball rule was then in vogue.

The home run, which is now generally accepted to be something Babe Ruth discovered, was no stranger to Anson's boys. In fact, one of them, Ed Williamson, collected three in one game

17

on May 30, 1884. Lots of sluggers have made three in a game since, but it's nice to know that it was a Chicago National who first thought about doing it.

Anson himself figures in the home-run production line. On August 5, 1884, he hit two homers. Next day he hit three more, or five for two games. Ty Cobb, usually regarded as baseball's greatest exponent of all time, managed to equal that mark forty-one years later. But no one has ever surpassed it, lively ball or not.

☻ VI ☻

THE ANSON INFLUENCE

A SURVEY OF CHICAGO'S BASEBALL IN ANSON'S TIME STRESSES the great personal popularity of the man. It has to, unless you are to suggest that the nature of a baseball fan who pays his money and takes his choice is vastly different now from what it was then.

Anson furnished five championships for Chicago in the twenty-one years he managed the club. All five were crowded into the first six years of his term. *Ergo,* Anson went through his final fifteen years as a manager without winning a title. Not only was there reflected no noticeable amount of sentiment that "something must be done"—as most assuredly there would be in these modern days—but when in 1898 the management was turned over to Tom Burns, straightway the team was hailed as the "Orphans." This was a rather obvious estimate of the great loss sustained when Pop Anson went away.

In his championship-winning years, Anson remained surrounded by such as Abner Dalrymple, George Gore, Mike Kelly, Ed Williamson, and Frank Flint. When these stalwarts had outlived their usefulness or had moved on to other fields, Anson had to be content for a five-year stretch with three second places in the league's final standings, and two thirds. After that the decline set in. From then on, the first division was rarely within sight of an Anson team at a season's end.

However, his 1897 club, on one day at least, flashed some of the power that was reminiscent of an old-time Anson offensive. It rose up and smote the Louisville club, hip and thigh. The final score was 36–7. You will search the records long and vainly to find another major-league score comparable to that.

If Anson's managerial efforts brought Chicago no more championships after 1886, it does not follow that he was not one to discover and develop new talent. He was. Definitely. That can be proven without much effort. Nor does this championship famine in his last fifteen years as a manager argue that Pop was letting any of his finds get away through any fault of his own.

One of the incidents in the middle stage of his career which definitely cramped his managerial style was the one year flare-up of the Players' League in 1890. This was a direct result of unrest which had been brewing among the players since 1887. In that year, the downtrodden and oppressed had formed the "brotherhood" as a possible means toward lifting their wage scale. No one became unduly alarmed about it at the time, and by 1888 there was such a feeling of good fellowship that Anson's White Stockings and a collection of other players from around the circuit went on an extended tour of the world. In the party was John M. Ward, one of the prime movers in the "brotherhood."

While Pop and his party were out of the country, some of the direct actionists who remained at home chose this as the proper time to draw up some radical rules grading players and players' salaries. They evolved a system which classified players from grade A to grade E and set a salary scale from $1,500 to $2,500. There followed what amounted to a revolt among the players. Certain outside interests, eager to get into the business, thought up the idea of starting a new league, and found many receptive listeners among the players. It was an ill-fated venture on more counts than one. The new league lasted but a year, yet in that time it was said to have cost both sides $500,000 or thereabouts.

All clubs in the National League were affected to some extent as the players jumped into the new circuit. Pop had to scramble so much to come up with a new team, most of whom were young and thus unbroken to major-league ways, that the time-honored White Stockings tag was taken off. Now they were Anson's "Colts."

20

Of those who skipped from Anson's care into the Players' League, most notable perhaps was Hugh Duffy. As a twenty-year-old he joined the White Stockings in 1888, batting .282. The following season he boosted the mark to .311 and showed definite signs of the greatness that was to be his before his career ended. When the Players' League held out its monetary bait, Duffy went over to its Chicago member. After the new league blew up with a bang, Duffy caught on with the Boston American Association team. He was there when a consolidation was effected as part of the peace terms when the baseball war was over. He was awarded to the Boston Nationals, and it was with this club that Duffy in 1894 pounded out the .438 batting average which is baseball's highest, never too seriously threatened by batsmen before him or since.

Though it took a baseball war to dislodge Duffy from Anson's team, Pop himself walked away from another great individual. That was William A. (Bill) Lange, an outfielder who, by any baseball standards, was one of the game's most remarkable exponents. In a six-year stretch in the nineties, Lange's batting averages ranged from .324 to .388.

A Californian, he was a giant in stature and weighed 220 pounds. He was very fast on his feet and quite agile. He was as great a base runner as the game ever knew, ranking with Billy Hamilton of his own time and the immortal Ty Cobb of a succeeding era. In the 1896 season Lange stole a hundred bases. Cobb's best on record was his ninety-six in the 1915 season.

Old settlers in Chicago still like to tell of a play Lange made in the outfield against Washington. The Colts were ahead 6–5, going into the ninth. The first Washington batsman up reached first in safety and was duly sacrificed to second. That brought up Kip Selbach, and he hit one out of sight—or so it seemed—of everyone but Lange. Bill raced back toward the fence. The man on second tore for the plate, never considering that the ball might be caught. The ball seemed destined to hit the fence or go over it; but all that hit the fence was Lange. At the very instant he crashed against it, and through it, he reached up and grabbed the ball.

For an average man that should have completed the play. But Lange wasn't the average man. He was a superman—and one day his deeds must surely merit him one of those plaques in Baseball's Hall of Fame. He scrambled out of the splintered boards and got that ball back to the infield. The Washington runner, who had left second before the catch, was unable to retrace his steps to keep from being an easy out on one of baseball's most astounding double plays.

There is a preponderance of evidence that Bill Lange was one of the greatest of all the ballplayers. For the present purpose there is presented one man's opinion, the man being A. G. Spalding, who had helped start it all, and who, in all the years after his retirement, kept a lively interest in the game's development.

One day in San Diego, California, Spalding was persuaded to make a selection of an all-time major-league baseball team. He listed five pitchers, three catchers, and two men for each of the other positions. His two selections for center field were Lange and Tris Speaker, whose notable career at Boston and at Cleveland earned him a place in Baseball's Hall of Fame.

"Both men," said Spalding, "could go back or to either side equally well. Both were lightning fast in handling ground balls. But no man I ever saw could go forward and get a low line drive like Lange. Because of that, all other things being equal, I would have to rate him above Speaker."

Lange retired from baseball at the very top of his game. Had he remained with the Chicago National League club, it is conceivable that he would have rated even higher on the hoof than the $10,000 Anson obtained for Mike Kelly, and later for John Clarkson, when he sold them to Boston.

These were astonishing prices for ballplayers at the time. They are mentioned here merely to establish that even in its early stages, the Chicago National League club was as handy with the big deal as it is to this day.

☒ VII ☒

HORSE AND BUGGY BASEBALL

IT WILL BE BROUGHT FORTH, NO DOUBT, THAT THE BALLPLAYERS of Anson's time, as well as those who dropped into that Chicago National League club's stage wait between Anson and Frank Chance, were not to be judged by any of the modern standards.

That is a mistake. For one thing, those savage hitters of the old days were not subject to the charity of any official scorers, as are all of the fair-haired boys of the present. There was no such thing in Anson's time, and for some time afterwards, as a ball "too hot to handle." In those good old days, nothing was too hot to handle. If the infielder didn't handle it, once having had his hands on it, he was charged with an error, even if it was smashed so fiercely that it carried him or part of him along in its flight. And unless a batsman hit the ball—as Willie Keeler aptly put it, "where they ain't"—he wasn't credited with a hit. The batsmen contended with the curve ball, the change of pace, and so on.

The baseball was dead, in the sense that it didn't contain the "rabbit" element which was introduced after Babe Ruth's home runs were found to be a ready means toward swelling gate receipts. Yet those old timers were able to knock that "lump of coal" beyond existing barriers every now and then.

In a game against Chicago, July 13, 1896, the famous Ed Delehanty of Philadelphia hit four home runs in a game. After he had hit the first three, Bill Lange, who was playing center field, shouted to the pitcher, Bill Terry, to wait a minute. Then Lange ran back to the clubhouse in the deepest part of center-

23

field, took up his stand there, and signaled for the game to go on. Lange was being funny. But Delehanty had a sense of humor, too. He hit the first pitch right between the clubhouse and the fence, and while Lange was searching for it, circled the bases.

When Lange found the ball eventually, he stuck it under the floor of the clubhouse, to be retrieved later as a souvenir. (This incident is mentioned just to indicate that Babe Ruth, who in the 1932 world series pointed to distant center field just before he slammed one of Charley Root's pitches over the spot, was not the first heavy-hitting opponent of a Chicago National League club who called his shot.)

If there were power hitters in those days, there was also the scientific type. They were called "place hitters." Keeler of the Baltimore Orioles was one of these. Anson himself was more or less of a place hitter.

In a game against Chicago, Keeler had been tapping the ball just over the infield. Lange decided to put a stop to that, so he sneaked in close to the inner defense and played there. Keeler promptly took a full cut, and when Lange got the rolling ball back, Keeler was on third base.

The condition of the playing fields and the contours of the ball parks were greatly different, of course, from what they are now. Infield surfaces were kept in good condition, but the outfields were inclined to be lumpy. They perhaps never got as bad as the small town outfield in which "Shoeless" Joe Jackson was discovered. It is related that the field patrolled by Jackson was quite a mess, what with uneven terrain, rocks, broken bottles, and whatnot. After Jackson, who played in his bare feet, had chased several drives, he gave up, came in to the bench, and announced that he wasn't going to play any more unless something was done to the outfield.

"Why don't you put on shoes, Joe?" asked his manager. "Then your feet won't hurt you."

"Who's talking about my feet?" demanded Jackson. "The ball's getting so wingy I can't throw it."

There were no great bleachers encroaching upon the foul lines or in the outfield in those early days. Consequently when a ball got past the outfielders it was good for the circuit, in many instances.

It was also more or less common practice for the pitchers to keep the ball around a batsman's shoulders. It was believed that this produced more fly balls than line drives or sharp bounders. Nowadays the low and outside pitch is standard practice, and times without number a pitcher, just clouted for a home run, will come up with the regulation alibi, "The pitch got away from me and went high."

Baseball in Anson's time, and for a while thereafter, was not exactly the big business it is now. Chicago's crowds ranged from three to five thousand on weekdays and might double that on Saturdays, Sundays, and holidays. Then, as now, the size of the crowd depended in great measure on how well the home club happened to be going, and what the opposition was.

The crowd was principally the sterner sex, though a few gals would appear now and then. An effort was made to encourage interest by setting aside one day a week as Ladies' Day, and eventually it helped make fans of them. However, Ladies' Day in the Anson era was not to be compared with the feature of the same name as it flourished under the Wrigley banner years later.

Salaries of the players, even after the $1,500–$2,500 regulations had brought about the ill-fated insurrection and the Players' League, didn't increase apace. Lange, admittedly one of baseball's greatest stars, was paid $3,000 for a seven-month season, and that was considered to be all the traffic would bear.

Besides being a great ballplayer, Lange was not a bad businessman. Some of his activities compare favorably with the familiar holdout tactics of the great ones who came after him. He was accustomed to collect $200 from club president James A. Hart to defray traveling expenses between Chicago and San Francisco.

In 1896 Lange coached Stanford University's baseball team in the spring. This was the year in which Jim Corbett and Bob Fitzsimmons were scheduled to fight at Carson City, Nevada. Lange was very anxious to see Corbett, his fellow townsman,

25

tangle with "Ruby Robert." So he simply went on a strike. On March 5 he received a telegram ordering him to report at once at Hot Springs, Arkansas, for training. Lange promptly wired back that he wouldn't report unless he got $500 more for the season, figuring this would be sufficient to halt baseball proceedings until he had seen Corbett and Fitzsimmons.

To his surprise there was a quick return wire, accepting his ultimatum. However, there were conditions attached: one, that he report at once—which was the one thing he was trying to avoid; the other, that he refrain from mentioning it to anyone, and above all to any newspapermen. President Hart didn't want any of his other players getting delusions of grandeur.

Lange was not at the end of his resources yet. On March 12 he sprained his ankle—or produced a reasonable facsimile thereof. By a strange coincidence a campus correspondent at Stanford managed to get this news to the Associated Press. After giving that service ample time to get the news to Chicago, Lange wired Hart that the ankle was coming along nicely, and that he would be able to report in about a week, in good condition. This he did, though feeling a trifle low after having witnessed Fitzsimmons locate the Corbett solar plexus with a well-directed punch in the fourteenth round, after which Gentleman Jim was never again quite the same.

It was during the 1898 season the Chicago club met up with their first full-fledged collegiate ballplayer, equipped with a degree and all that sort of thing. (They were to encounter many others, many of them to their dismay, later on, but this was the first.) He was Tod Murphy, who had been shortstop for Yale University and who had joined the New York club upon graduation.

He broke in against Chicago. In the course of the game, Lange was on first base with two out. Big Bill stole second, and when he found Murphy standing there, covering the bag, Lange upset him. The ball went to center field, and Lange went on to third.

When he reached third and looked around, there was Murphy, coming on the dead run.

Lange prepared to do battle, but to his surprise Murphy halted ten feet away and said, "I'm sorry I was on the base line, Mr. Lange. I'll see that it doesn't occur again."

When Lange told his teammates that, they were agreed that a high-class collegiate training must be a wonderful thing.

Later in the game Lange was again on first base. This time Pop Anson followed with a safety to center. Lange tore around second base, where Murphy was again standing. Bill's idea was to get to third as rapidly as possible. He was delayed slightly. Something hit him very suddenly in the pit of the stomach and knocked the breath out of him. As Bill gamely tried to stagger into third, he was thrown out easily.

"I'm sorry, Mr. Lange," called Murphy. "I'll see to it that it doesn't happen again."

☻ VIII ☻

WHITE SOX GET AROUND

DURING THE FIRST YEARS OF POP ANSON'S RULE HIS WHITE Stockings, after gaining their championships, had no new baseball worlds to conquer. At the end of the 1885 season, however, a postseason engagement of seven games was arranged with the St. Louis club.

This first of all the "world series" which ever involved a Chicago National League club presented some features which modern addicts will find strange indeed. One game—the second—was halted in the eighth inning and declared forfeit to the White Stockings, 9–0.

There had been constant squawking on the part of the St. Louis club over decisions by Umpire Sullivan. In the sixth inning, while the White Stockings were in the midst of a three-run rally, Ed Williamson sent a slow, spinning roller foul of the first base line. The ball was deflected by a clump of turf, bounced against the base, and was ruled a fair ball. The St. Louis club protested furiously that it was not fair but foul, and after getting nowhere with the argument, the team was withdrawn from the field, Umpire Sullivan declaring the game forfeited to Chicago.

A St. Louis sports writer of the time had this to say of the incident:

"Seeing that Sullivan was determined to have Chicago win, St. Louis wisely determined to withdraw its team from the field, as forfeiting the game was much more acceptable than playing for nine innings only to be robbed."

This may have been postseason baseball's first *non sequitur,* as well as its first forfeited game.

The series, while involving only the clubs of Chicago and St. Louis, opened in the former city. But that was the last any of Anson's followers saw of it in their home town. The next three games were played in St. Louis. After that the show went on the road, playing one day in Pittsburgh and winding up with the final two games in Cincinnati.

(It could have been worse, of course. In 1887 Detroit, National League champions, played St. Louis, Association champions. This one needed fifteen games—no less. It began normally enough, in St. Louis, and then went to Detroit. After that, Pittsburgh, Brooklyn, New York, Philadelphia, Boston, Philadelphia again, and then, wonder of wonders, a double-header, Washington in the morning, Baltimore in the afternoon. Back to Brooklyn, to Detroit, to Chicago, and the grand finale, Detroit.)

This should have been a world series to end all world series, but apparently it was not. At the end of the 1886 season, Chicago and St. Louis, whose first venture had resulted in three victories for each, with one tie, tried it again, both being champions in their respective leagues. This time St. Louis was returned the winner, four games to two. Oddly enough (in the light of what had gone before and what was to come the next year) this 1886 postseason series was played exclusively in Chicago and St. Louis, three games in each city.

Beyond being the first interleague championship games ever involving the Chicago National League club, these brushes with St. Louis stirred up an influence on its playing fortunes which has remained in the Chicago baseball air to this day. For the St. Louis American Association team was managed by Charles A. Comiskey. With baseball organizations playing under the Comiskey banner neither Anson's teams nor those which have come after him have ever had very much luck.

Comiskey entered Chicago when the American League was founded. By design as well as coincidence he hired for his first manager, Clark Griffith, who had been one of Anson's greatest pitchers and who was to remain in the American League as one of its foremost leaders, whether player, manager, magnate, or sometime power right near the throne.

Griffith had been pitching in the minors for a few years before he joined Anson's Colts in 1894—the same year Duffy was hitting his memorable .438 for Boston. In the half dozen seasons Griffith worked for the Chicago Nationals, he put together a great string of seasonal victories. In none of those six years did he win less than twenty games, and in two of them he won twenty-five.

It should be noted that he was pitching under conditions not a great deal different from those now in vogue. In 1893, the year before Griffith joined Anson, the pitching distance was set at 60.5 feet, and the "box" changed to the rubber slab against which the pitcher was obliged to keep his rear foot. In 1894 bunts rolling foul became strikes. In 1895 bats were not to exceed forty-two inches in length and the diameter was set at two and three-quarters inches. Foul tips became strikes and the infield fly came into the rules. In 1899, Griffith's last year with the Colts, the balk rule was introduced. Pitchers were now required to throw to first base if a feint was made in that direction.

Hardly had Griffith jumped over to the American League than baseball's designers came up with a five-sided home plate, that umpires might have less trouble judging which pitch was a ball and which was a strike. (There were witnesses available as late as the final game of the 1945 world series prepared to swear that it hasn't helped the umpire's vision a single bit.)

While Comiskey deprived the Chicago Nationals of a brilliant pitcher and of an individual of undoubted managerial talent, that wasn't all he took in getting his American League club under way. The name of White Stockings, which had been discarded for Colts, and subsequently for Orphans, appealed to Comiskey. So he simply adopted it for his club, with headline writers presently shortening it to White Sox.

Nothing much the National Leaguers of Chicago have been able to do since in the way of intracity baseball competition has been able to keep the White Sox from flaunting the title as proudly as Anson's original wearers ever did.

Since 1905, when the city series between Cubs and White Sox was inaugurated, the Comiskey forces have won nineteen of these series, while losing but six. One series—the first—ended in a tie. In games played, the Sox have won ninety-six, the Cubs sixty-two.

Any time—as must often be the case—the Comiskey name arises to plague the Cub followers, they can blame it all on Pop Anson. If he hadn't challenged the original Comiskey in St. Louis in 1885, who knows?

However, if there is any tendency to blame him, it will be in a nice way. For among all the many baseball heroes Chicago has known since the game began, none has ever threatened seriously Adrian C. Anson's claim to lasting fame.

The end of Anson's managerial career at Chicago was brought about by a difference of opinion between him and James A. Hart, the directing force of the club. Hart felt that Anson's usefulness as a player, and therefore as a manager, was at an end. Anson, slowed down but still capable of batting .300, argued otherwise, and one word led to another. As usual the club president had his way, and Anson was out.

His dismissal—for that is what it amounted to—did not rest well with Chicago fans. Anson's popularity was tremendous. Apart from his batting ability, his qualities of leadership and, above all, his excellent character made him a man apart in the rough and tumble game that baseball was in those days. An analyst of the times outlined Anson's four chief characteristics as integrity, sobriety, personal purity, and dignity.

Following his break with the team which he led so long, Anson attempted the thankless task of trying to lift the New York Giants, who had flattened out under the ownership of Andy Friedman. Part of the 1898 season was enough to convince him that this had been an unwise choice, and on that note Anson's active participation in baseball ended.

At the time he abandoned the game, or the game abandoned

him, Anson was reputed wealthy. He invested some of his capital in a billiard room and for a time the place was crowded. Then business became bad, and this was the beginning of a long series of misfortunes.

The stage interested him for a time, and Pop Anson's name meant something at many a vaudeville box office. It meant something in Chicago politics too, for a time. He served as city clerk for two years and polled many votes when he made a bid for the office of sheriff.

However, his personal fortune diminished one way or another, and he struck financial bottom when the mortgage on his home was foreclosed.

Memory of Anson's baseball heroics and of his sterling character gave rise to two movements to aid him. A citizens' committee was proposed to organize a huge testimonial for him. A. G. Spalding, now a most successful business manager, sent for the man he had sponsored in professional baseball, and outlined the project to him.

Anson listened politely and then made reply. "When a man as healthy as I am needs charity, I will let you know," he said, and bade Spalding good-by.

The National League, presided over by John K. Tener, who had been one of Anson's pitchers, then conceived the idea of establishing a pension for him. Anson rejected that as bluntly as he had turned down Spalding's plan.

In 1923 however, the National League, and fans generally, erected a monument in Oakwood Cemetery and dedicated it to the memory of the Chicago National League club's number one player-manager, past, present, or to come.

⊖ IX ⊖

THE GAME OF CHANCE

Pop Anson left Chicago's baseball scene one year too soon to welcome another young man from California who was destined to take his place among the Chicago Nationals' immortals. For it was in the year 1898, while Tom Burns was managing the club, that Frank Leroy Chance, not yet twenty-one, reported for duty. He was a gangling youngster who hoped to make his mark as a catcher. He did not. However, if he were among the ordinary catchers, it is difficult to find anything else in the game of baseball at which he was not extraordinary.

Chicago's baseball past and its present (as of 1898) was hooked up in the arrival of Chance. He had been noticed, playing college and semipro baseball in California, by Bill Lange, and recommended by him as a major-league prospect.

Chance played his first game for Chicago on April 29, 1898, against Louisville. He was the catcher. The pitcher was Clark Griffith, then a hurling force to be reckoned with, and who was later to become a manager and ultimately a magnate in the American League.

Opposing Griffith for a time that day was "Chick" Fraser, and though the Chicago team hit him hard and often, winning 16–2, it was not so very many years before Chance, then manager of the Cubs, made a deal which brought Fraser into a Chicago uniform.

Playing first base for Louisville that day was another awkward youngster, who was as much miscast at first base as Chance himself was as a catcher. The Louisville first baseman was "Hans"

Wagner, who was to become one of the greatest of all time short-stops, batsmen, and base runners.

Chance passed through the managerial terms of Burns, and next, Tom Loftus, uneventfully. Neither of these managers displayed any signs of sparking the club to a semblance of championship class, so owner James A. Hart summoned Frank Selee to take over in 1902. Selee had been a championship-winning specialist at Boston. He won no championships with the Cubs, though by 1903 the club had improved sufficiently to finish third. Next year it was second, behind the New York Giants, but in 1905 dropped back to third.

This closed out Selee's stay as manager. If Chicago remembers at all that he ever managed its National League club, it probably is because of the fact that he was in charge just before Chance took over, or that he changed the catcher into a first baseman.

In 1905, after operating the club for fourteen years, Hart was moved to sell his interest to Charles W. Murphy, sent in from Cincinnati with the backing of Charles P. Taft. As soon as control passed to Murphy, one of his first moves was to appoint Frank "Husk" Chance as manager.

They were to be a winning combination not only for Chicago but for the entire National League. As long as Chance and Murphy were in business as a companionable pair, there seemed to be little they couldn't accomplish. However, before the course of Murphy was run he was involved in one form of bickering or another with Chance, with league associates, with his own players, and with his paying public. Ultimately the National League moved in and forced him to sell his interests.

Of the team which was to bring Chicago its first world's championship, as well as its first National League titles since Anson's string in the eighties, Chance, the catcher, was the first to join up. By 1903, when Husk had been made over into a first baseman, three others who were to make baseball history had already checked in. They were Joe Tinker, Johnny Evers, and Johnny Kling.

Catcher Kling had come in from St. Joseph during the 1900

season. Shortstop Tinker arrived from Portland in the northwest during 1902. The same year in came from Troy, New York the fiery little man, Evers, to be the second baseman.

In 1905 a deal was made with the Cincinnati club which gave the Cubs third baseman Harry Steinfeldt and a giant pitcher, Orval Overall, who had been a baseball and football hero at the University of California, where Chance himself had spent a semester or two before answering baseball's call. About the same time a deal was made with Brooklyn whereby outfielder Jimmy Sheckard became a Cub in exchange for a bit of cash and four players, outfielders Maloney and McCarthy, third baseman Casey, and pitcher Briggs. Both of these deals were closed by the energetic Murphy, who just couldn't wait to get a winner—and didn't have to, very long.

Frank "Wildfire" Schulte arrived from Syracuse and played twenty games in the 1904 season. This same year found Mordecai Brown coming in quietly enough after having served a year with St. Louis. Pitchers Carl Lundgren and Jack Pfeister, outfielders Arthur Hofman and Jimmy Slagle rounded out the cast; and Chance was ready, when the 1906 season began, to give Murphy service.

This was the team which will be recalled as long as baseball is played. Before it fell apart, it won four League and two world's championships. It finished second to Pittsburgh in 1909, and second to New York in 1911. This stretch from 1906 to 1911 inclusive represented the years in which Chance was justly termed the "Peerless Leader."

These were the years in which the flawless infield was coming up with so many double plays against the hated New York Giants (and everybody else) that Franklin P. Adams, then writing in the New York *Evening Mail,* was moved to indite a bit of verse entitled "Baseball's Sad Lexicon." It came to be as familiar as Jack Norworth's song, "Take Me Out To The Ball Game." Adams, a baseball fan then as now, stood the rally-killing efforts of that Cub infield just so long. Then he sat himself down and wrote:

These are the saddest of possible words—
Tinker to Evers to Chance
Trio of bear cubs and fleeter than birds,
Tinker to Evers to Chance
Thoughtlessly pricking our gonfallon bubble,
Making a Giant hit into a double,
Words that are weighty with nothing but trouble—
Tinker to Evers to Chance.

This illustrious trio, inseparable in baseball's memories as they were on the playing field, are in Baseball's Hall of Fame as a unit—Tinker to Evers to Chance.

⊖ X ⊖

A RECORD IS MADE

ALL OPPOSITION WAS SWEPT AWAY BEFORE THE RUSH OF THE
Chicago Cubs in the 1906 season. At its conclusion,
Chance's team had piled up 116 victories against but 36 defeats.
Baseball had never before known such a seasonal record; nor
has it been equaled since, even by the incredible New York
Yankees of the Miller Huggins and the Joe McCarthy regimes.

The Cubs finished twenty games ahead of their nearest pursuer
in that National League race, the New York Giants. Mordecai
Brown, known also as "Miner," led the league's pitchers with
twenty-six victories and six defeats. Harry Steinfeldt topped the
club's hitters with a .327 mark.

It would have been nice if Chance, as Pop Anson before him,
had been able to lead the way with his bat in that championship
year. He had topped Cub hitters in the three previous seasons
with averages ranging from .310 to .326, but this was Steinfeldt's
year. Harry was funny that way. He was funny in other ways, too,
for that matter, having given up a career with Al Field's Minstrels in the early nineties while touring Texas. He had dabbled
a bit in baseball and, while on tour with the minstrels, was persuaded to help out the strong local nine of the town in which the
show was billed.

Thus began a rather notable baseball career; for Steinfeldt
stayed with baseball, enduring such things as the blowup of a
club in Texas, a draft by Detroit and subsequent sale to Cincinnati. There he was involved in an endless series of squabbles

with Garry Hermann over contracts. He remained idle for nearly two seasons when the arguing got out of control.

Eventually Steinfeldt did some playing for the Reds, withal halfheartedly, but Hermann was very glad indeed when Charles Webb Murphy came and took him away—hardly as glad, perhaps, as Murphy was to get him, though he has been the least publicized of all that memorable Cub infield.

While Steinfeldt was leading the club's hitters and Brown its pitchers, the others were booming along at such a rate practically no one in Chicago could see much sense in playing the world series that year. True, there was plenty of civic pride in this particular series, since it was Chicago's very own. The White Sox, under the direction of Fielder Jones, had turned loose with a splurge of nineteen victories in September and gained the American League championship. By coincidence, it was a New York club, the Highlanders, which pulled in second in this racing, too, just as the Giants had wound up behind the Cubs.

The Sox, from Ed Hahn who led off, through Ed Walsh, Nick Altrock, Doc White, Frank Owen, or whoever happened to be the pitcher, were definitely of the sort who couldn't hit their way out of a paper bag in that 1906 season. Their club's average was a very modest .228. Calling them "hitless wonders" was an understatement. This was what the up, but not yet coming, American League had the nerve to cast against Chance's Cubs, who had just won more games than any other baseball club ever did in a single year of play. And who, only the previous fall, had cleaned up the Sox, four games to one, with practically the same casts involved.

To make the plight of the White Sox even worse, George Davis, their regular shortstop, was injured before the series was to begin. This forced Jones to make a few hasty changes. He moved his regular third baseman, Lee Tannehill, to short; and an obscure utility infielder, George Rohe, was stationed at third base.

If the high and mighty Cubs had ever heard of Rohe before the series, they gave no indication of it. But they didn't have long to wait to know too much about him.

38

Brown, the ranking pitcher of the Cubs, opened the series, opposing Nick Altrock. As pitching performances go, there wasn't much to choose between them. Each allowed but four hits. But Altrock had Rohe, and all Brown had was the Cubs. It was Rohe's triple which decided the game in favor of the White Sox, 2–1.

Well, despite the fact that the Cubs had gone into the series one-to-three favorites in the betting, and few takers, no one was unduly alarmed about that first defeat. The next day would take care of everything—as indeed it did. Having left their own familiar West Side park, the Cubs proceeded to put on a batting demonstration at Comiskey Park which would have been given even more attention were it not for the fact that this day, October 10, 1906, was the one on which Ed Reulbach elected to pitch a one-hitter.

The hit was made by first baseman John "Jiggs" Donahue. There was ample reason to recall it in the fall of 1945 when Claude Passeau, of another set of championship-winning Cubs, flung a one-hit shutout in the faces of the Detroit Tigers. Until Passeau came through with his brilliant job, Reulbach's name had stood all alone in world series pitching history as the one who had come nearest to perfection.

Donahue's hit was a single. The lone Sox run was scored by Pat Dougherty, who drew one of the six passes Reulbach issued, and made his way around in the fifth inning.

The Cubs lit on Doc White for three runs in the second inning, and established a lead which grew until the final 7–1 was attained. Owen, who pitched the last six innings, was responsible for three runs.

Until now Walsh, the master of the spitball, had not appeared in the series. Manager Jones called on him to work the third game, for which the teams had returned to the Cubs' West Side park. Big Ed just missed equaling Reulbach's effort of the day before. Two hits were all the Cubs made off him, "Circus Solly" Hofman getting one and Wildfire Schulte the other. Walsh, so much on the theatrical side that Charlie Dryden once characterized him as the only man who could strut while standing still, scored a 3–0 shutout victory, and the White Sox led in the series, two games to one.

If the Cubs' batting spree in the second game had been overshadowed by Reulbach's one-hit pitching, then Walsh's fine effort in this game had to share the plaudits of the 13,750 witnesses with the erstwhile unknown Rohe. The stopgap performer had come through with another triple, this one off Jack Pfeister in the sixth inning, breaking a 0–0 tie and helping the Sox to their three runs. Pfeister pitched an excellent game but for the menacing Rohe, since four hits were all he had allowed.

Thus, at the end of three games, with the grand total of nine hits to their credit, the Sox had scored two victories. By this time Cubs and Cub followers were beginning to appreciate the meaning of that "hitless wonders" appellation.

Chance called on Miner Brown for the fourth game, and his number one man was again opposed by Altrock. This time Rohe's bat did not come to the aid of Nick, nor did those of any of the other Sox save Hahn and Pat Dougherty, who split two singles between them as Brown registered the 1–0 victory which squared the series. At that, Altrock kept on even terms until the seventh inning when Chance managed to get around with the game's only run. This was strictly a play-for-one-run game, Steinfeldt having sacrificed twice and Tinker three times, as the Cubs strove to cope with the team which had the patent rights on the system of making a little hitting go a long, long way.

Until now the pitching on both sides had been uniformly excellent, but when the fifth game was reached, the hitters (and the erstwhile "hitless wonders") began to take charge. Led by Frank Isbell, who broke out with a rash of four doubles, and with all hands save Dougherty, Billy Sullivan, and the pitchers participating, the Sox rocked Reulbach, Pfeister, and Overall for twelve hits. Though the Cubs made but a half dozen hits off Walsh and White, they were able to turn them into as many runs, the Sox contributing six errors to the cause as they went along. But a four-run fourth inning cinched the game for the

40

Sox, who took the verdict, 8–6, and thus needed but one more victory to become world's champions.

This they gained the next afternoon, 8–3. So well had they liked their sudden emergence from the "hitless wonders" estate, they kept right at it throughout the final game. All told there were fourteen Sox hits gained from Brown and Overall, and after the first two innings in which seven Sox runs were scored, the game was simply one of going through the motions. Doc White, in gaining the deciding victory, had an easy time of it but was careful enough to restrict the Cubs to seven hits, just the same.

Thus ended Chicago's first and only combination world and city series, one of the greatest upsets of the "dope" in baseball history. For purposes of comparison with what was to come later, it might be well to note that the largest crowd at any one of the six games was the 23,257 who watched the fifth game. The total attendance for the six games was 99,846, and the total receipts $106,550.00 Each winning White Sox was rewarded with $1,257.56, while each losing Cub drew $417.54.

Oh, yes—you might also want to know that the series, important as it was, was handled by just two umpires, Jim Johnstone of the National League and Silk O'Laughlin of the American League.

⊖ XI ⊖

CUBS GO ALL THE WAY

IN THE TOTAL OF GAMES WON IN 1907, CHANCE'S SECOND YEAR at the helm, the Cubs dropped slightly off the blistering pace they had set in 1906. However, their second consecutive championship was gained with 107 victories and 45 defeats.

Once again the Cubs merely breezed through their National League opposition, holding a lead of seventeen and a half games over Pittsburgh at the season's end. Mordecai Brown once more led the league's pitchers with a twenty-and-six record this time around.

No terrific hitting marked the Cubs' surge through their own league race. Frank Chance's .293 topped the club, a long way off the .350 pace Honus Wagner of Pittsburgh had set as the 1907 National League standard.

The world series of 1907, which was to provide the Cubs with their first world's championship, brought them to grips with Hughey Jennings and his Detroit Tigers. In the Tiger cast was the sensational young batsman, Tyrus Raymond Cobb, who had sprung into prominence that season by leading the American League hitters with a .350 mark, as the first evidence of what grew to be a Cobb habit. Coming up just ahead of Cobb was "Wahoo" Sam Crawford, who was no puny wielder of a bat, either.

The Cubs could offer no such formidable hitters as these. On the other hand, they could offer such pitching as neither Cobb nor Crawford had been required to face in the race in which they had just barely outlasted Connie Mack's Athletics.

42

The series began in Chicago, before an attendance of 24,377. Hank O'Day of the National League and Jack Sheridan of the American League were the umpires, baseball's powers that be not yet having recognized the need of four, or even three umpires—to say nothing of the extra pair who now sit around world series as alternates, just in case any one of the starting quartet pulls up lame.

There was work for Umpire O'Day in this game; not as much perhaps as he was to have in a game against the Giants in the Polo Grounds almost a year later—but enough. For it became Umpire Hank's duty to call a halt to proceedings at the end of the twelfth inning, darkness having come upon the scene, while the score was tied at 3–3.

In this game the Cubs got the only break they were to need in the entire series. It turned up in the ninth inning while the Tigers were leading, 3–2. In this inning one Cub run had scored, but Wild Bill Donovan had the final Cub struck out, apparently leaving a runner stranded on third with the tying run. However, the Tiger catcher, Charley "Butch" Schmidt, failed to hang on to the third strike. In came the run; the game was tied; and that's what Donovan had to settle for, with some disgust; while Ed Reulbach, who finished the game for the Cubs was perfectly content to take it.

Orval Overall, who had opened for the Cubs, pitched shutout ball in all but one of the nine innings he worked. In the eighth the Tigers mauled him for three runs, to take a 3–1 lead, forcing the Cubs to come from behind and score two in the ninth, the last with the aid of Schmidt's misplay, for the tie.

After that break in the first game, the Cubs didn't need anything but their own unaided efforts to go through the next four games, winning all to register the first world's championship victory in which the losing club failed to win a ball game.

In 1914, shortly after the Chance era came to a close, George Stallings, the Miracle Man, was able to guide his Boston Braves through a four-straight championship flight past Connie Mack's great Athletic team. But until then everybody thought the 1907 adventure of the Cubs was something out of this world.

Jack Pfeister conquered George Mullins, 3–1, in a routine second game, and the series stand in Chicago came to an end when Reulbach beat Ed Siever, 5–1, in the third game, with Ed Killian taking over for Detroit in the fourth inning when Siever was knocked out in a three-run Cub uprising. Attendance at this game dropped to 13,114, but the worst was yet to come as far as patronage was concerned.

The wobbling Tigers, with Schmidt in a state of total catching collapse, didn't have much to bring their home-town fans crowding into the ball park by this time. No more than 11,306 checked in for the fourth game, and they had little to cheer. For while the Tigers gained a one-run lead off Overall in the fourth, the Cubs came back with two off Donovan in the fifth, added three to that in the seventh, and coasted to a 6–1 victory.

As far as the Tigers were concerned, the series struck bottom in more ways than one in the fifth and final game. The crowd totaled but 7,370. Mordecai Brown pitched the series' only shutout, beating Mullen, 2–0, and allowed seven hits.

Manager Jennings was so disturbed at the Cubs' fourteen stolen bases in the first four games that he benched Schmidt and replaced him with a youngster, Jimmy Archer. That didn't help much. The Cubs stole four more off Archer. This was no nice way to treat a young man who was to find his way across league borders and be one of them ere their championship days were done.

The American League's newest sensation, Cobb, had to be content with no hits in the first game, and but one each in the last four for an average of .200. Crawford wasn't much more of a problem since his batting attempts yielded him but a .238 average. Steinfeldt's .470 led the Cub hitters, who produced a .257 average as a team.

In both attendance and gate receipts, this first of the many Cub-Tiger world series fell below the venture between Cubs and White Sox the previous year. Due allowance being made for the

44

fact that there were six games in the latter, the 78,068 total attendance, and $101,728.50 total receipts were low, indeed.

An interesting financial side light was provided by the respective owners of the two teams. At the series end, William H. Yawkey, whose Tigers had lost ingloriously, donated $15,000 of the club's share to the players' pool. Charles Webb Murphy, a careful man with a buck, pried himself loose from $10,000 of the club's share and gave it to his players—the first world's champions in Chicago National League history.

What with the money they earned, and the money they had thrust upon them, each winning Cub gained $2,250.00. Each losing Tiger, thanks to Yawkey's generous gesture, emerged with a cut of $1,945.96. This was enough to soothe a lot of baseball's wounds in those days.

The Cubs, champions of all they surveyed, marked time then until 1908, a year which was to be featured by some of the strangest of all their adventures, incidents which in the aggregate, set up a record that only the Cubs themselves, in the Wrigley era a quarter of a century or more later, were to match.

⊗ XII ⊗

TINKER TO EVERS TO CHANCE

THE YEAR 1908, WHICH BROUGHT ANOTHER WORLD'S CHAMpionship to the Chicago Cubs, might well be termed a Johnny Evers' year. The tiny Trojan, who fought with friend and foe alike—it is related he went through a stretch without deigning to speak to Joe Tinker, his next door neighbor of the infield—was all things to all the National League this season.

He was top hitter of the club with an even .300, but that was the least of his accomplishments. He gained everlasting fame in late September, when the Cubs were playing in the Polo Grounds.

The game went into the ninth inning, tied at 1–1. Moose McCormick, who specialized in pinch hitting for the Giants, had reached third, and Fred Merkle was on first base, two being out. Al Bridwell, next man at bat, lined a clean hit to center, and McCormick trotted home with what seemed to be the winning run. The crowd began to pour on the field, acclaiming the victorious Giants.

Merkle, as many ballplayers before him had been doing under similar circumstances, didn't bother to run down and touch second, but made his way directly from first base to the clubhouse. Other players had been getting away with this before without a challenge, but not while Johnny Evers was on the job.

The fiery little man set up a howl for the baseball. How he succeeded in getting it, or whether the one he did get was the one Bridwell had hit to center field, no one knows for sure. There are as many versions of what happened as there were witnesses. At all events, Evers obtained a ball, having first gained the eye and ear of Umpire Hank O'Day, and proceeded to step on second base, claiming a force-out of Merkle. O'Day concurred, and since Merkle was declared forced out at second, that nullified Bridwell's hit, cancelled McCormick's run, ended the inning, and left the game still a 1–1 tie.

Under ordinary circumstances, after the raging Giants had been quieted down, the game would have continued. But to continue was now impossible. The crowd was all over the field, and mad enough by this time to tear Evers limb from limb. There was nothing for the umpires to do but call it a tie, and let it go at that. In a somewhat calmer setting later on, it was agreed to play the game over, the day after the championship season ended.

To get the complete picture of Evers' generalship in this hour of the Cubs' greatest distress, it is necessary to go back nineteen days before that memorable September 23. Then the Cubs were playing Pittsburgh. A Pittsburgh runner, much as Merkle did, went on about his business after what seemed to be a game-winning hit, without the formality of touching second base. Umpire O'Day had been present then, too. And Evers had raved and ranted about the possible force-out, but to no avail. O'Day's quick answer, which failed to turn away the Evers wrath that time, had been that the run would have scored anyhow.

Later on, when he had time to reflect, O'Day realized that this had been a mistaken idea. Being a good umpire—if there be such thing—he resolved to have his head up for a similar happening in the future. Consequently, when Merkle's absent-mindedness led him astray from the straight and narrow path from first base to second, it is probable that Umpire O'Day was just as cognizant of the lapse as was Evers. When he ruled Merkle out on the delayed force play, made with or without the original baseball, the entire National League became a party to the play.

John McGraw, the Giants' manager, no slowpoke at slinging biting words, led the Giants' drive on Umpire O'Day, claiming that the Giants had won the game, and the Evers hocus-pocus was simply what a stage illusionist would term "misdirection."

A frontal attack by the Cubs was being directed at the same

47

time by Chance, the Peerless Leader, who had thought up quickly another complication to add to the situation. It was the Giants' home field. The home club according to baseball law is supposed to preserve law and order, or else.... The "or else," Chance maintained, was that the game be declared forfeit to his Cubs, 9–0, inasmuch as order was not restored.

Umpire O'Day didn't see eye to eye with Chance nor with McGraw. The best—and the most—he would do was to call the whole thing off for the day. That put the situation squarely in the lap of Harry Pulliam, the National League president. McGraw carried his claim to the president, and lost. When Pulliam ordered the game to be replayed the day after the regular season ended, McGraw appealed to the League's Board of Directors.

They upheld President Pulliam, and both Cubs and Giants had to await October 8 and the play-off game with some misgivings. Part of their fears had to do with Pittsburgh, which was very much in the race and was to remain so until the Cubs defeated them in the season's final Sunday game in Chicago. The Giants had yet to clean up a three-game series with Boston. This they were able to do without too much strain.

In the meanwhile, an attempt or two was made to bribe Bill Klem, one of the umpires scheduled to handle the play-off game. Bill, a sterling character, raised his own particular brand of hell about this, as only Bill Klem could.

The Giants' ball park, as might have been expected, was crowded with the largest number of patrons who had ever witnessed a game up to that time. Estimates place the number at 30,000 with thousands of others turned away. Estimates also say that practically all of the 30,000 didn't care what happened so long as it happened to those hated Cubs, and especially to Evers, Tinker, and Chance—Evers because he was the cause of it all, Tinker because one of the versions of the delayed force-out of Merkle was that it was Tinker who had wrestled with Giant pitcher Joe McGinnity for the original ball. McGinnity

48

Johnny Evers

Joe Tinker

Frank Chance

Mordecai Brown

was of the opinion that such a bit of anti-Giant evidence should be thrown as far from the scene as the stout arm of the "Iron Man" could heave it.

There was another good reason for Giant fans to dislike Joe Tinker. Of all those who played baseball at the time, he was the only one the great Christy Mathewson couldn't take charge of when the pressure was on. The Cubs' shortstop hit Matty as if he owned him, perhaps not as high and as far away as a latter day Giant, Mel Ott, was to hit a latter day Cub, Larry French. But hard enough, for all practical purposes.

New York fandom didn't like Chance on general principles. But for him and his ball club, the Giants might have had championships year after year, as indeed they were to have not so very long after Chance had passed on.

Matty had won thirty-seven games in the National League that season, and he had been given sufficient rest to start this crucial contest and even to cope with Tinker. Chance chose his left-hander, Jack Pfeister, who was generally successful at handling the Giants. But he didn't handle them very well this day. Indeed, he might have blown game and championship for the Cubs before the game was well under way, but for some confused base running by Buck Herzog, who was filling in for the Giants' regular second baseman, Larry Doyle.

Pfeister was wild when he started the game. He hit Fred Tenney with a pitch and walked Herzog. Roger Bresnahan fanned, but Johnny Kling dropped the third strike. Now, Bresnahan was automatically out, since there was a man on first base. Herzog did not have to run. But that was just what he did and having reached the vicinity of second base, he found to his dismay that Tenney was still there, wondering what was coming off. He found out, hurriedly. Kling dashed into the diamond with the ball, and having Herzog trapped, tossed to Chance who went through the formality of tagging out the bewildered Buck.

"Turkey" Mike Donlin then doubled to score Tenney, and when Cy Seymour walked, it looked as if the inning might go on indefinitely if Pfeister stayed on the mound. Chance summoned

Miner Brown from the bull pen at this point. The old reliable fanned Art Devlin to end the inning.

Matty proceeded steadily enough through the first two innings, but in the third up came Tinker. He slammed a hard drive to center field. Seymour didn't do a major-league job of judging its flight. By the time Cy had retrieved the ball, Tinker was on third base, and Matty, experienced campaigner though he was, showed signs of being irked with it all.

Kling didn't soothe his feelings when he singled, scoring Tinker with the tying run. Brown moved Kling along with a sacrifice, but Jimmy Sheckard flied out. Just when it seemed as if Matty was again himself, his control escaped him. Evers walked, having had plenty to say before, during, and after.

Then came the crash of doubles from the bats of the Franks, Schulte and Chance, and three more runs were in. It didn't really matter that Matty struck out Steinfeldt to end the inning. The Giants were licked. They did get a run in the seventh on a sacrifice fly, but that was scant returns for an inning which had beheld the bases filled before a man was out.

The Cubs were National League champions for the third successive time. This equaled the record established in the eighties by Pop Anson, and tied at intervals by Boston, Baltimore, and Pittsburgh.

☻ XIII ☻

HOLDING THOSE TIGERS

FOR THEIR THIRD SUCCESSIVE CHAMPIONSHIP, THE CUBS ALSO
turned up with the National League's most successful
pitcher, once more. This time it was Ed Reulbach, with a twenty-
four-and-seven record. That entitled him to pitch the opening
game of the 1908 world series, in which Hughey Jennings and his
Detroit Tigers were back for more—and were obliged without
much delay.

The Cubs might have been reasonably suspected of being
tired of it all after the stirring episode with the New York Giants,
but the Tigers weren't any well-rested crew themselves. They
hadn't known until the American League's final day whether
they were to be champions or not. A victory over the Chicago
White Sox qualified them, however.

While Reulbach started the ball game against the Tigers' Ed
Killian, neither was around at the finish. Killian folded first, departing in the third inning when the Cubs scored four runs.
Reulbach was untroubled until the seventh. Then a mass attack
by the Tigers put him to rout and brought in Orval Overall to
get the side out, as the Cub lead was cut to 5–4.

Miner Brown came out to pitch the eighth, and the Tigers
promptly put across two runs to take the lead. They held it only
until the Cubs came to bat in their half of the ninth. Before Ed
Summers was able to retire the last man, five runs trooped across,
giving the Cubs the ball game, 10–6.

There were twenty-four hits recorded in this game, the Cubs

51

getting fourteen. Unlike free-hitting engagements of later years, a double was the longest wallop of the twenty-four.

Bill Donovan worked the second game of the series, being pitted against Overall, whose one-third inning of exercise on opening day had tuned him up for an excellent effort. The husky Californian scattered four hits among the Tigers, beating them 6–1. Donovan was reached for only seven hits, but one of them was Joe Tinker's homer, a *rara avis* in those world series days. (If you don't think so, remember please that this was the only homer in three successive world series in which the Cubs had participated.)

Jack Pfeister was subjected to an old-fashioned going over by the Tigers in the eight innings Manager Frank Chance tolerated him in the third game, the lone victory scored by Detroit in two years of endeavor, 8–3 being the final accounting. Foremost in the array of hitters was Ty Cobb, who had his biggest day with three singles, a double, and two stolen bases. This wholesale production was very helpful to Ty's series record, for evil days were to come upon him.

The first of these was the very next afternoon when Miner Brown came through with a 3–0 shutout victory, holding the Tigers to three singles and Sam Crawford's double. Cobb was among the hitters present but not voting on that day. His bat was no more effective than those of pitchers Ed Summers and George Winters, who tried and failed to keep pace with Brown.

Nor was he any more in evidence the next day when Orval Overall dashed the Tigers' final hopes to earth, going Brown one better. He limited Detroit to two singles, neither of which went to Cobb, and Matty McIntyre's double, winning 2–0.

In this final game, as throughout the series, Frank Chance led his club in batting. His three singles in this game rounded out an impressive .421 for the series. Frank Schulte with .389 and Johnny Evers with .350 weren't exactly dormant during the five games.

Butch Schmidt, the Tiger catcher, even with a year's reflection, was still unable to find ways and means of halting the Cub base runners. They stole four bases in the opening game and came back in the next two to swipe three in each. They lifted their series total of stolen bases to fourteen in the fourth game, but in the fifth and last, they stole nary a base.

No one would have paid any attention to Cub base running in the last game anyhow, for it was in it that Bill Donovan stole a base. No other pitcher ever thought of doing that in a world series game. It was all the more remarkable an exploit since in a game of the 1907 series Wild Bill had been thrown out at first by Frank Schulte on what should have been a clean single to right, which should give a general idea of Donovan's speed afoot.

In these two successive world's championships gained at the expense of Detroit, Chance's Cubs contributed their share to their own and baseball's records.

They were now the first team to win two world's titles in a row.

They played their last series game against the Tigers before a crowd (?) of 6,210, which was a record of sorts. In the present times, there are probably that many people before one hot-dog stand in any ball park in which a series game is played. Or so it has seemed to many who have craved quick service.

As a crowd-gathering spectacle, this second annual romp of the Cubs past the Tigers was a bit of a bust. It played to but 62,232 in the five games, with receipts being $94,975. Each winning Cub drew $1,317.58, each losing Tiger $870.00. There was no boost to the Tiger pool by a grateful owner this year, but out of the greatness of his heart, Charles W. Murphy, the Cub owner, kicked in with an extra $800.00.

It might have been more, but Owner Murphy was having some troubles of his own, just then. Though it seems fantastic, considering the way in which fans had remained away in such numbers, there was a ticket scandal connected with this series. Owner Murphy was so much in the middle that he was openly charged with collusion by National League officials. The $800 added to the players' pool was said to have represented money for unsold reserved seats.

Perhaps it was just Murphy's prophetic vision, for this was

the last Chicago Cub team that was going to win a world's championship for him or anyone else for a long, long time. How long, no one yet knows, for while Cubs have been trying it, off and on, none of them have been able to do so, as yet, since 1908.

After the trio of National League championships, Chance's Cubs didn't cool off a bit. They didn't win a pennant in 1909, not because they weren't a great ball club—as their 104 victories prove—but because Fred Clarke's Pittsburgh Pirates were better. For the Pirates of that year were able to account for 110 games won, the second highest mark in major-league history, and the equal of the 1927 New York Yankees' figure—best on record in the American League. So the 1909 world series was in good National League hands, even if the Cubs didn't make it.

Hans Wagner and associate Pirates, who included the three-game-winning young sensation, Babe Adams, went right along and disposed of the Detroit Tigers, if not as promptly as Chance's Cubs were wont to do, at least to the general National League satisfaction.

The Cubs were right back for more in 1910, the final year of their greatness under Chance. They finished 13 games ahead of the Giants, once more passing the 100-victory mark, to collect 104.

Arthur Hofman, who led the Cub hitters with a modest .285 in 1909, continued to show the way through 1910, finishing with a .325 average. In spite of this, however, he had to yield to a new sensation, the right fielder, Frank Schulte.

Schulte in that 1910 season pounded out ten home runs and tied Fred Beck of Boston for league leadership in that department. Ten, mind you, ten! Now, don't start snickering—or at least don't start until you ponder over this item, gleaned from a sports record sheet which presented case histories of the Cubs in 1915. In treating of the high lights of Schulte's career, it set forth the following: "Schulte holds a record to be proud of—he has never failed to make one or more home runs every year he has played!" It is hard to reconcile that estimate with the current rage for home runs, but there it is.

54

While Hofman, Schulte, and the other Cubs were regaining championship estate, there was a complete upheaval of contenders in the American League. The Detroit Tigers were no longer a factor in the race. In their place, a new combination destined to be one of baseball's best was coming to light under the capable direction of Connie Mack. A perfect proportion of seasoned players and brilliant youngsters made the Athletics into a club which ran away and hid from all pursuers, finishing fourteen and a half games ahead of the New York Yankees.

However, the Cubs, back in their winning ways, were baseball's reigning sensation as they approached the 1910 world series. There were not very many who conceded the Athletics much hope for victory—which was judgment about as bad as judgment gets in baseball.

⊗ XIV ⊗

MEETING MR. MACK

FOR THE FIRST TIME IN THEIR MANY WORLD SERIES ADVEN-
tures, the Cubs were forced to get along in the 1910 event
without the services of Johnny Evers. A broken leg kept him
out of the action, and his place at second base was taken by Heinie
Zimmerman.

Now Zim in his own right was quite a character, even for a
club which has always specialized in rounding up quaint personages—they ran the scale, you know, from first search on Rube
Waddell to last look at Dizzy Dean, with a Lou Novikoff in
between. But Zim, who played his baseball by ear mostly, was
not then, nor thereafter, any man to fit in between Joe Tinker
and Frank Chance. Even F.P.A. would have had trouble reducing him to poetry of motion.

Zim was not the smooth defensive artisan that Evers had been.
He was capable of doing a job at second base, at third, or even
at shortstop, if need be. But there could not possibly be the perfection of association that had existed in the Tinker-Evers-Chance
combination. These three understood each other so well that they
were able to anticipate plays. They had played together so long
and under such trying conditions that it was unfair to expect
anyone but a baseball genius to step in and keep the continuity.

Zim was a robust hitter and a fairly efficient fielder, but he was
no mental giant, and again it is unfair to complain about that,
because Evers, the little man from Troy, was as brainy as baseball players ever become.

Evers' absence, however, may not have been the reason why

the Athletics overpowered the Cubs, winning the series four games to one. As a matter of fact, the Athletics were shy one of their own regulars, since Rube Oldring, the center fielder, was also on the side lines with a broken leg when the series began in Philadelphia.

If he were a man given to making excuses, Mack might have listed another absentee. Eddie Plank, one of baseball's greatest left-handers, had come up with a sore arm. This forced Mack to rely upon Chief Bender and Jack Coombs for all his series pitching, while the Cubs brought out the old familiars, Miner Brown, Ed Reulbach, Orval Overall, and Jack Pfeister, with comparative newcomers, Harry McIntyre, Lew Richie, and King Cole.

But in spite of this impressive list of Cub pitchers there wasn't much the Athletics, young and old, left undone to the Peerless Leader's pitching staff. As a club they collected fifty-six hits and thirty-five runs in the five games, for a team batting average of .317. Individually, Eddie Collins batted .429 and stole four bases, which must have caused the Cubs to wonder why the American League remained excited about Ty Cobb. Frank Baker, who hadn't yet gained his "Home Run" nickname, turned in a .409 average. And so it went right on down the line, with even the pitchers doing some hitting.

The series opened at Philadelphia, with Bender opposing Overall. The Chief was in rare form. The three scattered singles he allowed kept the Cubs runless until the ninth inning, when Tinker finally found his way across. By that time the Athletics had four runs, getting two in the second and one in the third. They had crowded six of their seven hits into these innings, with the result that Overall was yanked in favor of McIntyre, to appear no more in the series.

The series also produced another three-game winner, Coombs turning the trick for the Athletics, though the sequence of games in which he appeared was a bit unusual. Coombs made his debut in the second game, and Chance sent Brown out for the Cubs. The Athletics were glad to see the Miner. In the seven innings he remained, they whacked him for thirteen hits. Brownie staggered through the seventh, though the home club piled up six of its runs in that inning. This rally blew the game completely apart, for until then the score was but 3–2, with the Athletics leading. It wound up 9–3, and the American Leaguers had a flying start towards the world's championship.

The teams traveled to Chicago to play the third game. Since there was one day's idleness in between, Coombs was trotted right out again by Manager Mack. Colby Jack was even better on his second time out than the first. Six hits were all the Cubs made, and five runs. Coombs was a trifle unsteady at the start, three of the Cub runs being made in the first two innings; but they helped not at all, for Ed Reulbach was being clouted for an equal number of runs over the same period.

McIntyre took up the Cub pitching in the third, and he had only one man out when Pfeister came to his rescue. In that inning the Athletics collected five runs. They gained four more which they didn't need at Pfeister's expense in the seventh, and the game ended with a 12–5 score. The Athletics needed but one more to clinch the championship. In this third game they had mauled Cub pitching for fifteen hits, one of which was Danny Murphy's homer, the lone four-ply swat of the series.

Since all his old stand-bys had been so rudely treated in the first three games, Chance chose to start King Cole in the fourth game, and Bender gave it another try for the Athletics. Cole pitched well enough for eight innings, and then ran into some trouble. The Athletics had the bases filled and but one out when Ira Thomas hit into a double play—not Tinker to Evers to Chance, of course, but Cole to Archer to Chance.

However, the Athletics had a 3–2 lead, and it was a desperate situation for the Cubs. They were able to meet it squarely. In their half of the eighth they shoved the tying run across.

Brown replaced Cole at the start of the ninth. He kept the Athletics in check through two innings, the Cubs finally getting the 4–3 winning run in the tenth inning. The run was actually

"Jimmied" across, Archer doubling and Sheckard singling, with two out.

Since a day had elapsed between games three and four, Chicago weather being what it was, Coombs had been given as much as two days' rest when Manager Mack called upon him again, to finish up what was now an unequal struggle. Coombs was both willing and able. In this final game he scored a 7–2 victory over Brown, who was something of a work horse himself, having been in three of the last four games. The Athletics waited until the eighth inning to cut loose with the big blast in this game, scoring five runs.

The series attracted 124,312 with gate receipts reaching $173,980. In what was their last chance to share in world series loot, each of Chance's Cubs drew $1,375.16 as the loser's end. The Athletics collected $2,062.79 apiece.

Apart from the sensational batting, pitching, and defensive performance of the Athletics, and the broad hint that Chicago's greatest ball club was finally coming apart at the seams, this 1910 world series had another feature. It was the first time four umpires were assigned to keep the traffic in bounds. For the conquering American League, Tom Connolly and Jack Sheridan obliged, while Hank O'Day and Cy Rigler represented the National League.

This series was to be the last time for eight seasons that the Cubs were to gain much notice on the playing field, but that wasn't going to keep them from crashing into print in other ways, an old Cub habit.

⊗ XV ⊗

GOING, GOING, GONE

ECLINE SET IN GRADUALLY FOR THE CUBS IN 1911, WHILE John McGraw's New York Giants were literally running away with the National League championship, 347 stolen bases being a determining factor.

John Kling, one of the first of the four-time champions to join the Cubs, was also the first to depart, drifting away to Boston in 1911. Orval Overall, one of the "Big Four" of the Peerless Leader's pitchers, remained out of baseball that season and the next. When he did return in 1913, he merely went through the gesture of pitching before making his retirement permanent.

Chance himself had begun to near the end of his playing string in 1910, when he participated in about half of his club's games. In 1911 he appeared in but twenty-nine games.

The others of the Cubs' most famous team had some baseball of major-league quality left in them for a few more seasons. Some of them, indeed, were quite active through 1911, the principal one being Frank Schulte, who set a new National League record of twenty-one homers. This, along with a few other things, caused him to be given the Chalmers Award as the most valuable player in his league.

This was the first of the "Most Valuable" awards. It was discontinued after four years, but Cub followers will be happy to know that one of their boys was its first winner. Another one of their boys, Johnny Evers, took the award in its final year, but by that time Evers had gone on to Boston and another world's championship, with which the Cubs had nothing to do whatsoever.

As Cub history goes, much of 1911 was a restful year. But it was merely the calm before the storm—a series of storms, for that matter, which were going to burst forth in such fury in 1912 they were to carry away all semblance of championship class from the club.

Open warfare broke out between Chance and owner Murphy. The manager accused Murphy of having put over a fast one on him in the matter of a four-year contract deal. Chance climaxed his charge by quitting the team for a while, but later that trouble was patched up, and the Peerless Leader returned.

While the Cubs were struggling through the 1912 season, to wind up third eventually, some of their individuals gained passing fame. For the Giants, Rube Marquard was peeling off victory after victory until he had been credited with nineteen in a row. Seeking the twentieth, he went against the Cubs on July 8, Jimmy Lavender opposing him. That was the end of the Rube's victory march. The Cubs stopped it.

This was one of the few times in which it might be said that the Cub rooters—and there were some 25,000 of them at the ball park—were actually pulling for the erstwhile hated Giants to win a ball game.

Marquard's nineteen straight games were something to talk about. The Giants were more than a dozen games ahead of the Cubs in the pennant race, and it was natural that there was Marquard sentiment abroad in the Cubs' park, treasonable though that seemed to be.

If the crowd was anxious that Marquard win, some of the Cubs themselves, and especially the veterans, were quite determined that he would not. Johnny Evers and Joe Tinker were flaming, and Jimmy Archer, who was to catch the youngster, Jimmy Lavender, gave him a pep talk before the game began.

The Cubs were on top all the way. They scored twice in the second inning. Hits by Heinie Zimmerman and Tommy Leach began it. Vic Saier bounced to Heinie Groh, who tried to tag

Leach and start a double play. Leach evaded him and after a chase, Groh tried to settle for Saier at first. His throw was too late. Fred Merkle made a belated attempt to get Leach, and on the throw Zimmerman scooted for the plate and scored.

When Evers bunted safely and the bases were filled, it looked bad for Marquard, but Rube came through in fine style. He fanned Archer and Lavender and had two strikes on Jimmy Sheckard when a wild pitch was loosed. On it Leach scored. Sheckard then fanned, but the Cubs had two runs and a lead they did not relinquish.

The Giants scored a run in the third, but Marquard's defense collapsed in the fourth and again in the sixth, the Cubs scoring twice in each inning. Marquard left the game in the seventh when "Josh" Devore batted for him, and one more Cub run was scored off Jeff Tesreau, the final accounting being 7–2 in the Cubs' favor.

Earlier in the year—April 20, to be exact—Jimmy Sheckard broke up a game against the Reds in the tenth inning by hitting one out of the park. But Jimmy forgot himself after passing second base, and headed for the clubhouse instead of completing his round of the bases. It took some time to get that one straightened out and made official.

At the season's end, with no world series needing them, the Cubs were moved to engage the White Sox in a city series, with the usual results. This should have been a city series to end all city series, but it kept coming back intermittently until 1942 when the project was abandoned, perhaps until a situation such as 1906 is repeated, and Cubs and White Sox win pennants in their respective leagues.

This was to have been a normal, best four out of seven series. But there never has been anything normal when Cubs and White Sox meet. Complications set in at once. The first game was called at the end of nine innings, the score being 0–0. The Cubs made exactly one hit off Ed Walsh—it was Joe Tinker who got it. The Sox hit Jimmy Lavender safely six times but didn't score.

The next game was also productive of no decision. It was

called after twelve innings, the score being 3–3. Larry Cheney went all the way for the Cubs, with Eddie Cicotte and Walsh (of course) pitching for the Sox.

Walsh took the next day off, oddly enough, and Doc White was unable to best Lavender, the Cubs winning 5–4. They were so encouraged at this they came right back the next day, Ed Reulbach besting Walsh, 4–2. The Cubs made it three in a row in the fifth game, beating Cicotte and Lange, 8–1, Cheney registering his second victory.

Thus the Cubs needed but one more victory to cinch the city championship. They didn't make it in the sixth game, though it went eleven innings before the Sox put over a 5–4 victory. Walsh, the ever-ready, took the verdict over Lavender. The Cubs had a 4–2 lead going into the eighth inning of the seventh game, then folded up with the Sox scoring four runs to help toward an ultimate 7–5 win.

This was getting a bit irksome, so the Cubs went forth in the eighth game and held the advantage all the way through to the ninth. This inning began with them leading 5–4. It ended with Lew Richie and Lavender getting belted for four runs. Walsh worked for the Sox in the last half of the ninth, so that was that. The Cubs lost 8–5. The series was squared at three games each.

So far the competition had been reasonably close, but the final game of the series was something else again. Walsh was back to pitch, and Lavender started for the Cubs. He lasted two innings. Then came a succession of Cub pitchers, Smith, Reulbach, Lefty Leifeld (who had been obtained from Pittsburgh in a trade for Art Hofman that year), and finally big Fred Toney. The White Sox had no respect for any of them, save perhaps Toney. By the time he appeared the Sox had made sixteen hits and sixteen runs, and may well have been exhausted from their own efforts.

Since this was to be the last time he was to have the opportunity of pitching against the Peerless Leader's Cubs, Walsh was better than ever. He allowed five scattered singles and won, 16–0. A grateful Charles A. Comiskey gave Big Ed a check for

$1,500 for services rendered above and beyond the call of duty in that city series.

The Chicago owner, Charles A. Murphy, having made an announcement September 28 that Chance would not manage the club in 1913, was now ready to chase any and all of the men who had been making baseball history, save when they were involved with the Chicago White Sox. Whether he realized that some of his machinations were to lead ultimately to his being ousted himself was something else again.

Throughout his playing career, Chance had the unhappy faculty of getting himself hit on the head with pitched balls. He suffered great pains as a result of this, and eventually it was decided to operate on him for a supposed blood clot.

It was while he was hospitalized that owner Murphy came through with a statement denouncing the Cubs as strayers from the straight and narrow path of training. Among other things, he said that the Cubs of 1913 would have to get along without their rum ration.

Chance arose from his bed of pain and denounced Murphy for this, while defending his players as normally sober and industrious, if not always of championship stature or even of major-league competency. But it was not until the formal parting of the ways had come that Chance really reached the heights in blistering statements about Murphy.

He characterized the club owner as one who would not spend money for ballplayers or for the improvement of the ball park. He maintained that Murphy would not send scouts to the Class AA's or to the Class A's but into leagues of lower classification, so that any eventual purchases would cost but little.

"No manager can be a success without competent players," stormed Chance, "and some of these I have are anything but skilled. In all the time I have been with this club I have had to fight to get the players I wanted. Murphy has not spent one third as much for players as have other magnates. How can he expect to win championships without ballplayers?"

Again Chance maintained that he had argued with Murphy

64

that other owners were paying out money, and that Murphy had replied: "If they want to be suckers and pay it, they can, but I won't."

In his final blast at the Cubs' owner, Chance insisted that this reflected the conditions under which he had been forced to operate for the last three years of his stay. Nor was that all. The Peerless Leader went into details of his personal arrangement with Murphy.

"The years we won pennants and when we set a record of 116 games won, I was getting $5,500 a season," he said. "At the same time John McGraw was getting $18,000 and Fred Clarke $15,000. I had to threaten to quit in order to get my salary lifted to $10,000. Murphy would argue that I had some stock in the club and ought to be satisfied with that. Well, I bought that stock and I worked hard for it.

"I wasn't the only one having money troubles with Murphy. Every winter my ballplayers would come to me and show me letters they would get from Murphy when they asked for salary increases."

As a farewell statement, Chance brought up Murphy's oft-quoted promise to give the Cub fans a new ball park. "I'll bet $1,000 he never does," said the Peerless Leader.

If the bet had been made, Chance would have won it.

In letting Chance go, Murphy made it known that the Peerless Leader had resigned. Chicago's baseball fans, always eager to participate in a good row, thought otherwise. However, Chance was on his way, presumably heading toward Cincinnati, where the first member of the Tinker-to-Evers-to-Chance trio was also dispatched in the winter of 1912.

Tinker went to the Reds in a wholesale trade which involved some of his own Cub teammates and five from Cincinnati. Of these, outfielder Mike Mitchell, a fine hitter, was the most notable player involved as far as records go. He hit an occasional home run and was a handy performer in the outfield. For Cub historical purposes, the only name in the group who came to Chicago from Cincinnati which need be remembered is John "Red" Corriden. Red, an infielder, was no Tinker at shortstop.

His playing career through 1913–15 left no distinct footprints on the sands of Cubs' time; but when he returned in another deal, fifteen years later, to become a coach, Red Corriden was quite a figure.

Miner Brown and Ed Reulbach were also on their way before another Cub season began, and of all the old champions, that left only Johnny Evers and Frank Schulte around and about. It seemed logical, even to owner Murphy, that the successor to Chance as manager should be Evers. And it was so ordered, thereby bringing about one of the unhappiest years of all in the long and brilliant career of the little Trojan. Third place was the best Evers could do in 1913 with a club that was in the process of complete reorganization.

Heinie Zimmerman, who had long since taken over Harry Steinfeldt's place at third base, succeeded in leading the club's hitters with a .296 mark. This made him the Cubs' batting leader for the fourth year in a row. Since 1894, when Pop Anson got out of the habit of topping the club's hitters year after year, and Bill Lange took up the practice, Zimmerman's four-year leadership is the most consistent Cub batting effort on record.

When the Cubs finished in third place in 1913, Murphy didn't care much for that. He decided the thing to do was to bounce Evers and install Hank O'Day as manager. Hank, better known as an umpire, had been trying himself out as a manager at Cincinnati during 1912.

Cub fans didn't think very well of Evers getting the bum's rush so soon after Chance had been given same. But when Murphy began to rig up a deal which would send Evers to Boston, and the Trojan announced that he would jump to the Federal League, which was then in the formation process, the entire National League began to get peeved. The very idea of one of the National League's brightest stars being practically forced to go to the outlaw league was too much. A meeting was scheduled for Cincinnati in February 1914, and Murphy was ordered to come in and give himself up.

Present at the meeting were President John K. Tener of the

66

National League, Harry Ackerlund of Pittsburgh, who had acquired $40,000 worth of stock Frank Chance once held in the Cubs, John Conway Toole, the National League's legal adviser, and Charles Taft, who had aimed Murphy at the Cub franchise in the first place. It seemed no more than fair then that Taft should buy Murphy's share of the club, estimated at 53 per cent, for a sum reported to be $750,000. All of this seemed to settle everything, and Evers, the cause of it all, showed up with the Boston Braves after all.

It was well that he did, too, for it was in this 1914 season that the Braves, under the leadership of George Stallings, the Miracle Man, set a new record for world series execution, downing the famed Philadelphia Athletics in four straight games. Thus did Johnny Evers, at the close of his playing career, square matters with the club which had humbled himself and the Peerless Leader's other mighty Cubs in the series of 1910.

There at Boston there was no Joe Tinker on one side of Evers, no Frank Chance on the other. But at his right side was "Rabbit" Maranville, who was one day to lend his hilarious touch to some of the doings of the Cubs, especially in a season when the club needed not one manager, but three, to get through the schedule.

☻ XVI ☻

CUBS ON THE MOVE

DURING THE BASEBALL SEASONS OF 1914 AND 1915 IT IS questionable whether the activities of the Cubs drawing salaries from the ball club were of as much interest as those who had gone elsewhere. Outstanding among these were Frank Chance, the Peerless Leader, and Joe Tinker, who, according to F. P. A.'s jingle, started all those double plays.

Chance, though aimed at Cincinnati when the break with owner Charles W. Murphy came, detoured and wound up instead in New York. There he took up the management of the American League club. His New York record, for the purposes of tracing the histories of men who had Cub backgrounds, was not nearly as interesting as the fact that he succeeded as manager Hugh Duffy, who had once been under Pop Anson's care and got away.

Chance remained as manager in New York until September, 1915, when he resigned. He resumed his baseball activity in California later on as manager of the Los Angeles club, the secretary of which at the time was Charles "Boots" Weber, who was to be something of a factor many years afterward in the war councils of the Chicago Cubs.

The Pacific Coast League, of which Los Angeles was a member, was a go-as-you-please sort of an organization when Chance dropped into it. The man who had led the Cubs through so many battles on the field and off it couldn't understand that way of doing baseball business.

When his club came to San Francisco to play its first series, it registered in the same hotel Coast League clubs were in the habit of patronizing. This was a theatrical hotel, peopled principally by vaudevillians and denizens of the bright lights. As like as not, at three o'clock in the morning, some act playing Pantages' or the Sullivan and Considine circuit might decide to rehearse a new number. Indeed, there is reason to believe that the standard gag—"The only house rule is that you mustn't smoke hop in the elevators"—stemmed from that hotel.

Chance, on his first trip in, went to a theater in the evening with Weber, and it was perhaps one o'clock when they got back to their rooms. Tap dancers were going through routines in the lobby. A tenor was trying to make Enrico Caruso sound like a bum. In the corridor of Chance's floor an Indian-club act was practicing a few new routines.

Chance didn't even bother to go to his room.

"Get my club the hell out of here ... *now!*" he roared at Weber. And sometime between then and morning such of the Los Angeles club as were to be found in their rooms were moved a few blocks away to a hotel where, by comparison, all was as silent as the tomb.

Chance was about to essay another major-league managerial effort, this one with the White Sox, when his death intervened. The man who would have been one of his coaches did the best he could that year as manager of the White Sox through the 1924 season. The man was Johnny Evers.

Tinker, the third Cub immortal, who had started for Cincinnati about the same time Chance did, didn't get along very well there. He was sold to Brooklyn during 1913, and when he demanded $2,000 of the purchase price, and owner Garry Hermann offered instead a stein of beer and a cask of pickles, Tinker straightway jumped to the Federal League, then about to get under way. It is nice to note that Tinker, who became manager of the Chicago Whales in the ill-fated Federal League and won a pennant in 1915, was joined there by Mordecai Brown.

In returning to Chicago via the Federal League route, Tinker became acquainted with owner Charles H. Weeghman, who had developed a dairy-lunch business into a hefty bank roll. When the Federal League folded after a stormy two years, Weeghman was more anxious to remain in baseball than were very many of the other "angels" whose wings had been singed in trying to buck the old, established, organized baseball firm.

The Cubs' franchise was being operated on what amounted to a remote-control system, ownership being vested in Charles Taft of Cincinnati. As the Federal League collapsed, Weeghman made his move toward securing control of the Cub franchise. Various sums are reported as the purchase price of a controlling interest in the Cubs at the end of the year 1915. One of those is $500,000, the story going that Weeghman turned that amount in cash over to Taft, shook hands with him, and became the proprietor.

He had a ball park, located at Clark and Addison Streets, where the Whales had played their home games. The Cubs were still operating on the West Side, where they had been since the days of Bill Lange. So Weeghman's first major move was to install the Cubs in his own park; and Tinker, who had done very well by him as manager of the Federal League champions, was given charge of the team for the 1916 season. He supplanted Roger Bresnahan who had followed Hank O'Day as managerial changes came thick and fast.

Tinker came no closer to a championship than had any of the others since Chance. But he did have in his employ one Cy Williams, who played the outfield and occasionally wound up and hammered a ball over the fence. In this 1916 season Cy pounded out twelve such hits, and became the National League's home-run champion for that year.

This was well enough, to be sure. Yet it is rather certain that more than one tried-and-true Cub fan of not too short a memory contemplated that record, and as he cried in his beer, gave voice to such sentiments as, "Twelve home runs! Why, Schulte would have hit that many with his sleeve in one of his good years!"

Tinker went the way of all the other Cub managers since Chance at the end of that one season; and Fred Mitchell took over. Mitchell's career, somewhat longer than seemed to be par for the course in those days, lasted through the 1920 season.

In some respects it was an eventful period in the Cub history, not only for Mitchell but for the club's entire future. For this was the stage in which the past was definitely linked up with the present. Mitchell was unable to get the Cubs higher than fifth place in his first season, but those 1917 Cubs were to figure in one game which has a place apart in the pitching records of all major-league baseball.

On May 2, the Cincinnati Reds were in Chicago for a series with the Cubs. That day's pitching assignment called for Fred Toney of the Reds to oppose Jim "Hippo" Vaughn of the Cubs. There is a question which was the heftier, but if their combined weights be placed at 450 pounds, the estimate will probably not be too small. Toney was a right-hander; Vaughn operated with the left.

There were some 3,500 persons present in the Cubs' ball park that day. There were 350,000 who wished they had been in the vicinity when they learned from the newspapers next day what had taken place. For Toney and Vaughn went through nine innings of baseball in which neither man allowed a hit or a run. In the tenth inning, when Vaughn weakened sufficiently to allow two hits and one run, Toney refused to yield, and thus recorded his ten-inning, 1–0, no-hit, no-run victory.

In the first nine innings both pitchers were on absolutely even terms. Toney walked Cy Williams in the second, and again in the fifth. Vaughn walked Heinie Groh twice, but Heinie was doubled up each time.

Earl "Greasy" Neale, who was to gain fame later as a football coach, collegiate and professional, had some distinction in the first nine innings of this memorable game. Neale, batting against Vaughn, was the only Red able to hit a ball out of the infield.

When the game turned into the tenth inning, Vaughn got past the first man without trouble. Then Larry Kopf rolled one between Fred Merkle and Larry Doyle, and into right field for the game's first hit. A line fly Hal Chase sent Williams' way

71

slipped from Cy's clutches, an error being charged, and Kopf made his way around to third in the confusion.

At this point Jim Thorpe, the famous Indian athlete, took his turn at bat. He hadn't been doing much in his previous tries, and he really didn't do much now. His tap in front of the plate bounced fairly high. Thorpe, who could run, if he couldn't hit major-league curve-ball pitching, was away like a flash. Vaughn came lumbering in and pounced on the ball. He took a quick look at the flying Thorpe and reached the decision that while he mightn't be able to throw him out, he might be able to get Kopf, who was tearing for the plate. That was all right, except that catcher Art Wilson wasn't let in on the decision soon enough. He was expecting Vaughn to make the orthodox toss to first base, and too late he attempted to stop the ball Vaughn had fired toward the plate. The ball got away, and Kopf scored.

This play brought up some fine discussion of the scoring proprieties, whether there should be an error on the play, or whether Thorpe should be credited with a hit. The official verdict was in Thorpe's favor, and that's how it happened that Hippo Vaughn of the Cubs, who pitched a no-hit, no-run game for the regulation nine innings, permitting but twenty-seven men to face him and keeping all but one from hitting a ball out of the infield in that time, was the two-hit loser in what has to be accepted as major-league baseball's greatest pitching duel.

Once again, the Chicago Cubs, for better or for worse, had figured in baseball's enduring records.

☙ XVII ☙

A CHAMPIONSHIP OF SORTS

SHORTLY AFTER THE 1917 SEASON HAD ENDED WITH THE CUBS settling for fifth place, the most important deal of the club's existence—up to that time—was completed. It brought from Philadelphia the famous battery of Grover Cleveland Alexander and Bill Killefer.

Two of the Cubs' second-division players, Mike Prendergast and "Pickles" Dilhoefer, went along, but the principal item involved was money. A popular estimate was that the Cubs shelled out $60,000. It might have been more; it might have been less. However, the financial records of the Cubs of this period were so entangled, it may be just as well to say that the transaction was a big deal for the Cubs, and let it go at that.

Alex went off to war after he had worked three games for the Cubs in 1918. Of these he was able to win two. Those Cubs who hadn't gone off to war and such replacements as were brought in from the minor leagues squared away and won the National League championship.

This was the year in which the "Work or Fight" order halted all baseball right after Labor Day. The major leagues were given permission to play a world series immediately following the curtailed season. And that is how the Cubs happened to meet Babe Ruth for the first time—and Ed Barrow. To say nothing of George Whiteman, who had been hastily snatched from the minor leagues by the Boston Red Sox. He not only helped them into the world series, but more than helped them win it with the aid of several hard and timely hits.

73

The Cubs, in years to come, were to see a lot more of Ruth and of Barrow. But Whiteman didn't trouble them again. He came up to the Red Sox because their regulars, or some of them, were away at war. When these players returned, Whiteman went back whence he had come. However he had his moments, which is more than can be said for most of the stopgap players of that war year of 1918.

The Babe Ruth of 1918 hadn't quite made up his mind (or had it made up for him by Manager Barrow) whether he was a left-hand pitcher or a left-hand hitting outfielder. In the American League race he had appeared in ninety-five games in the outfield. He was recognized as a menace by Manager Mitchell of the Cubs, who sat up nights figuring out ways to curb the Babe's talents.

Mitchell had at his disposal two left-hand pitchers. One was Hippo Vaughn, the same who had engaged in that memorable struggle with Fred Toney the year before. The other was George Tyler. Tyler had been a member of the Boston Braves pitching corps during 1914, and figured in the four-game sweep over the Athletics in a somewhat luckless capacity. He had started a game in order to give Bill James and Dick Rudolph a breathing spell, and had done well enough. However, he gave way to a pinch hitter after ten innings, and James came into action to become the winning pitcher of record when the Braves finally got the winning run across in the twelfth. Unlike ice hockey, there is no point in baseball's record for the assist on the pitching play which went from Tyler to James, who scored the victory.

Possessed of these two skilled left-handed craftsmen, Mitchell was reasonably sure that if he could work them in nearly every game of the series it would be unlikely that Barrow would install the Babe in the outfield for the games in which he wasn't pitching. Mitchell was going right along with one of baseball's most mystifying, yet widely accepted theories, that a left-hand batsman is at a disadvantage against a left-hand pitcher. By the same reckoning a right-hand batsman ought to be out of luck against right-hand pitching, but apparently the theory doesn't go that far.

In his world series planning Mitchell was unable to figure out any way in which he could keep Ruth from starting as a pitcher—and that was the Cubs' hard luck. The Babe beat them twice. He opened the series at Chicago, beating Vaughn, 1–0, and allowing but six hits. The game's lone run was scored by Dave Shean, who made his way around in the fourth inning.

Bullet Joe Bush wasn't as successful as Ruth when he worked the second game, and Tyler beat him 3–1, squaring the series. The notable feature of this game was an error by Whiteman. It was to be the only one charged against the Red Sox in the entire series.

Boston went on top in the third game, Carl Mays submarining his way to a 2–1 victory. It was Vaughn again for the Cubs, and while he allowed but seven hits, as Mays did, the Red Sox managed to get two runs out of them in the fourth inning.

The fourth game found the series moved to Boston. Ruth was the Red Sox pitcher, and Tyler was in for his second time in the series. The Cubs fared a little better against the Babe on this second time around. They were able to put over two runs in their half of the eighth, and tie the score at 2–2. This was drawing things too fine for the Red Sox, so they hammered over a run in their half to take the lead.

When the ninth inning opened, Barrow switched Ruth to the outfield, and Bush worked the final inning. Since the winning run had been scored while the Babe was the pitcher of record, credit for the victory went to him.

Ruth had entered the tussle with the Cubs with what billiardists would call an "unfinished run" of thirteen scoreless innings. This represented his closing chore against the New York Giants in 1916. Since he worked a shutout against the Cubs in the first game, and went seven innings his next time out before being scored upon, his world series string of consecutive scoreless innings was twenty-nine. This exceeded by one, the existing record established by Christy Mathewson; and thus, if in a negative fashion, the Cubs added one more peeve to the great number New York Giant fans already held against them.

Vaughn was unbeatable in the fifth game of the series, scattering five hits, to win 3–0. Sad Sam Jones was nicked for a run in the first and two more in the last.

The series came to an end the next day when Mays hurled a three-hitter, winning over Tyler and Claude Hendrix, 2–1. The Red Sox furnished Mays with two runs in the second inning, and those were all he needed.

This wartime world series had some financial aspects which for a time overshadowed all the splendid pitching. The now accepted plan of having second, third, and fourth place clubs in each major league share to some degree in world series receipts, was adopted in 1918 for the first time. It caused a long howl to go up from Cubs and Red Sox alike. The howls increased when the attendance didn't come up to anticipated standards, especially at Chicago where Comiskey Park had been borrowed for the occasion. Even the contending ballplayer with the least financial savvy could see that the individual winner's or loser's share was almost certain to set a new low for world series wealth distribution.

After the fifth game the players went on a strike; but they came back, as strikers generally do, and played out the string.

Their first guess was eminently correct. The total attendance was 128,483, with the receipts $179,619. Each winning Boston player collected $890. Each losing Chicago player picked up $535. That was hardly enough to tide over any Cub against the stretch of eleven years before the club was to figure in another world series.

In more respects than one, this 1918 series was one which proved beyond reasonable doubt the wisdom of the axiom, "Take nothing for granted in baseball."

It is extremely doubtful that any exultant Red Sox fan suspected that the time was not far off when the greatest players in their championship array were to be sold to New York, there to go on to heights undreamed of in baseball. Ruth, who many

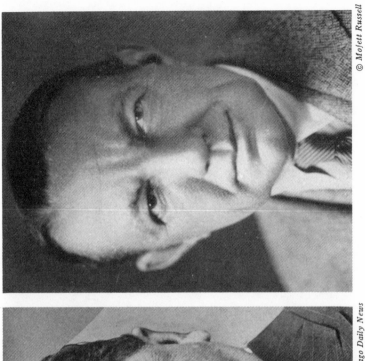

William Wrigley, Jr.

William Veeck

Jim Vaughn, Cubs' Greatest Left-Hander

believe made possible the Yankee Stadium, the pitchers, Bush, Mays, and Jones, catcher Wally Schang, and shortstop Everett Scott were all to find their way to New York and there make baseball history.

It is just as doubtful if any Cub fan, in the doldrums because another so near and yet so far chapter had been written into the quest for a world's championship, suspected that, in truth, a new era, and the greatest, was just around the corner. Few realized that there was enrolled in the Cubs' list of stockholders one man who was destined to pick up the organization which had now struck bottom and lift it to unprecedented heights. Yet that was what was in store.

The Wrigley era had begun. Now it was to flourish.

☻ XVIII ☻

ENTER WM. WRIGLEY, JR.

SOME TIME DURING THE YEAR 1915, WILLIAM WRIGLEY, JR., gum magnate, was on his way back from Cincinnati to Chicago and became involved in a parlor-car discussion which had to do with baseball in general and Chicago National League baseball in particular. Wrigley, one of Chicago's foremost citizens, took quite a bit of good-natured ribbing because his city didn't seem able to convince any of its men with money that the Cubs were a good investment.

"How does it happen that a Cincinnati man has to bank-roll the club?" Wrigley was asked.

He replied that he didn't know, but that he might look into it.

"You ought to do something about it," persisted one of the party.

"Perhaps I will, if the opportunity arises," Wrigley said.

The Cubs at this stage were mixed up, as were all other major-league clubs, in the war with the outlaw Federal League. After the passing of Charles W. Murphy, controlling interest in the Cubs had returned to Charles P. Taft of Cincinnati. In 1914 two Chicagoans, John R. Thompson and Charles McCulloch, had offered Taft $650,000 for the club, but no deal was made. Later on an effort was made to interest J. Ogden Armour in owning the club, but he wasn't having any, just then.

At the blowup of the Federal League, Charles A. Weeghman, the chief stockholder of the Chicago Whales, and one of his baseball associates, William M. Walker, decided to try to buy the Cubs.

78

But first—as the radio commercial announcer would have it—a brief message from the sponsor. Weeghman and Walker, one through dairy-lunch rooms, the other through wholesaling fish, had funds, but for the purpose of buying the Cubs, they wanted company. Weeghman sought out Armour and suggested that he put up $500,000. Armour couldn't see that proposition, but he agreed to be one of ten who would put up $50,000 each.

How, why, or when Wrigley was persuaded by Armour to be one of the ten investors is not known. Wrigley consented to contribute his share to the pool and presently went to California, where he was enjoying life in Pasadena, when the ownership of the Cubs was transferred to the syndicate of Chicagoans, with Weeghman as the front man, on January 20, 1916.

Sometime between his original approach by Armour, at Weeghman's behest, and the closing of the sale of the club, Wrigley had doubled his original investment of $50,000. When it became known that he was interested in the Cubs, the theory was advanced that Wrigley was concerned primarily in advertising his gum, the sale of which had been the basis of his fortune. It is fair to assume that Wrigley did expect his gum to get some indirect advertising, but neither then nor thereafter has Wrigley gum been directly exploited through the medium of the Cubs. And this, despite the fact that in later years Chicago baseball writers covering the Cubs' spring training camp at Catalina Island were frowned upon by certain of the shopkeepers for threatening to bootleg in Avalon a brand of gum Wrigley didn't manufacture.

After a few springs, however, the good people of Avalon were willing to accept the Chicago baseball writers for what they were —as fine a collection of exhibits A to Z as Bob Casey would be able to find and impress between covers.

When the first meeting of the reorganized Cubs was held, Wrigley was represented by W. H. Stanley. He gave his consent to Weeghman's proposal that Wrigley be a director of the club. Then Stanley phoned Wrigley, advising him of what he had done.

"All right," said Wrigley. "Let it go. But I'll never go to a meeting."

Stanley, knowing Wrigley, said nothing, preferring to let nature take its course. Perhaps he suspected that he had just heard what may have been the all-time record for understatement.

The first definite impression Wrigley gave the syndicate of owners that he was taking an active interest in the Cubs' doings came in 1917, when he was able to sell the ball club the idea of training in California.

Weeghman eventually began to pull up lame in the furious financial pace he had been setting for himself. He was forced to do a lot of borrowing to keep going. Much of this was done from Wrigley, with Cub stock being used as collateral. When a financial crash hit Weeghman, Wrigley found himself possessed of the largest single block of shares in the club, though he did not possess control. He was beginning to take a lively interest in the club's affairs, however.

In December 1918, it was Wrigley who appeared at the directors' meeting and presented Weeghman's resignation as president of the club. Fred Mitchell, the Cubs' manager, was installed as president, and William L. Veeck was named vice-president and treasurer.

Wrigley had become acquainted with Veeck during the spring of 1918 when the Chicago baseball writers, of whom Veeck (as "Bill Bailey") was one, were invited to dinner at the Wrigley home at Pasadena. The club's affairs, artistic and financial, were getting a good going over by the baseball writers—who never have pulled any punches in dealing with the Cubs. Wrigley took it all in, but seemed most interested in Veeck's criticisms.

"Could you do any better?" inquired Wrigley.

"I certainly couldn't do any worse," said Veeck.

And thereby he moved himself into the Wrigley empire to become, before his death, one of the most important front-office men in that part of it known as the Chicago Cubs.

In the new line-up of inner office personnel, another baseball

80

writer, John O. Seys, was also included. He joined on as club secretary and later acquired a good deal of authority.

It was not long before the National League in looking over its bylaws found out that Mitchell, managing the Cubs on the field and signed to a player's contract, couldn't double as president. So in June, 1919, Mitchell moved out, and Bill Veeck became president of the club.

The year 1919 was to be an ill-fated one for Chicago's baseball, for it was in the fall of that year that the American League champion White Sox were defeated in the world series by Cincinnati, and the rumbling of "thrown" games began, which was to reach its climax not quite a year later when eight members of the team were banished forever from participation in organized baseball.

This scandal left the game in a bad way. Baseball personages in both leagues were agreed that something had to be done and quickly, lest public confidence in the sport be lost. A. D. Lasker, an advertising executive and a large shareholder in the Cubs, proposed that control of the game be placed in a triumvirate, with the most prominent men available to compose it. His idea found some acceptance and it also found some opposition.

Wrigley, who had quite a lot at stake in baseball by this time, then came forward with a compromise. He suggested that the three-man idea be scrapped and that one man be given complete authority over all leagues. His man was Kenesaw M. Landis, a federal judge. On November 12, 1920, a seven-year contract was signed with Landis to take charge of baseball. That charge he kept both wisely and well for the quarter-century of life there was left to him.

At the end of 1918 when Veeck took charge of the Cubs' finances, Wrigley, his sponsor, owned somewhat less than one half of the club's stock. Lasker was a heavy stockholder. He had headed the group which put up the last $150,000 when Weeghman was forming his syndicate. Lasker was never very enthusiastic over the choice of Veeck as president of the club, and said so frequently in his friendly arguments with Wrigley.

Through 1920 when Mitchell finished up his stay as manager of the Cubs, and through part of 1921 when Johnny Evers again essayed the management, only to be replaced by Bill Killefer, Lasker made no issue of the club's playing qualities—though there were those who did. But something Killefer did annoyed Lasker and he began to argue with Wrigley about the kind of a manager the Cubs had.

One word led to another, and finally Lasker made one of those "Either you buy me or I'll buy you" propositions. The first part of it appealed to Wrigley, who was now definitely committed to the baseball business. He bought 888 shares from Lasker, insisting that his friend retain a small block in order that he might be a member of the board of directors—and perhaps express an opinion of Killefer again.

These 888 shares, along with 500 bought from Armour the same year, gave Wrigley control of the Cubs. Then, for the first time, he began to think in terms of a championship. It was a long time coming, and both his ball club and his ball park were to be subjected to a complete overhauling before the Cubs next came down in front in the National League race.

⊜ XIX ⊜

WRIGLEY BUYS AN ISLAND

WITHIN TWO MONTHS OF THE DATE IN WHICH WRIGLEY came out in the open as the power behind the Cubs, he was at his winter home in Pasadena. The home had been sold him by David Blankenhorn, a realtor, and there is some evidence that Wrigley subsequently maintained a lively interest in the real-estate business.

At this time Catalina Island, across the channel from the Southern California mainland, was a resort of sorts. Wrigley had heard glowing tales about it from Joseph H. Patrick, one of his associates, but had never visited the place. The island at this time was owned by a family named Banning, and it was duly reported that they were faced with the necessity of raising a sizable sum of money—$700,000 being the accepted figure. Word of this got to Blankenhorn, and he in turn thought of Wrigley as a prospective purchaser, the idea being that the island could be developed into a huge real-estate development.

Wrigley was sold on the idea, and closed the deal for the island without ever having seen it. Nor was he in any great rush to see what he had bought. Indeed, several weeks elapsed before he made his first trip to the island.

He expressed amazement at its contours, dominated by mountainous peaks rising up out of the Pacific. His idea of an island, he admitted frankly enough, was a reasonably flat piece of land surrounded by water.

He remained overnight at the island. Upon arising in the morning both he and Mrs. Wrigley were captivated with the charm of the place. They resolved then and there that here was a project worthy of all their imagination, and all the drive of Wrigley. It is not related whether it was Wrigley, or one of his copy writers later on, who first breathed:

"In all the world, no place like this."

But whoever the author, truer words were never uttered. To be sure, the Catalina Island Wrigley gazed upon that morning, drenched in the sunlight of the Pacific, was not exactly a haven of comfort or a holiday seeker's bargain. Those phases were to come, and doubtless Wrigley visualized many, as his son and heir, Phillip K. Wrigley, was to visualize more.

Avalon, the capital city of the Wrigley island kingdom, was in 1919 no bargain as a municipality. It had no paved streets. It had no sewerage system. It had a poor electric light plant. Its only drinking water came from two wells, which were so inadequate most of the water had to be brought over from the mainland. Yet Wrigley was able to see in it a vast playground to which untold thousands would one day come on pleasure bent.

His first plan for the regeneration of Catalina was to commission D. M. Renton, a contractor, to put up 350 bungalows. Renton, after that first commission, was to remain for many years as a sort of major-domo over all Catalina. If the statement be made that he knew where every foot of wire, every inch of pipe, every board, and every nail was on Catalina, where it came from, and who handled it, that would be no exaggeration.

The one thing Wrigley was sure of from the start was that there was to be no tawdriness about Catalina, no cheapness or vain show. It wasn't going to be another Coney Island. With that in mind, he really began to spend money in remolding the island nearer to his heart's desire. His real-estate partners, Blankenhorn and Robert Hunter, demurred. They were of the opinion that lots could be sold without all this utopia formula. So Wrigley listened to them, disagreed with their ideas—and bought them out.

He had discovered, as he went along, that the transportation to and from the island was less than adequate. He went into

84

the steamship business. To the "fleet" was added the Goodrich line *Virginia*, originally built for service on the Great Lakes. It was renamed the *Avalon*. That wasn't shipping enough, so a new and larger steamer was built. That was the *Catalina*, the flagship of the Wrigley fleet.

Plying their course offshore in the marine gardens were glass-bottom boats. Wrigley had ideas about them, too. So he bought out the owner.

It was his plan to be able to sell to the native of California, and to the tourist, a Catalina "package." This would include transportation to and from the island, perhaps a meal or two while there, or hotel accommodations for those who wished to remain, and rights to various "tours" such as mountain rides and a cruise in the glass-bottom boat. To do all this, Wrigley had to add the hotel business to his growing list of enterprises.

Construction work on the island was keeping up apace. A huge reservoir was built back in the hills. A new hotel, the "Atwater," was erected. Row after row of bungalettes in two sectors, one known as Island Villa, the other as Villa Park, came into being. And on the side of one of the loveliest of Catalina's hills there arose Wrigley's own magnificent home, from which he could gaze down upon the wonders of his "magic isle."

Somewhere, somehow, in the midst of all this face-lifting process, Wrigley's crew of designers put in a golf course, nine holes at first, later to become eighteen of the most agonizing kind for the duffer, along canyons, through canyons, over canyons. And at long last the thought came to him, why not have a baseball field here, too?

It was on that baseball field in the spring following Wrigley's taking over the Cubs as his very own, that the club did its training for the first time. Catalina Island was to be its permanent spring-training camp, the annual visits being halted only when World War II broke loose and Catalina Island, as well as Wrigley's Gum, went off to war. There on a splendid baseball field, in the shadows of Catalina's mountains, Bill Killefer assembled his squad in the spring of 1922.

Killefer instituted the most arduous system of road work ever designed to make a sorely tried ballplayer wish he had taken up some other means of livelihood. For Catalina, as related, runs very much to uphill and downdale. Save for the picturesque bay on which the town of Avalon is situated, sundry coves here and there, and a comparatively late development, the airport, Catalina's contours were made by nature for wild goats rather than for ballplayers.

There are still men alive who went to that first camp with Bill Killefer who will swear that once Bill looked them over on the flat, he knew they weren't all major-league ballplayers, and so they might as well try to be mountain goats. Day after day he forced them to run up those hills and down, until Charles Leo "Gabby" Hartnett, fresh up from Worcester that spring but even then in good voice, cried aloud in anguish, "I hope they've got those turns banked in the National League infields, for one of my legs is shorter than the other from trying to navigate these damned hills."

Neither Killefer's training nor Killefer's ball club bothered the National League much in that 1922 season, unless you happen to be one who worries about the Phillies. On August 25 the Cubs engaged them at Wrigley Field. The final score was Cubs, 26, Phillies, 23. There were twenty-six hits for the Phillies, twenty-three for the Cubs. In one inning, the second, the Cubs scored ten runs. That was just the windup. The main event came in the fourth. In it the Cubs scored fourteen.

That was almost enough action for an entire season, but the club had enough energy left to beat the White Sox in the city series, four games to two. Cubs haven't been so accustomed to triumphs over their cross-city rivals that they should be denied due credit when such an overturning of Chicago baseball dope takes place.

For all of the Wrigley influence, the fresh viewpoint, and above all the fresh money, the Cubs struggled through 1923 and 1924 as a run of the mine major-league club. In their own peculiar way, however, they did contribute to one of the game's records

86

in 1924. On August 1, Dazzy Vance of Brooklyn fanned the last man in the first inning and the next six who came up in order in the next two innings.

Attempts were being made right along to arrange deals, for Wrigley wanted a winner, come what may. But it has been proven often enough in both major leagues that it isn't always possible to assemble a championship-winning team however large the bank roll of the team's owner may be. Wrigley was not the first wealthy magnate to find that out. Nor was he the last.

A chance for a bit of business did come the way of the Bills, Veeck and Killefer, shortly after the close of the 1924 season which had found the club finishing in a not too imposing fifth place.

They were at Pittsburgh attending a dinner for Barney Dreyfuss, owner of the Pirates. Barney coveted Vic Aldridge, one of the Cub pitchers, and said so.

"All right," said Veeck. "I'll give you Aldridge and I'll take Maranville and Grimm."

"That Maranville and that Grimm drive me crazy," said Barney. "Always cutting up, always making the jokes. But if I let Grimm go, I have no first baseman. Maybe I can have Niehaus, no?"

Niehaus, the Wrigley Field programs said, was a first baseman.

Veeck pretended to be weighing that proposition for a while and asked to withdraw for a conference with Killefer, though fearful all the time Dreyfuss would change his mind.

When he rejoined Barney, Veeck had decided to press his luck.

"You can have Niehaus, too," he said, "but you'll have to throw in Cooper."

"That Cooper, that Maranville, and that Grimm all drive me crazy," said Dreyfuss. "A deal it is."

And that's how Rabbit Maranville and Charlie Grimm came to the Cubs. Cooper came, too, but his comings and goings with the Cubs are relatively unimportant.

Veeck was not to know then, of course, that he had just made a deal for two who were to be managers of the club. Maranville, who was to lead the club for a brief but hilarious term, and Grimm, who was to be one of the most popular ballplayers ever to appear in Chicago, and who was one day to be hammering at the managerial championship records of Pop Anson and Frank Chance.

To Veeck, at the moment, Maranville was a shortstop the Cubs could use, and Grimm was a flashy-fielding first baseman and a gifted entertainer. He was a left-hand hitter, but unlike most of that ilk, he actually thrived on left-hand pitching—left-hand pitching that is, save the sort served up by Walter "Dutch" Ruether, a nomad of the major leagues, who is currently on duty scouting up new material for Grimm, the manager.

It is related that Grimm, in all his years of batting against Ruether, considered that day a success in which he secured more than a hard foul. One afternoon while Dutch was working for Brooklyn, Grimm's bat came in contact with a pitch, and the ball popped rather high in the air. The second baseman had to go back on the grass to take it. As Grimm turned to go back to the dugout, Ruether came over to the line and spoke to him.

"Guess I'll have to start dusting you off," he said. "It looks as if you're starting to get to me."

If Bill Veeck didn't suspect the managerial talent there was bound up in Grimm, he must have had some ideas that Maranville was a born leader. He was, indeed—a leader in fun and frolic, whose escapades are an endless source of material for baseball raconteurs.

Maranville was a playful little fellow. He was at home balancing on the ledge of a New York hotel, high above the street, while attempting to snare some pigeons, or dropping a paper laundry bag full of water out of a St. Louis hotel window to land with some tidal wave effects very close to where secretary John Seys was seated, getting himself a breath of fresh air and wondering, perchance, what Maranville was up to now.

But withal Maranville was a great ballplayer when he found

time to play. He had been great with the Boston Braves. He had been great with the Pirates. Unfortunately, the comical side is the one that will be exposed—which is all right, in a way, since playing records at best are apt to get boresome, and Maranville's personal history never will.

When Grimm and Maranville moved on to Chicago, they must have left some heartbroken teammates at Pittsburgh, notably "Cotton" Tierney, who was a character in his own right. Perhaps even a pitcher, who shall remain nameless, sighed at the passing of Grimm and Maranville from the Pirates. For the pitcher was the unwitting hero of one of the finer touches of the Pirate humor of that period, as the following episode culled from the reminiscences of Grimm would indicate.

The Pirates were playing St. Louis, and the day was terribly hot. The pitcher, who liked a snort or two as well as the next man, had been restricted by Manager George Gibson to water and nothing else—or else. The pitcher didn't like it much, but orders were orders. He was sent out to work and did a fine job of it, though each inning as he came back to the dugout he gave the hated water bucket a lot of attention.

When the game turned into the seventh inning, the pitcher made up his mind to take steps. He reached the box and picked up the ball. The catcher crouched and gave him a sign. The pitcher just stood there. The catcher tried another sign. No move from the pitcher. Right through the repertoire of battery signals went the catcher. The pitcher remained in a state of suspended animation. By this time Manager Gibson was getting mad. He yelled at Grimm who was nearest him.

"Go over there and see what in hell's wrong," he ordered.

Grimm sauntered over and made inquiry.

"I'll not throw another ball until I get a shot of liquor," said the pitcher.

There was nothing Grimm could do about that, so he just stood there, too. Presently the catcher came out. Cotton Tierney joined the party. At last Maranville jogged in to ask what was coming off.

"He won't pitch unless he has a shot," explained Grimm.

"It ain't a bad idea," said Maranville. "Anybody got one with him?"

Now Grimm, who was no cop then and isn't now, never has revealed which Pirate had a pint, or what was left of one, in the hip pocket of his uniform.

"All I will say," says Grimm, "is that we huddled around the pitcher, who bent over out of sight. He had his snort. Maybe somebody else had a snort. Anyhow the meeting broke up. We went back to our positions. The pitcher picked up the ball, and for the rest of that inning the Cardinals didn't get a hard foul off him."

When the inning was over, Grimm was first into the dugout. Manager Gibson was waiting for him.

"What was the matter out there?" he wanted to know.

Maranville, who had arrived a step behind Grimm, had the reply.

"The guy's supporter was binding him," he said, "and he didn't know what to do about it out there in front of all those people."

That was the Maranville, who on July 7, 1925, found himself suddenly appointed manager, Bill Killefer having decided there was no use suffering any longer.

The bewildering managerial changes of 1925 are best related by an eyewitness, Grimm himself, who was the field captain of the Cubs at the time.

"We were playing a game in Chicago," Grimm says, "the last before we went on a road trip into the east. Killefer came to me before the game and said that he wanted to win that one more than he wanted anything else in the world. He said it was going to be his last ball game. He didn't tell me why, and I didn't ask him. We went out and won it, 1–0.

"That night on the train I made it my business to look things over. Killefer wasn't around, but nothing had been said to anyone about his leaving the club.

"When we arrived in New York, Bill Veeck called us all into a meeting in the ball room. I guess I had an idea what was coming off, but I'm sure no one else did, and least of all Maranville. Veeck told us that there was going to be a change in managers, and then called up the Rabbit, asking us to meet the new manager. This was the first intimation Maranville had of it, and he was just as surprised as the next one.

"As I look back now, I'm not sure whether Maranville was to be a fixture, or whether he was just appointed to finish out the season.

"I never did know when Veeck began negotiations with Joe McCarthy, though I'm pretty sure they had reached an understanding long before that 1925 season closed. On the face of it though, Rabbit had a chance, and he seemed to appreciate it, at first."

Maranville appreciated it so much that when the Cubs won their first game under his direction, he led a celebration which could hardly have been noisier than if the Cubs had just won a world's championship. Some of the ardor of Rabbit and his co-celebrators cooled off late at night when they lost a decision to a taxicab driver in Times Square.

The brief reign of Maranville the manager became louder and funnier as it went along, and it was but a matter of days before Veeck gave up on him and ordered traveling secretary John Seys to send him home. There had been numerous brushes between Maranville and Seys, and the latter was very happy when the incident closed on a hilarious farewell note.

To finish out the schedule, George Gibson, who was now acting as coach of the club, took over the management relinquished by the man he had tried to manage at Pittsburgh not so very long before.

The Cubs in this year of the three managers finished in eighth place. Never before, and not since, have they sunk so low. Yet even this misfit collection was able to come through with an incredible accomplishment.

They defeated the White Sox in the city series, four games to one, in the games in which decisions were reached. They settled for a tie in the opening game of the series, a contest that was in some respects one of baseball's most remarkable.

The game opened with Grover Cleveland Alexander pitching against Ted Blankenship. It closed after nineteen innings had been played, with the same two still in action and the score tied 2–2. The Sox were away to a two-run lead in the third, with the Cubs picking up one in the fourth and one in the fifth. Of the two rival pitchers, Alex furnished the more unusual performance, for the Sox got to him for twenty hits and yet were unable, in eighteen of the nineteen innings, to get a run across.

Cooper, the ballast in the Grimm-Maranville deal, pitched the second game for the Cubs and won 2–1, Ted Lyons being the loser. "Sheriff" Fred Blake bested "Red" Faber in the third game, 8–2, and not until the fourth game were the Sox able to put across a victory. Then Blankenship came back to win 7–2, over Percy Jones and Guy Bush.

The Cubs staked Tony Kaufman to two runs in the fourth inning of the fifth game, and he coasted to a 3–1, five-hit victory. The finishing touch was given by Cooper in the sixth game when he won 7–4, over "Rubber Arm" Connally and Blankenship.

The Cub hitters in that series were led by Grimm with .417.

One other bit of information about that 1925 city series. One of the American League umpires was Clarence "Pants" Rowland. Eight years before, in 1917, as manager of the White Sox, he gained for Chicago the only world's championship that had come its way since Frank Chance's Cubs had lost their touch. A few years later Rowland was to attach himself to the Wrigley forces and take in considerable territory before his course was run.

With this most convincing defeat of the White Sox that any Cub team has ever gained, the year 1925 closed. But the city series triumph was not enough to keep Wrigley and Veeck from recalling that in the National League race their club had finished a bad last. They made a pledge that never again would the Cubs suffer that indignity.

That pledge has been kept.

⊖ XX ⊖

JOE McCARTHY CHECKS IN

FROM TIME TO TIME, AS THE HISTORY OF THE CUBS UNFOLDS, the existence of parallels has been pointed out. Now, at the outset of the 1926 season, when the club was committed to a policy of escaping from the second division hurriedly, another one of these parallels must be noted. This one, of course, is sheer coincidence. But parallel it is, just the same.

President Bill Veeck, who abandoned a successful newspaper career to join forces with William Wrigley, Jr., and the Cubs, had started his journalistic life among the scribes at Louisville— the same Louisville, four members of whose club had been drummed out of baseball "for the good of the game" by President Wm. H. Hulbert in 1877; the same Louisville whose team had been given that awful 36–7 drubbing by Pop Anson's club in 1897; the same Louisville whose American Association club in 1925 and for several seasons prior had been capably managed by Joseph V. McCarthy.

In his seven years as a Cub executive, as well as in his baseball-writing days for the Chicago *Evening American* before that, Bill Veeck's acquaintance with ballplayers in major leagues and in minors was perhaps as large as anyone's. From one and all who had ever played for, or had any dealings with, Joe McCarthy, Veeck had been unable to run across one who didn't have a boost for the Louisville manager.

They were agreed that he knew baseball and that he knew men and how to handle them. No one put a rap on him, which, in a sport which seems to thrive on second guessing, must have

93

amazed Veeck, the seeker after information. McCarthy had never been a major-league ballplayer. The Class AA as an infielder had been the extent of his climbing before his playing career was ended and he turned to managing.

It was taking a long chance then to bring up this comparative unknown to big league ways, and give him custody of a ball club that wanted a championship more than it wanted anything else. Yet that was what Bill Veeck did. Thus entered into the Cubs' life a manager who will be ranked with the greatest of all time, though it must be admitted much of the McCarthy managerial record was made at New York and in the American League—but the Cubs must be scored an assist on the play. He didn't remain the Cubs' manager more than five years, but as he said himself, from his loftier eminence as a collector of American League and world championships for the New York Yankees:

"That was about par for the course. Since 1900 only Chance stayed any longer than I did. Anyhow it worked out all right in the long run for all of us, didn't it?"

To McCarthy was handed the material left over from a club that had finished a hilarious last in the 1925 season. He welcomed the opportunity, not on the negative side that anything he did at all must be an improvement, but with positive confidence that he could make good with the resources of Wrigley and the backing of Veeck.

There were those on the ball club who had other ideas about the new manager. Long inured to haphazard management and overcome by their own sense of major-league importance, these players regarded McCarthy as a "busher," and they had to be shown. He was not long in showing them.

The ranking figure on the ball club was Alexander. In the 1919 season his 1.72 earned run average set a Cub pitching record that has never been equaled. Jim Vaughn's 1.74 the year before coming nearest to it. In the 1920 season Alex turned in a 1.91 earned run average. He led the Cub pitchers in seven successive seasons. Old Pete had been a great pitcher—and would be a great pitcher again, when he found the time.

94

It was one of baseball's tragedies that Alex had his own peculiar ideas on keeping in condition. McCarthy was not a hard taskmaster. He had been a ballplayer himself; he knew ballplayers. He knew that there were many skilled performers who had their moments when they batted against or pitched with John Barleycorn. He didn't care so much, one way or another, about that. All he asked was that his ballplayers be ready when game time came, so that they might give him the best they had when he asked for it.

Old Pete wasn't quite up to that a good part of the time. Several times McCarthy called on him and Old Pete wasn't ready. McCarthy had to make a quick judgment. He realized that Alexander, on his past pitching record, was one of the game's greatest heroes; and that getting rid of him by a "busher" in his first major-league managerial season might well bring down the wrath of Cub fandom. But to let Old Pete get away with it must of necessity lead to the question: Has this manager any guts? McCarthy had.

On June 22, 1926, Alexander was sold to St. Louis at the waiver price. All baseball knew then that McCarthy was managing the Cubs in fact as well as in name. There was no resentment shown by either the departing great pitcher or the remaining manager. Indeed, McCarthy likes to tell yarns to this day of his experience with Alexander.

One of these developed when McCarthy and his players met, as was their custom, to discuss ways and means of pitching to hitters of an opposing club with which a series was about to begin. One of the Cubs' misfits had been dealt to this club a short time before, and the point was raised whether it might not be advisable to change the Cubs' signals.

While the discussion was at its height, Old Pete, who had arrived late and promptly seemed to go to sleep in a chair, made neither sound nor gesture.

"We've got to change our battery signs," insisted one of the Cubs. "When So-and-so gets on second he'll be able to call every pitch."

There was a slight stir in Old Pete's corner.

"If he was *ever* going to get on second base, McCarthy wouldn't have let him go," said Alex—and took no further part in the meeting.

McCarthy's knowledge of American Association business, and especially its baseball standards, helped him in his building up of the Cubs. At Toledo in 1925, playing outfield, was the roly-poly, good-natured "Hack" Wilson. He had been planted there by the New York Giants, who for some reason had forgotten about him. McCarthy hadn't, and when the Cubs went to camp in 1926, Hack Wilson was a member of the cast.

Before he was to leave the club, which was soon after McCarthy did, this little round man was to hang up a National League home-run record which still stands, and a runs-batted-in record which all the batsmen of all time, National or American Leaguers, have been unable to equal.

Wilson was a high ball hitter on the field—and off it—but there wasn't a day in all the time McCarthy managed him that Hack wouldn't be on the job, ready to take his cuts when the baseball bell rang. He was in one scrape after another, but McCarthy forgave them all, because Wilson, for all his extracurricular activities, did give service on the ball field.

In one of the spring training junkets to California, the Cubs were playing exhibitions in Los Angeles. Hack got out of bounds one Saturday night, and McCarthy knew about it. The Cubs' manager was not one to maintain a house-detective system in running his ball club, and it could have been an accident that he found out about Wilson's being A.W.O.L. on this particular occasion. McCarthy happened to be on his way to church early Sunday morning when he saw Wilson zooming down the street in a car full of very, very jolly good fellows.

It was the custom for the Cubs, still in the training process, to go through lengthy batting and fielding drills before each exhibition game. Wilson, looking like anything but the well-trained athlete, was among the early arrivals at the park. He went

Rogers Hornsby

Hack Wilson

promptly to work, keeping as far away from McCarthy as he could.

When the game began Hack was at his post in center field. He was fairly dripping with perspiration, the day being unseasonably hot, and sweating it out was one of the best things Wilson did.

First time up Hack hit a home run that started the Cubs off on a rally. They kept on collecting runs until by the time the game was half over they had so many McCarthy mercifully removed his regulars—all but one—and sent in rookies. Wilson stayed in. Meanwhile he had hit his second home run. He was almost in a state of collapse now, but McCarthy gave no sign that anything was out of the ordinary.

In the seventh inning Hack teed off and hit one of the longest home runs that had ever been witnessed in the vicinity of Los Angeles. He was barely able to jog around the bases. When he returned to the dugout, McCarthy looked him over.

"Maybe you better go in now, Hack," he said, "or you'll be too tired to go riding again tonight."

Out of the American Association for McCarthy's first year with the Cubs came Riggs Stephenson, the "Old Hoss." He had served a four-year term in the American League with Cleveland before dropping back to the Association. There McCarthy recognized his hitting possibilities, and up came the Old Hoss to take his place in the Cub outfield.

The pitching staff also gained potential strength before the 1926 season opened. Charley Root, who had been out in the Pacific Coast League on option, was recalled. Pat Malone, who had been knocking around the minor leagues for several seasons, eventually landed with Minneapolis, and while toiling for that club, caught McCarthy's eye. Root and Malone joined up with such regulars as Percy Jones and "Sheriff" Blake.

Guy Bush had been recalled by the Cubs for 1925, but he had not yet acquired major-league polish. He wasn't as fearful of the big city as scout Jack Doyle, who found him in the deep south, says he was when first glimpsed. Doyle insists that Bush, upon learning that he had been sold to Chicago, hid out on several posses Doyle, the "Old Oriole," had sent to find him.

Nor was Bush as yet the glass of fashion and the mold of form he was to become when, as a most successful pitcher for the Cubs, he was to dress and look like something out of the "Sheik of Araby," or at very least, a Rudolph Valentino B picture. All that came later.

The Cubs might have had another outfielder for that 1926 season if McCarthy hadn't decided that his judgment of a ball-player was better than that of William Wrigley, Jr., who just owned the ball club. During 1925 while sojourning in California, Wrigley had become attached to Frank "Lefty" O'Doul, a splendid-hitting outfielder who was then with the Salt Lake club.

O'Doul, a native San Franciscan and one of the foremost salesmen of the "Native Son" formula, had come up to the Yankees in 1919 as a pitcher. The Native Son formula, in case you have forgotten, calls for a refusal to admit at all times and in all other places that there could be any sector of the land comparable with California. If you come from San Francisco, as O'Doul did, that's the greatest place on earth. If you come from Los Angeles, that's the greatest place on earth. There is a song, "I Love You, California," you know—and it's the Native Son's National Anthem. O'Doul remained for two seasons, featured chiefly by his being the life of the many parties which Babe Ruth organized. O'Doul was returned to San Francisco without having added anything to the Yankees' playing strength or having detracted therefrom. He was back in 1922 and then moved on to Boston, the Red Sox sending him out to Salt Lake in 1924.

O'Doul thrived on Coast League pitching. And Wrigley thought so well of him he one day asked Bill Lane, the Salt Lake owner, how much he wanted for the outfielder. Lane thought $15,000 would be about right, and Wrigley said it was a deal.

O'Doul showed up at camp with the Cubs at Catalina in the spring of 1926 but fouled out as far as McCarthy was concerned and was sent to Hollywood. Wrigley said not a word—then.

Later on, when O'Doul broke back into the National League,

and either led it in hitting or caused damage to some Cub pitching hopes, Wrigley would sigh:

"Oh, that O'Doul . . . my O'Doul!"

Even though the Cubs made the 1926 race with no O'Doul, they were able to get back into the first division. Hack Wilson led the league's home-run hitters with twenty-one, equaling the mark set by Frank Schulte fifteen years before. Hack also led in drawing bases on balls, getting sixty-nine, every one of which made him more irritated than the one which went before. For Hack dearly loved to swing a bat at anything which came within swinging range. It didn't make any difference to him who pitched, or how. Hack was in there taking his cuts, supremely confident that one of them would land.

A particular source of annoyance to the Cub hitters was Dazzy Vance of the Dodgers, who had fanned seven of them in a row in 1924. Daz, who affected an undershirt whose right sleeve was torn and flapped while he went through his pitching motion, specialized in striking out Cubs. But Wilson never conceded Daz anything. As soon as the Dodgers would come on the field on the days Vance was due to pitch, Hack, from across the field, would start hurling insults at the Dodger pitcher.

On the Cub squad as a utility player was the slightly built Clyde Beck. He once confided that Vance, in pitching to him, should be made to throw from second base.

One day at Wrigley Field, Vance was scheduled to work for the Dodgers, and Beck was to be in the Cubs' line-up. Just before the Dodgers came out for their warm-up, Wilson was in the Cubs' dugout rehearsing some new stuff to call Vance. Beck pleaded with him to keep the peace that day.

"I've got to hit against him," he protested, "and I don't want him stirred up any more than he usually is."

"Nuts," said Wilson. "The big bum can't break a pane of glass, and I can't wait to tell him so."

The Cubs were at batting practice when the Dodgers came out. Vance had just appeared when Hack let him have it, a complete new routine of sweet sentiment. Beck had been waiting his turn to take batting practice. But no more. He walked quietly back to the dugout and placed his bat under the bench.

"This isn't going to do me any good today," he said.

Following their 1926 season, the first under McCarthy, the Cubs went through a routine city series with the White Sox and lost four of the seven games played—which occasioned no surprise whatever.

⊗ XXI ⊗

THE CUBS PROGRESS

FOR THE 1927 RUNNING, MCCARTHY REACHED INTO THE AMER-
ican Association for another ballplayer to add to his cast.
That was shortstop Elwood "Woody" English, who came up from
Toledo for a reported $50,000 and gave the club a high-class
workman at another infield position. Grimm was a fixture at first
base, while various characters were appearing at second and third
base. Among them was "Sparky" Adams, who had been with the
club since 1922.

Adams had yet to do his best deed for the Cubs. That was to
come on November 28, 1927, after the club had again finished
fourth.

On the Pittsburgh Pirate roster at the time was right fielder
Hazen "Kiki" Cuyler. He had helped the Pirates through the
exciting world series of 1925, and it was one of his many hits
which eventually gave the decision to Pittsburgh. By 1927, however, when Donie Bush had succeeded to the Pirate management,
Cuyler for reasons never adequately explained was not Bush's
favorite ballplayer. He appeared in but eighty-five games, and in
the world series not at all. Not that it mattered much, for that
was the year in which the Yankees were crashing through with
one of their four-straight demonstrations in the world series, and
Cuyler was probably very happy he didn't get caught in the
traffic as did the playing Pirates.

McCarthy and Veeck decided to look into the Bush-Cuyler
feud and paid a visit to Pittsburgh to discuss it with Barney
Dreyfuss. Dreyfuss explained that Cuyler would probably be

traded, since he and Bush didn't get along, but that the manager wanted infielder Hugh Critz of the Reds.

"Won't Sparky Adams do just as well?" inquired Veeck.

Dreyfuss thought he might—if outfielder Pete Scott were included. The deal was closed. It took all of five minutes but gave the Cubs an outfielder who was to become one of the delights of Wrigley Field for many years to come.

In midseason another seasoned pitcher had been obtained when Hal Carlson was secured in a trade with the Phillies. Carlson was a normal, dependable pitcher in so far as opponents and fans who watched him were concerned. He had one eccentricity, however, which trainer Andy Lotshaw discovered. Whenever it was Carlson's turn to pitch, he would begin to complain of soreness in his arm. It wasn't that he was trying to avoid duty—far from it, for he was of the work-horse type. He just craved the services of the trainer and the rubbing table.

One day the Cubs were in the midst of a double-header and Carlson hadn't figured in McCarthy's original pitching plans. In between games McCarthy decided to switch to Carlson, who at once sought out trainer Lotshaw and asked for a quick rub to see if it would take out the soreness which had just developed in his arm.

Lotshaw had just started on a bottle of Coca Cola when the call came from Carlson, who had planted himself on the rubbing table, stripped to the waist. Lotshaw took a swig of the Coca Cola and approached the table carrying the bottle in his hand.

"Hal," he said, "I ain't seeming to get no place with the regular rub I been giving you. Today I got some new stuff I want to try. I hear it's mighty good."

"Try anything," said Carlson, "but hurry. I have to pitch the next game."

So, dousing the pitcher's arm and shoulder generously with the rest of the Coca Cola, Lotshaw proceeded to give Carlson a regulation rub, and sent him on his way. Carlson pitched and won his game. He was never better.

For the rest of his stay with the Cubs, until his untimely death in 1930, Carlson would have no other rub save that new stuff "Doc" Lotshaw had tried on him—but he never did find out that it was Coca Cola, that being one of the few secrets Doc Lotshaw ever kept for long.

Toward the close of the 1927 season yet another pitcher came the Cubs way. This was the left-hander, Art Nehf, who had been released unconditionally by Boston in August. Nehf had been a great pitcher for John McGraw in New York, and his ability, his personality, and his promise even at that late stage of his career, appealed to McCarthy. The Cubs' manager guessed right on Art Nehf.

Some of McCarthy's finds were already well established with Wrigley Field patrons while the 1927 season was in progress. Hack Wilson had pounded out a .321 average to lead the club's hitters in 1926, besides getting his twenty-one home runs. Old Hoss Stephenson took charge in 1927 with a .344 average, but Hack stepped up his home-run production to thirty, and shared the league's leadership with Cy Williams of the Phillies.

Hack also led the National League that year in striking out, being fanned seventy times. If he felt too badly over this—which is unlikely—he took consolation from the fact that in the same year Babe Ruth fanned eighty-nine times against American League pitching.

The hustling, heads-up type of baseball McCarthy had them playing appealed to Chicago's fans. Attendance went to 886,925 in 1926, and in 1927 it went beyond the million mark for the first time, totaling 1,163,347.

There were other contributing factors. Wrigley and Veeck had been as active in remodeling the ball park as McCarthy was in recasting the ball club. In 1923 the lower grandstand had been subjected to reconstruction. Through 1926 and 1927 the upper deck was the object of the construction gang's efforts.

Wrigley had in mind—as has his son and successor, the present Cub owner, Phillip K. Wrigley—the principle that the customer is always right. This meant that the patron who bought his way into a ball park was entitled to comfort. That comfort, believe it or not, had to include satisfaction with the caliber of baseball the Cubs were playing for him, as well as the neatness of his box, grandstand, or bleacher abiding place, or the spic and span nature of the concession stand where he might refresh himself while on the premises.

There were few complaints against the Cubs as the crowds increased to a new high through 1928. The club itself picked up momentum and took third place in the final National League standings.

It was still going strong through the city series of that year, vanquishing the White Sox in four out of seven games. Winning Cub pitchers were Pat Malone, Guy Bush, and Sheriff Blake (two), while the leading hitter was Hack Wilson with .407—a hint of the shape of Cub things to come.

At the end of the 1928 season, McCarthy, Veeck, and Wrigley, in that order, felt that one more player, preferably a strong-hitting second baseman, was needed to give the Cubs' championship stature. Such a second baseman was Rogers Hornsby, then at Boston, after a spectacular career as player and manager at St. Louis and New York.

As a member of the Cardinals, Hornsby had put together six successive National League batting championships, with averages ranging from .370 to .424. Pitchers in the league had not yet found any way to still his bat, and Hornsby himself wasn't giving any indication of being on the decline. True, he had left St. Louis after managing the Cardinals to the first world's championship of their careers. He was reported to have had trouble with the management at New York, his next abiding place. And now, all wasn't supposed to be serene at Boston, whence the Giants had sent him.

Hornsby then, was the player who might well give the Cubs that championship touch. So Veeck went forth to see what dealing could be done.

There wasn't a great deal of the "wait till I talk it over with the boss" about Veeck or McCarthy. When the deal with Boston was proposed, Wrigley didn't expect to hear from either until it was closed. However, the deal grew in magnitude as it was discussed. Eventually Veeck felt it wise to call up Wrigley and discuss with him some of the phases of the haggling that was going on.

"You want him, don't you?" asked Wrigley.

Veeck admitted that he did.

"McCarthy wants him, doesn't he?" asked Wrigley.

Veeck said he was sure about that, too.

"Well, I certainly want him," said Wrigley. "So get him."

Never a word about probable cost. That didn't enter into Wrigley's calculations, at all.

Veeck went back and closed the deal. The record books set forth that Rogers Hornsby came to the Cubs in exchange for five players and $200,000 cash. The five players is correct. They were second baseman Freddie Maguire, catcher "Doc" Leggett, and pitchers Percy Jones, Harry Seibold, and Bruce Cunningham.

The actual cash in the transaction was $120,000 and not $200,000. However, it was a sum greater than had been paid for any other ballplayer, up to that time. The estimated value of the five players was not a great deal. They had not done much for the Cubs, and they did not combine to make the Braves any more formidable than they had been before the trade was arranged.

Thus entered into the Cub ranks one of the greatest of all National League players, in name as well as in fact.

Here was a personality the like of which the Cubs had never known before. Not all of them were to adjust themselves to Hornsby's ways at once, or ever. He was the type who said what he thought, when he thought it. As player, manager, coach, or in whatever other position he has occupied in baseball or out of it, if he liked something, he said so, and if he disliked something, he said so. But in either case what he said went. He wasn't one to retract or to apologize. In his competitive years, tact was something Hornsby hadn't learned.

He was one more very high-salaried artist added to a cast which even then must have made up a pay roll perhaps as high as a major-league club's ever gets. But he was what McCarthy,

Veeck, and above all, Wrigley wanted. He was what they got at a price for which no complaint has yet been made.

The advent of Hornsby set the pennant bee buzzing in Chicago that winter and early spring. The Cubs had finished third in 1928, a bit behind the Giants, who in turn trailed the Cardinals at the finish by two games. However, the champion Cardinals had been set upon in the world series by those Yankee maulers and were slaughtered in four straight games, Babe Ruth winding up the one-sided show with three terrific homers in the fourth and final game.

It was National League history, by this time, that any one of its champions subjected to a going over in the world series by the Yankees was unlikely to recover from it in time to be much use in the following season. Pittsburgh, trounced in four straight by Ruth and Company in 1927, hadn't. So why should the Cardinals?

So the Cubs and their followers could see a pennant right ahead. No doubt Wrigley could, too, for he was with the first squad of Cubs who went to his beloved Catalina to start training that spring of 1929.

The trip across the channel was made on the *Catalina*. It was the custom of the ballplayers, or at least all of those who weren't subject to *mal de mer,* to sun themselves on the upper deck during the two hours it required to sail from the mainland to Avalon. Because of that, they were to witness an incident which had no ulterior meaning whatsoever, but which some of the veteran Cub busybodies were to remember in the days to come.

In their own way, a great many of those Cubs of the spring of 1929 had been heroes and were regarded as important as well as valuable baseball property. However, none of them had ever been invited to accompany Wrigley on the bridge of the *Catalina*. But Hornsby made it. First time out. He was up there with Wrigley and the captain of the steamer in plain sight of one and all.

Now Hornsby was the last man on that ship who would want himself to be considered the precedent-establisher. But that's the way it was. Everybody suspected then that of all who had wanted Hornsby as a member of the champions to be, it was Wrigley who had wanted him most.

Though Wrigley got what he had paid for, a championship, in the very first season Hornsby was with the Cubs, the road to the pennant wasn't smooth all the way. At the very outset Gabby Hartnett, the catching mainstay, hurt his throwing arm, and he was of little use the entire season. In July the Cubs were able to make a deal with the Braves for catcher Zack Taylor, and he filled in most capably the rest of the way, when Cub power and pitching enabled the club to shake the rest of the field. The championship race ended with the Cubs ten and a half games ahead of Pittsburgh, and leading the hitters was Hornsby with .380.

Charley Root's nineteen victories and six defeats were the most productive of the league's pitching for the season, though for the Cubs' purposes Pat Malone and Guy Bush were most effective.

Hack Wilson batted in 159 runs that year. He was so eagle-eyed at the plate that he fanned but eighty-three times, as contrasted with his ninety-four of the 1928 season when he set up a mark that was going to endure until another Cub, Dolph Camilli, came along six years later to equal it.

Hack went his own way, as usual. There is no evidence that he modeled his deportment or his appetites after Hornsby, though many of the other Cubs did, especially those who were convinced that Hornsby's hitting secret was an addiction to succulent steaks.

No matter in what town Hornsby found himself, he either knew, or found out very soon where the best steak was being broiled. In Los Angeles the first spring he was with the Cubs, he discovered a lunch wagon in an otherwise vacant lot not far from the hotel at which the club stayed. He made his discovery known, and night after night the hotel's dining room was remarkably free from Cubs as they rushed to the lunch wagon to get first search on the steaks.

When you are told that in the spring-training time it is the custom for the players to sign checks, the meals being on the club when the eating is done in the hotel, you will appreciate the strain this Hornsby steak diet must have put upon them. Especially when it is known that a great many of the Cubs of that time, however great their salaries, were very cagey about parting with any money unless the emergency was grave indeed.

That may have been the reason why many of those Cubs never did fully understand Hornsby, or he them. For Hornsby was definitely of the school of thought that "you can't take it with you." So was Hack Wilson, though his study of the subject was along lines greatly different from Hornsby's, as both reached the same conclusion.

Whatever their dietary or monetary standards, these Cubs were a ripsnorting team which played its baseball for all it was worth. Small wonder then that Chicago went completely overboard for it, setting up a seasonal attendance record of 1,489,632.

In this highly productive season it was more of a novelty for a game to be played, weekday or Sunday, without an overflow crowd on the field than with one.

There was another new phenomenon which didn't hurt the Cubs' home attendance any: the broadcasting of the home games. Broadcasting baseball from Wrigley Field began in 1925, and was continued over the protest of some of the Cubs' rival clubs in the west, notably St. Louis.

In the original broadcasting state, the pioneer announcer worked from a place within earshot of the press box. Some of the descriptions of plays and players that went out over the air were not always what the baseball writers were jotting down in their scorebooks, or creating into deathless prose on their portable typewriters.

It wasn't at Wrigley Field, but in Forbes Field, Pittsburgh, that Ring Lardner had his say on the subject of a baseball broadcast from within sound range of a press box. But it might well have been. Since Ring plied his writing trade along with Cubs and White Sox at one stage of his career, the incident might as well be set forth here.

Lardner was attending a world series game at Pittsburgh and

the luck of the draw placed him right next to Graham Mac-Namee, who was giving out with all his eloquence as only MacNamee could. About the fifth inning of the game, Lardner excused himself to Grantland Rice, who was his next-door neighbor on the other side.

"I am going back to the hotel," he said. "It is asking too much of me to keep track of two games, the one I am seeing out on the field and the one I am hearing."

The broadcasting of baseball out of Wrigley Field was something else again. Once started, it became a "must." At one time no less than five Chicago stations were on the air daily with the ball games. And it did help stir up trade for the Cubs, as the following figures make clear:

(1) From 1918–24 with a club that averaged fourth place in the National League standings, the Cubs for that seven-year period drew 3,585,439 patrons.

(2) From 1925–31 with a club that averaged fourth place in the National League standings, the Cubs for that seven-year period drew 7,845,700 patrons.

That represents a gain of 119 per cent. Over the same period the other seven clubs in the league gained 27 per cent in their home attendance.

There was one other factor in the increase of interest in the Cubs and their doings at Wrigley Field: Ladies' Day. Now this gesture of setting aside an afternoon each week in which the gentler sex might watch a ball game as guests of the club had been tried by the Chicago National League club as far back as the days of Pop Anson. But until Wrigley took over the Cubs, it was more or less a gesture.

Wrigley not only invited 'em out, he practically insisted on it. Since there has never been anyone concerned with the presentation of major-league baseball wiser to the ways of promotional advertising than the Wrigleys, not even a sale of nylons in early 1946 was as productive of mass turnouts of women as were these Ladies' Days at Wrigley Field.

They were booming in 1929, but it was not until June 6, 1930, that the peak was reached. On that day there were 51,556 persons in Wrigley Field, whose normal capacity wasn't quite 40,000. Of that 51,556 persons, 30,476 were ladies, guests of the management.

By that time the club was supplying its lady guests with tickets through three downtown outlets, since there was almost a panic each Friday when they all swarmed around the many gates of Wrigley Field on the "just show up and walk in" basis. By 1931 the club had to change the rules again, and ask the ladies to write in for a ticket, enclosing a self-addressed stamped envelope.

That cooled their ardor somewhat, but an average Ladies' Day at Wrigley Field still gets a notable quota of the gals who begin to shriek at the first foul ball and keep right on until the last man is retired.

The way Wrigley foresaw it, an adequate proportion of those ladies would come back to see ball games one day other than Fridays—and more often than not, bring the old man or the boy friend along with them.

Or even if they didn't, there were enough of them who appeared on Fridays and, having been admitted, as Doc Lotshaw put it, "free of gratis," were ready, willing, and anxious to pay the additional tariff and sit in box seats, of which Wrigley Field has more, proportionately, than any other ball park in the major leagues.

It was in this 1929 setting, and with that 1929 ball club that Wrigley gained his first objective, a National League championship. That was only half the battle. What Wrigley wanted most was a world's championship. And that, the Cubs set out to try to get for him on October 8, the series opening in Chicago.

⊗ XXII ⊗

THOSE CHAMPIONSHIP BLUES

ELEVEN YEARS HAD ELAPSED BETWEEN THE TIME FRED Mitchell's Cubs had lost the championship touch and the Cubs of Joe McCarthy had recaptured it.

Many stirring events had taken place in baseball in the interval. The Giants, for instance, had succeeded in winning four league championships in a row, breaking Frank Chance's record with the Cubs, and had put world's championships at the end of the first two.

Brooklyn's Leon Cadore and Boston's Joe Oeschger had gone twenty-six innings to a 1–1 tie for baseball's longest major-league game.

There had been an unassisted triple play in the 1920 world series by Cleveland's Bill Wambsganss, and a home run with the bases filled in the same year by Elmer Smith. All this against the Brooklyn Dodgers.

Baseball's first million-dollar gates for world series play had begun in 1923, and presently became commonplace. Similarly individual shares of winning players in the series went up and up until if a cut of more than $5,000 wasn't registered, some one of the athletes was bound to start wondering where the customers were.

It was during this eleven-year stretch that Babe Ruth lofted out his record sixty home runs as his 1927 season's work.

Many great events had come to pass since the Cubs had last faced an opponent from the American League with baseball's title at stake. But in the last analysis, things hadn't changed a bit for the Cubs in eleven years. Or even in nineteen, for it had been that long since they last met a team of Connie Mack's.

The Athletics had run away with the American League race, finishing eighteen games in front of the second place Yankees, who had begun to grow old not too gracefully. The Cubs' National League winning margin, ten and a half games over Pittsburgh, seemed modest by comparison.

Connie Mack was operating that season with two great pitchers, the left-hander, Bob Grove, and the right-hander, George Earnshaw. Not too far off the pace of either was another left-hander, Rube Walberg.

As the clubs prepared to open the series in Chicago, most of the speculation centered around which one of these three Connie would choose to open against the Cubs.

On the Athletics' pay roll and listed as a pitcher, was the veteran, Howard Ehmke. He had appeared in only fifty-five innings during the course of the campaign. To the amazement of all, and as it developed, to the utter befuddlement of the Cubs, it was neither Grove nor Earnshaw, but Ehmke who started the series—and probably finished it. For after striking out thirteen of the free-swinging Cubs and shutting them out until the last inning when they moved Kiki Cuyler across, Ehmke's 3–1 victory set the National Leaguers back on their heels. They were still rocking when the series came to an end, though it must be said that the hardy Athletics landed many another jolt on vulnerable Cub spots before the finish.

Charley Root, the Cubs' and the National League's leading pitcher for the year, drew the assignment against Ehmke. Root pitched a magnificent game, but when he left in the seventh for a pinch hitter, the Athletics had a run, which was enough to cost Root the game. A pair were added in the ninth off Guy Bush.

Jimmy Foxx crashed through with a home run for the Athletics, but the power of the Cubs, bound up in Rogers Hornsby and Hack Wilson, was stopped completely. Neither made a hit, and both furnished their share of Ehmke's thirteen strike-outs. Woody English, who doubled for one of his two hits, was the only Cub able to add an extra base to any of the eight safeties Ehmke allowed.

For the games at Wrigley Field, the city of Chicago had graciously consented to let the Cubs expand their bleacher seating arrangement above and beyond the outfield walls, and thus 50,740 were able to witness the downfall of the local prides.

In the second game the Cubs did not curb their passion for striking out, but they did do some more robust hitting against George Earnshaw than they had been able to do against Ehmke. However, even though they drove Big George out with a shower of three runs in the fifth, the Athletics had already pounded Pat Malone and Sheriff Blake for six runs, getting three in the third and again in the fourth.

When Earnshaw was taken out as a precautionary measure, Grove finished up the game, adding six strike-outs to the seven Earnshaw had registered, so that the Cubs again had fanned thirteen times in a world series ball game, proving that what had been a new record only the day before, now threatened to become a habit.

The final score of this game was 9–3 in the Athletics' favor, Hal Carlson having been tapped for a run in the seventh and two in the eighth.

Al Simmons, Foxx, and Jimmy Dykes led the attack on McCarthy's pitchers, with Foxx getting his second homer of the series, and Simmons his first. Simmons drove in four runs, Foxx three.

Hack Wilson came out of the ether in this game and secured three hits, none of which figured in the meager Cub scoring.

With the Athletics on top by two games, the series then turned to Philadelphia. Earnshaw was sent back into action again, and though he added ten more strike-outs to the growing number the Cubs were piling up, he wasn't able to make it three victories in a row for his side. Guy Bush was in command at all times, save when Bing Miller drove Mickey Cochrane over in the fifth inning to establish a 1–0 Athletic lead.

In the very next inning the Cubs swarmed all over Earnshaw

and scored three runs, Hornsby driving Bush home, and Cuyler getting English and Hornsby over with a timely hit.

This victory for the Cubs seemed to put a different aspect on the series. Certainly there was no reason to suspect in the early innings of the fourth game that the Cubs were not on their way to a one-sided victory which would even up the series.

Jack Quinn, a veteran right-hander, was hammered for seven hits in the first five innings, with the Cubs scoring two runs in the fourth. They picked up a cluster of five runs in the sixth while Rube Walberg was pitching, and added another off Ed Rommel in the seventh. There had been a home run for Charlie Grimm and a triple for Rogers Hornsby—and all the while Charley Root was firing his fast ball past the Athletics, having allowed but three hits in six innings. When the Athletics came to bat for their half of the seventh, the Cubs were leading, 8–0.

Al Simmons, first man up, slammed a fast ball out of the park. Someone was always doing that against Charley Root, especially in a world series game.

"That gives Al two for the series," chortled a Philadelphia sportswriter. "Ties him with Foxx."

Just that—nothing more.

How was even a Philadelphia sports writer to know that Al's homer was the first boulder, rolling down the mountainside, that was to start the avalanche?

Jimmy Foxx singled. So did Bing Miller. Jimmie Dykes singled, and Foxx scored. Oh, well, that made the score 8–2.

Joe Boley singled, scoring Miller. The score was now 8–3, there were two men on base and none out. Maybe this *was* a rally under way.

Connie Mack thought so, for he sent up George Burns to bat for Rommel. Burns lifted a pop up to Woody English. That was one out; but Max Bishop kept the rally going by singling, and Dykes scored the fourth Athletic run of the inning. Joe McCarthy thought it was time then to get Root out of there. Two left-hand hitters, Mule Haas and Mickey Cochrane, were next in line. The Cubs' manager played his percentage and sent out Art Nehf, the slim left-hander, to face these two.

While Nehf was taking his warm-up pitches, one of the returns from catcher Zach Taylor was a trifle high. Art looked up, and as the blazing sun got in his eyes, ducked hastily and the ball went on past him to be retrieved by one of the infielders.

No one paid much attention to that—then. What if the sun is in a direct line from pitcher to catcher? Let's see what the Mule will do to keep this inning alive. The Mule belted a line fly directly into center field. Hack Wilson saw it start, knew it was coming his way, and then proceeded to lose track of it entirely in the sun. The ball went right on by him. When it was finally run down and returned to the infield, there were enough runs across the plate to put the Athletics very much back in the ball game.

They stayed right in it. Cochrane hung around and drew a pass, whereupon Nehf's part in the show was over. He turned his pitching role over to Sheriff Blake, as Simmons came up for the second time. Al hit safely once more, a single this trip, which was promptly matched by Foxx, and the latter's hit put Cochrane across the plate with the tying run.

It looked now as if the Sheriff needed help, so out came Pat Malone to see what he could do. His first effort resulted in Miller's being nailed with a pitched ball, and the bases were filled.

In this spot, with 29,991 persons going fairly batty, Dykes launched a long, high fly to left field, close by the foul line. It looked as if Riggs Stephenson might get under it, but since Stevie's throwing arm wasn't much, there was no possible chance to halt the run scoring from third after the catch. Instead, the ball fell safely, and two runs, represented by Simmons and Foxx, rushed across. The Athletics led 10–8, having gone through the most furious rally any world series inning has ever recorded.

Really it didn't matter after that whether Malone fanned Boley, and Burns, who thus had the unusual fate of having furnished, as a pinch hitter, two of the three outs in the biggest world series inning of all time.

To finish up the ball game, Connie Mack had Bob Grove ready. He breezed through the last two innings. Not a Cub made a hit, and four of them struck out.

Malone came out to pitch the fifth game for the Cubs, and Ehmke, hero of the first game, was given another chance to distinguish himself.

President Herbert Hoover dropped in for this game, and was given a reception by the fans quite unlike any ever accorded any other President out to see a ball game. This, of course, was in 1929.

In the less than four innings Ehmke worked, he fanned no one. He was nicked for six hits, and two of them, sponsored by Grimm and Taylor, were useful in scoring Kiki Cuyler and Stephenson in the fourth inning, when Walberg was called upon to finish out the game.

Walberg held the Cubs safe the rest of the way, but the Athletics made no progress at all for eight innings against Malone. In that time they had been able to get but two hits. Malone seemed to be an even better bet to win by a shutout than Root had been in the fourth game, before the Athletics finally caught up with him.

Walter French batted for Walberg, leading off the Athletics' ninth, and Malone got rid of him. One down, and two to go.

Next came Max Bishop. He singled.

With the Athletic fans roaring for him to do something, Mule Haas gave it his best—a line fly across the right field barrier, and the score was tied.

Malone, never one to have his temper under control, didn't blow up with a bang at this break. He proceeded to retire Mickey Cochrane. Two down, one to go for a tie.

But Malone never did make it. Simmons doubled, and the winning run was on second. Foxx was passed intentionally, being regarded properly enough as more of a menace than Bing Miller. But the proprieties had ceased after that seventh inning in Root's game. *All* Athletics were a menace, and thus, when Miller doubled, scoring Simmons with the winning run, making it 3–2,

116

it was true that while the Cubs, from Wrigley down to the least known member of their great following, must have been disappointed, no one was surprised.

This series, and particularly the seventh inning of the fourth game, was made to order for the second guessers. They lost no time in getting to work. Wilson, the luckless center fielder who had lost a fly ball in the sun, was charged with having blown both game and series. McCarthy came in for his share of criticism because he was unable to stem that seventh inning rally. No one took time out to realize that the pitchers who had been subjected to the going over were the best McCarthy had.

There was scant satisfaction for Cubs to be derived from the fact that Wilson's .471 average led hitters on both sides in this memorable series.

Everybody in Chicago was mad—and kept getting madder.

Everybody had something to say—and said it.

⊗ XXIII ⊗

THERE'LL BE SOME CHANGES MADE

ALL WINTER LONG THAT 1929 WORLD SERIES WAS GIVEN A kicking around. That William Wrigley, Jr., was bitterly disappointed is putting it mildly. Whether there were words between him and Manager McCarthy, or between President Bill Veeck and McCarthy, no one can say for sure.

However, it can now be revealed here that on the way to the training camp at Catalina in the spring of 1930, McCarthy confided to one sports writer that win, lose, or draw, he would not be with the Cubs for longer than the current season—if that long. The sports writer was asked not to print it—and hasn't, until now.

The Cubs went through a rigorous training schedule and performed capably enough in the regular season to give rise to hopes that they would win another championship.

For all of the irritation shown over the 1929 world series disaster, the fans kept on coming out to Wrigley Field. Maybe they were now rolling lemons out on the field whenever Hack Wilson came to bat. Maybe, as was broadly hinted, Wilson didn't care much about Rogers Hornsby, or the other way around. The little round man was doing his darnedest to square himself with Joe McCarthy for any possible hurt the losing of that fly ball in the Philadelphia sun may have caused.

He finished up the season with 56 home runs, a National League record. He drove home 190 runs, a major-league record; and he drew 105 bases on balls.

Whether they accepted Wilson as the great ballplayer he

really was in those two years with the Cubs, or whether they came out simply to get some laughs, it is a matter of record that in 1930 the Cub attendance was 1,467,881, less than 20,000 drop from the all-time high of the year before, and Hack Wilson merited top billing.

Over in the American League, Bob Shawkey was acting as stopgap manager of the New York Yankees during 1930, following the death of Miller Huggins. The Yankees were going nowhere, and apparently neither was Shawkey. So one day, the sports writer who was keeping secret the fact that Joe McCarthy wasn't going to be with the Cubs for 1931 had an idea.

He ran across George Perry in New York, Perry being a confidant of Colonel Jacob Ruppert, the Yankee owner.

"Would the Colonel like to have Joe McCarthy manage his ball club?" Perry was asked.

"Are you nuts?" responded Perry. "Wrigley would never let him get away."

"If he did let him get away, would the Colonel want him?" the sports writer persisted.

"I'll find out," said Perry, and did. He announced that the Colonel had chased him out of the Ruppert brewery.

"He said Wrigley was a great friend of his," Perry said. "He said Wrigley would never let McCarthy go. He said I was crazy. He ran me out."

"But he didn't say he wouldn't take McCarthy if he could get him," persisted the sports writer.

"No," admitted Perry. "He didn't say that."

The sports writer took a trip up to Ruppert's brewery, told Colonel Ruppert what facts he had at his disposal, and subsequently returned to Chicago.

The Cubs were then in residence. The sports writer eased himself into the corner of the dugout where McCarthy was seated, and talked about pennant chances, the weather, and other things. Finally. . . .

"Would you like to manage the Yankees?"

"Who wouldn't?" asked McCarthy. "Why?"

"Oh, nothing," said the sports writer, and returned to his own business.

There have been a great many accounts of the manner in which Joe McCarthy made the switch from Chicago to New York, from the National League to the American. The one just related happens to be correct, and indeed, well-nigh complete—save for the following few details: There was a long-distance phone call to George Perry, telling him that if Colonel Ruppert ever let him back in the brewery, not to go out until he had established that McCarthy could be had. There was a mutual waiving of the priorities Bob Quinn of Boston seemed to have on McCarthy's services, if and when he ever left Chicago. There was an undisclosed meeting between Ruppert and Wrigley in which the latter gave his blessings to McCarthy's move.

In late September McCarthy's resignation as manager of the Cubs was accepted, Wrigley and Veeck having acceded to the mutterings of many disappointed fans.

Rogers Hornsby was placed in charge of the team, which yielded to a late season rush of the St. Louis Cardinals and finished second, two games behind the pennant winners.

It was while the Athletics were cleaning up the Cardinals in the world series that McCarthy's managerial deal with the Yankees reached the official announcement stage. But the Cubs had not seen the last of the manager who had restored them to winning ways after the lean years following Frank Chance's triumphant era.

The Cardinals and the Athletics were to monopolize the baseball headlines for the 1931 season. The best the Cubs could do was gain third place, but in 1932, driven hard by Hornsby, they began to perk up again.

There were tales told all season long of difficulties between Hornsby and his men, and of difficulties which were Hornsby's own. Always a horse-player, which he maintained was his own business, and which he certainly did not attempt to keep secret, Hornsby's activities with the bookmakers were brought into open discussion by some of the sports writers.

It is very improbable that any of these activities had much to do with his ultimate dismissal by Bill Veeck, and they certainly could not have disturbed John O. Seys, who had been a race writer in his newspaper days and maintained a conservative interest in the thoroughbreds throughout his lifetime.

There were tales told of money borrowed and money lent which were also advanced as reasons why the Cubs were in an uproar. Again, that had very little to do with Hornsby's inability to direct the Club to Veeck's satisfaction.

There is no question but that Veeck criticized Hornsby's judgment on the matter of handling pitchers, and Hornsby was never one to let such criticism go by unanswered. It was this, no doubt, which caused Veeck finally to throw the weight of his office into the argument; and when he pulled rank on the manager, that was the end of the manager.

As has been the case of many star ballplayers who have essayed managing, Hornsby was impatient with some of his material. His own playing standards were so high, and some things came so naturally and so easily to him that he was at a loss to understand why others were unable to grasp their lessons and remember them.

As a player and as a manager, Hornsby never failed to speak his mind out. Many of the Cubs didn't like that, and while some of them openly resented it, others preferred to sulk and feel very unhappy about it all.

It is pertinent to this story to mention that long after he had concluded his career in professional baseball, an older and a wiser Hornsby, still loving the game, became an instructor of youthful ballplayers in Chicago, under the direction of the *Daily News,* and his effort at starting off the youngsters along the right paths to baseball success is one of the soundest looking-forward movements baseball has had in many a year.

On August 2 Bill Veeck turned the management over to Charlie Grimm.

All the Cubs who didn't like Hornsby, or said they didn't, liked Grimm immensely, and pulled themselves together and went

on to win a pennant. Billy Herman, a newcomer from Louisville, took over the spot at second base where Hornsby once had
seemed master of all he surveyed.

This was not a great ball club which won the National League
pennant in 1932. But it must have been fate that it happened to
be the Cubs, for over in the American League Joe McCarthy had
found the range in his second year as manager. His Yankees won
107 games, turning back the bid of the Athletics for four straight
championships. This was something McCarthy was reserving
for himself, in the years to come.

By contrast, the Cubs' winning average was .584. Only
Hornsby's Cardinals, pennant winners in 1928, had ever gained
a National League championship with a lower figure. However,
those .578 Cardinals had outlasted the mighty Yankees in the
world series, so the Cubs and their fans were mildly hopeful that
history would repeat.

It didn't. McCarthy had a great ball club. It had tremendous
power; it had pitching; it had defensive strength. It had, from
Babe Ruth down to the lowliest of the uniformed group, as fine a
set of masters of the insult as the game has ever known.

And as it happened, the Cubs themselves had furnished some
of the best material for bench-jockeying. When Hornsby departed, the Cubs, many of whom were elated, ignored him in the
clubhouse vote on splitting the players' end of the series receipts.

Perhaps the Yankees would have overlooked that. But in
August the Cubs had rescued from the San Francisco Missions,
Mark Koenig, an infielder who had been with the Yankees for
six seasons. Koenig's play, particularly at bat through August and
September, was truly sensational. In thirty-three games he batted
.353, and many of his hits, from singles to homers, had been the
medium of winning badly needed games.

Indeed, there were many who felt that without Koenig, the
Cubs wouldn't have won the pennant at all. To him, in the distribution of world series loot, went a half share.

While the world series lasted, and any Cubs were within earshot, the Yankees refused to let them hear the last of that mis-

guided departure from generosity. There wasn't very much the Cubs could do about it by way of retaliation. Every time they turned around, Lou Gehrig or Babe Ruth was knocking a ball out of the lot. Or Tony Lazzeri was.

Even Lon Warneke, a first-full-season sensation among National League pitchers, was not immune. Though Warneke had won twenty-two games and lost but six in his own league, and had led it with a 2.37 earned-run average, the Yankees swept over him as they did any of the seven Cub pitchers who found their way in and out of the series.

Gehrig was the worst disturber of the Cubs' peace and quiet. He made nine hits for an average of .529 in the four games the series lasted. He had three home runs and a double. He walked twice. He scored nine runs himself and drove in eight more. Only once did he strike out.

Guy Bush was the first pitcher to get in the way of the Yankee blasts. He was driven out in the sixth inning of the first game. Burleigh Grimes lasted less than two, and Bob Smith finished up the game. Bush and Grimes fell heir to the heaviest pounding, the Yankees getting five in the sixth, and three in the seventh, as they rolled to a 12–6 win.

Warneke started the second game, and was the only Cub hurler in the entire series who finished what he started. But he had to yield, 5–2, to Vernon Gomez, and in the course of the production every Yankee save Gomez and Frank Crosetti made at least one safe hit. No one hit any home runs in this engagement, but Lou Gehrig's three hits, Bill Dickey's two, and a timely single by Ben Chapman, gave the Yankees runs to spare. They picked up two in the first inning to establish a lead, and went on from there.

These first two games were played at New York, and then the series moved to Wrigley Field. The Cubs were talking to themselves by this time, and were positively in awe of the Yankee power.

However, they were able to put up something of a battle in game three, actually having the score tied at 4–4 as late as the fourth inning. In the next the Yankees came through with two runs, and were not headed thereafter, winning 7–5.

This was the famous game in which Babe Ruth, legend has it, called his home-run shot against Charley Root. The Babe had been in good voice throughout the series, and especially in this game. The Cubs in their own way had hurled epithets at him, and a good time was being had by all.

Ruth came to bat in the fifth inning. Root fired a strike past him. The Babe held up one finger. Root let fly with another pitch. Another strike. Again the Babe held up a finger.

There are those who will always contend that what the Babe did this third time was point out toward the center field corner, as Root prepared to pitch.

They will contend further that as the pitch came up to him (and in this cannot be contradicted), that Ruth whaled away at it, and the last glimpse anyone in the park had of that baseball was when it dropped over the fence just beyond where the Babe had pointed.

That's the legend, and there are those who can add all sorts of flourishes to it.

Whether Ruth pointed at Root, pointed at the fence, or whether he remembered his manners and didn't point at all, but merely indicated that there were two strikes on him and he still had the big one left, is something that will not be debated here. Indeed, it will not be examined any more closely than the claims of *seven* separate persons, outside Wrigley Field after the game, each one exhibiting a baseball which he insisted was the one Ruth hit.

However it be told, or whatever its facts, it was and is a good story. So was the home run. So was the one Lou Gehrig made right after it. Or either of the other homers Ruth and Gehrig each made in the game. For that matter, for Cub purposes, there was nothing wrong with the home runs Gabby Hartnett and Kiki Cuyler each made in that game. Only no one ever tells about them, or elaborates upon them.

That Babe Ruth had a way with him, you know.

The closing game of the series was turned over to Johnny Allen as the Yankee pitcher. He was spotted to a run off Guy Bush in the opening inning, but as soon as the Cubs came to bat they proceeded to get to him for four runs and five hits before Manager McCarthy sent Wilcy Moore to the rescue.

Warneke, who relieved Bush in the first inning, was clouted for two runs in the third, and Jakie May held forth until the seventh. The Yankees made two off him in the sixth which gave them the lead, but the Cubs promptly tied it in their half.

In the seventh the Yankees wound up and let 'em have it for keeps, scoring four runs, to which they added another cluster of four in the ninth, off Bud Tinning and Grimes. The final score was 13–6.

Home-run production for this game was taken care of by Tony Lazzeri (two), Earl Combs, and for the lost cause of the Cubs, Frank Demaree.

Four straight victories for the Yankees, the first world series for the Cubs in which they had been unable to win at least one game. Joe McCarthy must have been satisfied with it, even if the Cubs were not.

And being baseball fans, many of the Cubs patrons who had been most violent in berating McCarthy for the way he ran the club in the 1929 world series, now exercised their second guessing prerogative and allowed that they always knew Wrigley and Veeck had made a mistake when they let McCarthy get away.

⊗ *XXIV* ⊗

SECOND GUESSERS TAKE OVER

IN THE YEARS IMMEDIATELY FOLLOWING THE WORLD SERIES disaster of 1932 the Cubs were to go through a long stretch in which something akin to chaos had come again.

The simpler form of club operation which had been in vogue during the William Wrigley–Bill Veeck era—the Cubs' most prosperous stretch—was abandoned in part when Wrigley's death occurred in early 1932.

Ownership of all the Wrigley properties, of which the Cubs were but one, passed on to his son, Phillip K. Wrigley, who had given no public evidence until then that the Cubs, or baseball, bothered him much one way or another. Besides, the amount of detail connected with the gum business, the Catalina affairs, a hotel in Arizona, and sundry other activities were more than enough to keep P. K. busy in his every waking moment. He was content to let Veeck go on with the front-office management of the Cubs, though then, and for many years prior to his father's death, P. K. had sat in conference with him and Veeck on baseball affairs.

Veeck was now more determined than ever to bring a world's championship to Chicago. The most direct route, he believed, after surveying the Yankee power in the world series, was through increased batting strength. That as much as anything is how the Cubs, prior to the 1933 season, happened to reach out and deal with Cincinnati for the colorful Babe Herman. The Babe's eccentricities, real or imaginary, while associated with the Brooklyn Dodgers, had gained him wide attention. But he could hit a baseball, and the Cubs were willing to take a chance that one day he might slam a ball to the outfield and suddenly break for third base instead of first.

Veeck was not fated to know whether Babe Herman was what the Cubs needed or not. The most forceful of all Cub presidents up to that time died during 1933—and with his passing, there settled upon the Cubs a period of inner operations so strange that they challenged, at times, even the most unpredictable of Babe Herman's base running antics for first place in the "What's coming off next?" class.

To get Herman, four players and a sizable amount of cash had gone to Cincinnati. Where he definitely fits into the Cub picture is that his deal was the first of many in the next several years which were to establish the Cubs, in the minds of the second guessers at least, as being utterly lacking in judgment or luck, or perhaps both. Neither his bat nor his personality was to avail the Cubs much in 1933. The best the club could do was finish in third place, the Giants having resumed their winning ways that year.

The Babe's flair for the eccentric was not particularly noticeable during his stay with the Cubs. Indeed, in his weirdest flights he was not able to match some of the antics of another outfielder, a youngster, who was to join the Cubs in the spring of 1934. (But more of that young man later.) If any biographer ever gets around to the writing of Babe Herman, His Life and Times, it is possible that the only incident which will be taken from his Cub career is one which had as its setting a ball park in San Antonio.

The Cubs were there for a spring exhibition game or two on their way back from Catalina Island. In that particular year baseball in San Antonio was being played in a park which had a very short right field fence. It was so short that a marker was placed on it, halfway out toward center field. Baseballs hit over the fence between that marker and the right field foul line went for two bases. Those hit over the fence on the other side of the marker were ruled home runs. Beyond the fence was a row of residences, each with a yard. Then came a street, more residences, more yards, and another street.

At a not too critical point in the game, Herman came to bat, got a pitch inside and to his fancy. He really teed off on that one. It soared over the right field fence, over the first row of houses and the first street, and landed upon the roof of one of the houses in the second row. It is doubtful if Babe Ruth, Lou Gehrig, Hack Wilson, or any of the other long-distance hitters in all baseball history ever knocked one any farther than that drive of Babe Herman's.

You have guessed it. It cleared the ball park fence on the wrong side of the marker. It went for just two bases. Things like that could happen only to Babe Herman.

When Veeck's death occurred, the presidential chair was taken over by William H. Walker. He was a holdover from the Federal League days and had joined the party when Charles Weeghman had taken over. Walker's holdings in the Cubs were of some size. His was to be an eventful term of office, though it was comparatively brief.

When the Cubs fell behind in the 1933 pennant race, there was the usual uproar in Chicago. During the season there was ample reason to suspect that the club had lost much of its customer appeal. The home attendance for the year was but 594,879, a drop of almost 400,000 from the pennant-winning season previous. And they didn't all stay away because they didn't like Babe Herman.

In an effort to stir up the club and fans alike, a deal of tremendous proportions was engineered with the Phillies, whose right fielder, Chuck Klein, had been adjudged the league's most valuable player in 1932. His .368 average led the National League hitters in 1933, so Klein was a natural for the Cubs' purchasing department. He came to Chicago in exchange for three players, one of them Mark Koenig, and a sum of cash estimated at $65,000.

Again the Cubs' ill luck in the matter of player deals was manifested. Early in his career with them Klein became afflicted with the muscular knots known as a "charley horse." It was so resistant to all the ministrations of trainer Doc Lotshaw that that worthy finally confided to Manager Grimm he was afraid Chuck's ailment was "chronicle." No charley horse in all base-ball history could compare with the knots Doc Lotshaw could tie in the English language.

A mildly profane man, Lotshaw seldom invoked the Deity. He was asked about that one day by a curious interviewer who wanted to know if Doc didn't believe in God.

"In course," said Lotshaw. "What do you think I am—an amethyst?"

There was some talk each spring of attempting to get Doc Lotshaw a match with Sam Goldwyn, but somehow it always fell through.

But to return to Klein—

In his years with the Phillies while he had been using his bat against the Cubs, they had no worthy left-hand pitcher to send against him. Perhaps left-handed pitching didn't disturb Chuck's calm while he was a Philly. Very early in his stay with the Cubs, however, it was found out that he was far from a .368 hitter or even a .300 hitter against left-handed pitching.

Doubtless his ailments bothered him, but the erstwhile free and easy Klein was also disturbed by the pressure that was on him as a member of a high-pressure club such as the Cubs. He said so very frankly, pointing out that while he had been with the Phillies no one paid much attention whether he hit or didn't hit.

"Here," he said, "they watch you on every pitch."

It did make a difference. Klein finished his first year with the Cubs with a .301 average, more than thirty-five points lower than any other annual mark he had made in his six years with the Phillies.

He didn't help the Cubs to a pennant that year. They finished third once more, as the Cardinals' Gas House Gang rollicked their way to the title.

Klein, according to the exacting standards of the Cub followers, was a bit of a bust. Yet the deal for him and its aftermath didn't create anywhere near as much furor pro and con as did another transaction with the Phillies in the middle of the 1934 season.

Late in 1933 the Cubs had acquired from Sacramento first baseman Dolph Camilli. He began the 1934 season as the regular first baseman and was doing reasonably well. Then on the afternoon of June 11 it became known suddenly that Camilli had been traded to the Phillies for Don Hurst.

To this day there are Cub fans who are trying to find out what brought on that one. Its repercussions were such that eventually William Walker, the club's president, was carried away. His stock was purchased by Wrigley, who became the actual working head of the organization.

Again it seems proper to take testimony from an eyewitness in treating of this incredible deal. Grimm, the Cubs' manager, had discussed with Walker several weeks earlier the possibility of getting another first baseman. Camilli was striking out a lot—he managed to lead the league in that department some years—and there were some fielding flaws which Grimm, the stylist, detected. However, no particular first baseman was considered.

One afternoon when the Cubs were not scheduled, Grimm and his family visted the Century of Progress. Returning to his home late that afternoon, Grimm answered a phone call from a Chicago newspaperman who wanted to know if it was true that Camilli had been traded for Hurst.

"It was news to me," says Grimm, "but I was in a helluva spot. If he had been, and I said he hadn't, I'd be a liar. If I said I didn't know anything about it, he'd think I was either lying or was an awful dummy. So I had to stall, and explained that I had just come in and I'd call him right back and so on. Then I had a helluva time trying to find Walker. I finally got his chauffeur on the phone and asked him. The chauffeur confirmed the deal and then very graciously permitted me to talk to Walker.

"We had some words about it, but there was nothing I could do, then. If there is any blame coming over the deal I'm as much in it as Walker was.

"Walker was a tough man to get along with. He was a fan first and a president afterwards. I don't know how many times he fired me after we'd lose a game. Then we'd get together for dinner and everything would be straightened out until we lost another one. Then he'd fire me again.

"It got so for a time I was afraid to go to the phone at night after we blew one. If Lillian, my wife, answered the phone and said it was Walker, I'd tell her to get the trunk packed, 'cause here we'd go again."

Camilli eventually went on to Brooklyn from the Phillies and had many fine seasons. Each time he hit a home run or distinguished himself otherwise, there were Cub fans who resumed talking to themselves about his having been traded for Hurst— a perfectly harmless sort—especially to opposing pitchers—who wouldn't go a step out of his way lest he might harm a baseball innocently rolling on its way to a base hit.

The Chicago sports writers were pulling no punches now as they second-guessed right along on everything the Cubs did—or did not. Writers in other major-league cities, and even as far off as Los Angeles, where the Wrigleys had owned the club since 1921, joined in the general clamor. They made a great deal of the fact that the Cubs, whoever ran them, or whoever played with them, possessed one degree of consistency. Even when they were right, they were wrong.

Four times since 1908, it was pointed out, the Cubs had been able to win National League pennants, yet each time they collapsed under world series pressure. But until 1932 no club had been able to drub them in four straight world series games.

If anyone of the best friends and severest critics were reminded of the fact that Pittsburgh, St. Louis, and even one of Connie Mack's storied Athletic teams had also blown four straight games in the world series, they didn't mention it.

Contemporary critics of the Cubs' fortunes were maintaining that the club was operating on a "win or else" basis. It is difficult to reconcile that belief with the facts gleaned from a survey of either of the Wrigleys' personal activities with respect to the club.

In many cases the hostile criticism was inspired by writers who earlier had let their own enthusiasm mislead them into seeing possibilities in players which the players didn't really possess at all. Rather than admit their own bad judgment, the sports writers proceeded to put the blast on ownership, management, and players who had let them down. There is no one quite as irritable as a sports writer who has taken what he considers a very comfortable seat on the end of a very long limb and suddenly has that limb collapse under him.

These factors undoubtedly had their effect on making the Cubs the one team in Chicago toward whose activities no fan was neutral. He was either for the Cubs or against them. No middle of the road here; not after 1932; not as late as 1945. In sports page, radio, taproom, or greenroom discussion, there was no "so what?" attitude toward the Cubs. This mystery grows deeper when it is contrasted with the limited expression of sentiment for or against Chicago's other major-league club, the White Sox. A long line of White Sox failures since the baseball tragedy of the 1919 world series never has roused any Chicago fan or sports writer to a fever pitch, demanding that something be done. It could be, of course, that the White Sox followers have been too busy investigating what's wrong with the Cubs, or advancing their own theories, of which there have been almost as many as there are fans in Chicago.

P. K. Wrigley's own idea with regard to this phenomenon is that fan opinion, and to some extent press opinion, has been based on the premise that his club was designed to exploit the gum business, which doesn't happen to be true, and that there has been a tremendous fortune ever available for Cub use.

"People imagine," he says, "that because the Wrigley Gum Company shows profits, that money should be the ball club's for the asking. I imagine they felt the same way about Colonel Ruppert's running the Yankees as a means of exploiting his brewery, or Powel Crossley running the Reds to exploit his radio properties.

"However, there are a great many stockholders in the Wrigley

132

Gum Company who would be the first to complain if any of their money was used in baseball. So none of it ever has been used for that purpose, or ever will.

"We aim to have the Cubs pay their own way, just as if they were my only interest. In this the Cubs are no different from any other major-league club whose owners have no outside interests.

"Actually the Cubs do make their way on their own, too; but it is hard to get anyone to believe that this is so."

It has been related that Colonel Ruppert was most exacting in his demands from the Yankees. In the closing weeks of the 1932 season, when the Yankees were in front by seventeen games or so, and needed only another win or two to cinch the pennant, they came to Detroit and lost the first game of a series there.

That night Manager Joe McCarthy was called on the long-distance phone by Colonel Jake.

"Can't you do something about this, McCarthy?" pleaded the Yankee owner. "I can't stand this strain!"

Colonel Jake, whose club had a lead then of sixteen games with something like eighteen left to be played, was a piker in his demands compared with some of those who watched the Cubs, talked about them, or wrote about them. Especially the last. . . .

A distinguished member of the craft was accompanying the team on an eastern trip, which began in Boston. The Cubs scored a run in the first inning. The Cub pitcher, facing the Boston lead-off man, cut loose with his first pitch, high and outside—a called ball. The distinguished author petulantly slammed his scoring pencil against the floor of the Braves' press coop.

"There they go!" he stormed. "Quitting already! I don't know what I've ever done in my life to be forced to watch this sort of thing, day after day."

It's too bad he didn't linger longer. For this was all in the days before Dizzy Dean, before Lou Novikoff, and before Manager Jimmy Wilson and the bewildering line-up changes.

☙ XXV ☙

RULE BY COMMITTEE

WHEN THE DEPARTURE OF WILLIAM WALKER FROM THE presidential chair thrust P. K. Wrigley into the very midst of the baseball business, he was regarded as a stranger in a strange land. Very few knew that he had held an active interest in the doings of his club for many years, and that he was in regular attendance at all discussions of Cub plans and policies. His father and Bill Veeck were the accepted factors in running the club's business affairs, but while remaining in the background, P. K. had free voice in all matters—and used it, though the general public remained unaware of this fact.

P. K. Wrigley had ideas and many of them. He had associates and many of them too, with or without portfolio. As he took the recognized leadership some observers were of the opinion that he had surrounded himself with a complete squad of yes men. That was not strictly true. There were in the group, which included club executives, advertising men, radiomen, and their various friends, many who answered to the popular description of yes men. But a well-oiled hinge in the neck was something that did not appeal to Wrigley one bit. What he was striving for, from the moment he took over the Cubs, was a compact organization which would run the baseball property, make its own decisions, and not bother him with every minute detail. Unhappily it was many years before he was to have his hopes realized.

Nominal head of the executive staff below Wrigley was Charles ("Boots") Weber who had been brought in from Los Angeles, and who in all the time he functioned for the Cubs, was looking forward to the time when he would be able to return to his beloved California. Weber was not one to make many decisions without first consulting the Big Boss.

He was, perhaps, not as cautious as an executive of the Wrigley Hotel property in Arizona, who once communicated with P. K. long-distance to find out what he should do about some kitchenware which had become lost, strayed, or stolen. But Boots was cautious enough about getting his neck out very far.

When chided by P. K. over his unwillingness to make decisions, Weber's stock reply was: "If I were twenty years younger—"

No other major-league club owner has ever gone as far afield as P. K. Wrigley in determination to satisfy his patrons. He has had the game surveyed as a business, as a sport, and as an amusement enterprise. He has had the players subjected to all sorts of tests short of having each and every one psychoanalyzed. It is a pity the surveys did not go that far, for every now and then there appeared on the pay roll some rugged individualist who would have given the greatest of all the psychoanalysts something of a workout.

Season after season, game after game, pitch after pitch, individual Cub reactions were studied, graded, classified, and filed away for future reference. Motion pictures were taken of them in action. In time there was a complete knowledge of what sort of pitches a given Cub could hit and what sort he could not. There seemed to be some debate whether the weak became strong and the strong became stronger after all this, but the work went on just the same.

Sports writers had quite a time dwelling upon what practical value, if any, was forthcoming from all the work of the "professors" who were reducing hardy ballplayers to statistical tables and laboratory specimens. Some of the ballplayers openly sneered at some of the projects.

The surveys went on. If they had no other value they called attention to the fact that there were Cubs to be written and talked about. It is barely possible that this had a promotional publicity value in the long stretches when the players' actual skill on the field did not merit much sustained attention.

If any of the carping critics had been so minded, they might have discovered that there was merit in these Cub statistical surveys.

At the end of each season, there is a more complete record of each player's activity available for study than any of the rival clubs possess. The Cubs' management is not content with the routine records of batting and fielding and pitching averages. It knows, in record form, how a batsman has conducted himself during the season, when runners are in scoring position and when the bases are empty; it knows what he has done when he has batted in the close games as well as in the one-sided games; it knows how he has reacted at the plate when a tying or winning run is in scoring position; it knows, in brief, just how valuable an asset he has been to the club, and what sort of a competitor he is.

These records, kept in minute detail by a statistician who accompanies the Cubs throughout the season, are able to show what a batsman does against various types of pitching, in various ball parks, and under all kinds of conditions. They show the efficiency, or lack of it, of the pitchers and the fielders under all possible circumstances.

If the clinical surveys were something that baffled the critics of the Cubs, the club's relationship with Los Angeles was equally mystifying—or so many of the contemporary critics wrote. To them such things as prices for players bought from Los Angeles were simply the transfer of money from one Wrigley pocket to another.

In reality, if the Cubs wanted a player from Los Angeles they had to bid as high as and sometimes higher than other clubs seeking the same player. The Los Angeles club was just as fussy about protecting the interests of its minority stockholders as the Cubs.

If the financial operations of these two clubs were distinct— for all of popular belief to the contrary—not all the rest of the pattern was. Many of William Wrigley's baseball salesmanship ideas which had been introduced in Chicago were tried in Los Angeles as well. One of them—Ladies' Day—was the cause of a near revolution in the Pacific Coast League when rival owners refused to see eye to eye with Wrigley on this idea.

Where Wrigley Field, Chicago, was content to set aside Friday as the one day in the week on which the ladies might see games free of charge, in Los Angeles Wrigley went all out. Every day was Ladies' Day. This promptly brought a loud protest from the other seven Pacific Coast League clubs. They were accustomed to getting a share of admission prices paid by ladies on all but one day of each week. As the ladies were now seeing their baseball free any time they took a notion to visit the ball park, and as each visiting club's share of the proceeds was diminished, there was considerable hell raised all around. It wasn't the first time there had been hell raised over a Wrigley promotional idea, nor was it to be the last.

There is no record, however, that the other Pacific Coast League magnates forced William Wrigley to back away from his novel plan until he was content to do so of his own accord.

Outside of Los Angeles the Cubs had no interest until recent years in what could be termed a farm. Nor had they many working agreements with minor-league clubs.

They did possess a scouting system of sorts. The principal scouts were Clarence Rowland and Jack Doyle. Rowland had become a scout after a varied baseball career in the American and sundry minor leagues. He had been manager of the world's championship Chicago White Sox team of 1917. Subsequently he tried himself out as an umpire. He was around and about Reading when Bill Jurges, greatest of all Cub shortstops, was getting his final minor-league tune-up before prancing into the National League to stay for a long, long time.

Early in life Rowland mastered the fine art of being all things to all people. Wherever he was or whatever he was doing, he never strayed very far away from the big boss or from anyone who looked as if he might have the ear of the big boss. He sat in on most of the councils of the Cubs and agreed with everybody, always. The Cubs had great confidence in him, and some of their major transactions were consummated only after Rowland had blazed the trail.

Doyle was a scout of an entirely different tribe. He was a grizzled relic of baseball's knock 'em down and drag 'em out days. He had played with the famous old Baltimore Orioles in the nineties and toward the end of his career had made a pass at being the Cubs' first baseman.

He had the range of the country in his scouting expeditions. He was not the accomplished user of the long-distance phone Rowland was, while away from the home base. Early in his career Doyle had found out that one lasted longer if one kept as far away from the front office as he could. Doyle, the Old Oriole, flew home only when ordered to do so.

He seldom volunteered any information unless it was asked of him. He was rated a good scout. His prize discovery was Gabby Hartnett. He might stand on that if he never located another ballplayer for the Cubs. However, he did find many others, such as Guy Bush. He turned down many more, but some of them managed to find their way into the Cub fold for all of that.

One of his discoveries was a minor-league pitcher who seemed to have all that it takes for success in the majors. He was acquired by the Cubs and given every chance to fit himself into the club, but never quite did so. The case puzzled Doyle no little until one day in the Polo Grounds he found his own answer.

The Old Oriole was seated in a box right beside the Cubs' dugout. It happened to be the first time Doyle had seen his find pitching against major opposition. The Giants began to crowd the pitcher early, and soon he was in more trouble than he could handle. When relief arrived Doyle's man came in to the dugout, apparently very happy about escaping with his life.

Meanwhile the Old Oriole was getting a going over by his neighbor at this latest failure of Doyle's find.

"I know what's wrong with him at last," volunteered Doyle.

138

"Well, for the Lord's sake lean over that rail and tell Grimm," advised the neighbor.

"Won't do any good," said Doyle. "It's too late now. Grimm can't do anything about it. Nobody can do anything about it. That fellow ought to be a great pitcher. He never will be. He has a weak puss . . . and I never noticed it until just now."

The pitcher never did make good with the Cubs, nor was he of any aid and comfort to other major-league clubs which held him temporarily, and finally he drifted out of baseball entirely.

The search for young talent up and down the land brought many strange characters into the Cubs' landing nets. One of them was the young outfielder mentioned already as a possible rival for Babe Herman. This was an affable youngster and a polished gentleman. He seemed able to hit and run and throw. He was a fine fielder. He also played the ukulele.

The Cubs were not to find that out until the first night he spent in the hotel at Catalina when he reported for spring training. They were to find out other things about him later on. He made good with the club, after a fashion, and played with it for some time. Thereafter he made the rounds of the National and American Leagues as well as most of the Class AA's.

With the start he had he really might have made Babe Herman look to his laurels as an eccentric, but somewhere along the line the young man snapped out of his daydreaming and went on to become a very useful ballplayer.

The Cubs will remember him chiefly for a series of incidents which took place on an eastern road trip, beginning in Baker Bowl, the place the Phillies once called home. He was assigned to right field in the final game of the series. About the fourth inning three Phillies came to bat and went out very quickly. The Cubs jogged in to the dugout—all save our hero. Head down, hand on hips, he was still standing at his post in right field when the Phillies' guardian of that territory arrived and nudged him out of there. The Philly said not too politely that it was bad enough to have one of them out there at a time, but it was asking entirely too much for both to be there at the same time. Our hero sprinted to the dugout, being razzed unmercifully by such non-combatant Phillies and fans who were awake at the time.

The next afternoon the Cubs were at Brooklyn. During the progress of the series there, a game turned up in which Danny Taylor was on second base for the Dodgers in a late inning of the game, with none out and the score tied.

A Dodger batsman lifted a short fly to left field, where our hero was stationed for the time being. He came romping in gracefully and made the catch without trouble. Then to the utter astonishment of everyone, he turned and threw the ball out to Kiki Cuyler, who was playing center field and who was a long way out at that. Taylor had chosen this moment to become a little absent-minded himself, and he neglected entirely to tag up and scoot for third base, though every Dodger fan in the park was yelling for him to do so.

When the series with the Dodgers ended, the Cubs took up next day with the Giants at the Polo Grounds. Our hero was a bit late. He missed batting practice entirely and fielding practice as well. He did get there in time for the game and presented an explanation which Manager Grimm accepted as good and sufficient, all things considered. Our hero had gone all the way to the ball park in Brooklyn. No one had told him the Cubs had moved on to the Polo Grounds.

He was a conscientious lad, was this strange young character. When he was told something he never forgot it. He had been told off after forgetting how many were out in that game in Baker Bowl. He resolved to be on the alert thereafter. No one would catch him napping again. He would be the first man off the field each inning, or the first man on it, as the case might be. That—and only that—can account for an incident in the second game with the Giants.

The Cubs, as visitors, went to bat first. Carl Hubbell, pitching for the Giants, was having one of his very best days, so two Cubs went out rapidly. As the second one went down swinging vainly at Hubbell's pitch, our hero leaped from his seat in the dugout on the third base side of the Polo Grounds and dashed rapidly into left field, not stopping until Joe Moore told him to get the hell out of there until Hub got the next man out.

There is every reason to believe that this display of "early foot" by a comparative newcomer was what discouraged Babe Herman in his career as an eccentric character during this period. Since as a player the Babe neither helped the Cubs much nor hindered them through 1933 and 1934, he was made part of a huge trade engineered with Pittsburgh at the 1934 season's close. The Cubs had finished in third place, and as usual everyone in Chicago was protesting that something must be done.

The Cubs were in dire need of a capable and durable left-handed pitcher. They had not possessed such a one in many a season, actually since Hippo Vaughn's time, though Art Nehf had his moments in the late twenties. Larry French was the left-hander the Cubs wanted. He came to them along with outfielder Fred Lindstrom, and between them they helped greatly in bringing another pennant to the Cubs.

French was a work horse among pitchers. Lindstrom, who had been a brilliant infielder with the Giants, transferred to the out-field after a time and did well there, too. He was a smart ball-player, and when he did come to the Cubs, there were those who felt that it was about time; for in his prep school days Lindstrom had been a coming wonder on a Chicago high school team, but the Giants had seen him first.

Lindstrom and French brought two new and well-trained voices to the Cubs' clubhouse discussions of ways and means. The entire playing organization by that time was so much on the every-man-for-himself basis that no one bothered much when Larry and Lindy cut in for a say or two.

To get these two Pirates, the Cubs had to yield Babe Herman and give up as well their veteran pitcher, Guy Bush, and one more, Big Jim Weaver, whose chief distinction was that he had grown about as tall as any major-league pitcher ever gets.

Lindstrom took over center field as his very own. Beside him ranged Chuck Klein and a newcomer, Augie Galan. The latter had been brought up from San Francisco as an infielder but had been changed over by Manager Grimm after one season. Little Augie might have been one of baseball's greatest outfielders if it had not been for a discouraging series of physical mishaps which seemed to dog his trail through the major leagues. As it was he became a great lead-off man and one who batted smartly and ran the bases with rare judgment. He fitted in well in the organization within the organization, which had among its charter members Bill Jurges and Billy Herman, and to which Lindstrom and French were initiated without delay.

⊗ XXVI ⊗

THE THREE-YEAR PLAN

THE CONSISTENCY THE CUBS HAD BEEN SHOWING IN LOSING world series as rapidly as they got into them, was now being matched by their faculty for gaining a National League pennant every three years. They had won in 1929, paused until 1932, and won again. Now in 1935 they came roaring through the stretch in September putting together an incredible string of twenty-one straight victories, many of them with sensational finishes. Their final victory, storybook style, was the one which clinched the pennant; and it was gained in St. Louis when Phil Cavarretta delivered the home-run shot that settled the last fighting hope of the Gas House Gang.

In gaining twenty victories Bill Lee led the club's pitchers, since but six defeats were charged against him. But Lon Warneke, working early and often, with a twenty-and-thirteen record for the season was the Cubs' master workman.

The world series opponents were the Detroit Tigers, who had not been on the Cubs' calling list since 1908. The meeting of Cubs and Tigers posed a problem for all the forecasters. The Tigers had been in four previous world series and had lost them all. The Cubs were making their fifth try after blowing four in a row. It was in the record, however, that the only world's championships the Cubs had ever won were at the expense of Detroit Tigers. Much was made of that in the Chicago press—and elsewhere.

Though but three years had elapsed since their last appearance in baseball's big show, the Cubs' line-up had changed greatly.

The outfield was now made up of Augie Galan, Fred Lindstrom, and Frank Demaree. Chuck Klein was in and out of right field, according to the response made by his aches and pains to the ministrations of Doc Lotshaw and sundry other advisers, some of them with degrees.

Fixtures in the infield—or so it seemed then—were Phil Cavarretta at first, Billy Herman at second, Bill Jurges at short, and Stanley Hack at third. This was an infield which might have challenged the artistry of Tinker to Evers to Chance, with Steinfeldt thrown in for good measure.

Gabby Hartnett was the Cubs' catcher, single games or doubleheaders, it made no difference.

The pitchers, besides Warneke and Lee, were French, the left-hander, the veteran Charley Root, and "Tex" Carleton, who had been obtained from St. Louis. He specialized in beating the Boston Braves. Unhappily there were no Braves in the 1935 world series.

It seemed like a throwback to 1908, when Warneke opened the series in Detroit and restricted the Tigers to four scattered hits. He won 3–0. So completely was he the Tigers' master that Warneke himself handled eight fielding chances to equal a series record. The Tigers were not hitting Warneke often, nor were they hitting him with any semblance of authority.

"Schoolboy" Rowe was the Detroit pitcher and he came through with an excellent game. However, he was reached for a homer by Frank Demaree and allowed six other hits. Two of them were by Hartnett who drove in a run.

The year before most of these Tigers had participated in a wild and woolly series with St. Louis. The Deans, Dizzy and Paul, each won two games. Joe Medwick was banished by Commissioner Landis after the fans had rioted following a mix-up between Medwick and Marvin Owen, the Tigers' third baseman.

It was at this series incidentally, that Commissioner Landis, from observation of "Pepper" Martin, finally found out after years of trying—as he admitted later—how to spit tobacco juice through his teeth. But what the Commissioner learned in part

© *Chicago Sun*

Lon Warneke

Gabby Hartnett

then, and was soon to learn in its entirety, was just what free style language professional ballplayers could pass back and forth.

It was generally conceded that in the seventh and deciding game, which Dizzy Dean won 11–0, the Gas House Gang had roughhoused and rough talked the Tigers into submission. At least this was the Cubs' impression, and it gave them ideas.

They opened with a withering blast of insults, centering their attack upon Hank Greenberg, the Tigers' first baseman. It was a mix-up at the home plate in the second game rather than any words of the Cubs, which finally cut down Hank. He had contributed a home run as his share of the Tigers' 8–3 victory in that game, but later on, in a slide into the plate, he was blocked off heavily and forcibly by catcher Gabby Hartnett. In the crash Greenberg's arm was injured so badly that he was unable to participate in the remainder of the action.

Charley Root started that second game. He was just what the Tigers ordered. He had to be removed in the first inning before he was able to retire a man. Four Tigers hit safely and they were on their way to a four-run inning before Root made his escape. Roy Henshaw, tiny and left-handed, next took up the burden, but he was driven out in the fourth when three more Detroit runs scored. Fabian Kowalik finished out the game, the Cubs not bothering Tommy Bridges, the Tiger pitcher, to any great extent.

During this game the Cubs' conversationalists turned some of their attention to one of the American League umpires, George Moriarty. He was something of a public speaker himself, and epithets flew over the place so freely that Commissioner Landis felt it necessary to call a meeting at his Chicago office before the third game began, and draw up a new code of world series house rules.

In a strictly informal aside, much later on, Commissioner Landis had this to say of his cross-examination of the Cubs and Umpire Moriarty:

"In my time in this world I have always prided myself on a command of lurid expressions. I must confess that I learned from these young men some variations of the language even I didn't know existed."

Whatever private chuckling he may have done over the incident, it was a severe Commissioner Landis who bound over the Cubs and Moriarty to keep the peace for the rest of the series. They did, too—after a fashion. ᾿

Because of Greenberg's injury Manager Mickey Cochrane had to make some quick changes in his line-up for the third game. He moved Owen from third base to first, and Owen's regular post was taken over by Herman Clifton, a utility infielder.

It may have been Cochrane's own worriment over these changes and the two changed-over infielders' unfamiliarity with the new jobs, but the fact remains that these three, Cochrane, Owen, and Clifton were the only Tigers who didn't share in a twelve-hit batting attack which gave the third game to Detroit, 6–5.

Bill Lee started for the Cubs, opposing Elden Auker, who was speared for two runs by the Cubs in the second inning. Another was added in the fifth, Lee holding the Tigers safe all the while. There was a run for the Tigers in the sixth, but going into the eighth the Cubs' 3–1 lead seemed safe enough. Probably would have been, if this were not a world series game, in which, as far as the Cubs are concerned, things rarely are what they seem.

The roof fell in on Lee in the eighth. By the time Lon Warneke came shuffling to his rescue, a four-run inning was under way. It was against a Tiger 5–3 lead that the Cubs launched their ninth inning rally. Two pinch hitters, Chuck Klein for Bill Jurges, and Ken O'Dea for Warneke, each came through, two runs tallied, and the score was tied.

Larry French went out to do or die for the cause of the Cubs. He died in the eleventh, the Tigers getting home with the run that broke up the game, 6–5, and gave them an edge in the series.

Tex Carleton worked so deliberately in the fourth game that it required two hours and twenty-eight minutes, though but three runs were scored in it. Cautious and capable though he was, Tex lost a heartbreaker to Alvin Crowder. The Tigers won 2–1, Gabby

146

Hartnett's homer being the lone Chicago tally. The homer's only importance was that it gave Carleton a temporary lead in the second inning. The Tigers tied it in the next, and the game remained that way until the sixth when an unearned run gave Detroit the victory margin.

Warneke reported for duty in the fifth game and once again he was pitted against Schoolboy Rowe. Long, lean, lanky Lon was still the master of the Tigers. The Cubs, no longer too stout-hearted, seemed to sense this and were less tense than usual.

Fred Lindstrom was benched for this game and Chuck Klein was in the outfield. His homer gave the Cubs one of their three runs, and his single was part of a third inning rally which gave Warneke a two-run lead. Billy Herman also drove home a run in this inning.

Two-thirds of the way through the game Warneke appeared to have his second shutout victory of the series in hand. In the press box assembled experts were thumbing record books to see what, if anything, Lon had left unfinished in 1932, and whether he was threatening Babe Ruth's record for consecutive scoreless innings in world series play.

Down at the edge of the dugout, where Manager Charlie Grimm had taken his stance, there seemed to be excitement of some sort. Behind the plate Gabby Hartnett, always a theatrical figure, was putting on something that was definitely not an act. But out in the pitcher's box Warneke, who was the cause of all the concern, seemed no different than he had been a pitch or several pitches ago. But that was just to the unpracticed eye.

Hartnett, who had caught every Warneke pitch since Lon broke in with the Cubs, sensed that something was wrong with the pitcher's arm. There followed a consultation and Warneke, protesting all the way, was led to the dugout as time was called.

Box-seat patrons near the dugout could near the voices of Warneke and Grimm raised as the argument continued. Warneke admitted that something had gone wrong with his arm but insisted that he wanted to keep going on with the game.

"This is a world series game, Charlie," he pleaded. "I can finish it up. I'm right enough for that."

"I don't give a damn if it's *the* world series," yelled Grimm. "Your arm is more important than any ball game."

So out came Warneke and in went Bill Lee. He held the Tigers in check the rest of the way, the Cubs winning 3–1. But with the injury to Warneke's arm went their next to last hope of winning the series.

They did carry the battle to the Tigers next day when the show resumed in the Detroit ball park. Warneke was through. Lee had been used up the day before. Root had not shown too much in his efforts, so it had to be Carleton with two days' rest or French with three. Grimm chose French, who drew the well-rested Bridges, curve-ball specialist as his opponent. They were on even terms for three innings when the Tigers scored once and took the lead. The Cubs came back in the fifth, scored twice, and went ahead only to have the score tied again in the sixth. That was the way the game stood when the Cubs came to bat in the ninth inning.

Stanley Hack opened the inning with a long shot to center field and raced all the way around to third base. Three chances were now afforded the Cubs to get that precious run home with what was in the line-up then. Other variations were possible by the use of pinch hitters.

Bill Jurges followed Hack to bat. A hit, a long fly to the outfield, even a slow roller to the infield would do it. Jurges wasn't up to any of these. He fanned ingloriously, waving in vain at the Bridges curve.

Next came French, the pitcher who had been hammered for ten safeties, but who had managed to be no worse than even. Pinch hitter for him? Grimm decided not. French batted for himself, and his best was a dribbler to Bridges, who saw to it that Hack remained anchored at third and then tossed French out at first base.

Now but one chance was left—Augie Galan. The most little Augie could do was a long fly to the outfield. Had that long fly opened the inning instead of closing it. . . . Hack remained at third base, now in the guise of the regular custodian of the post, rather than a base runner not long since a menace to all Detroit.

Bridges' magnificent job at turning back the Cubs' bid for that all-important run touched off Tiger enthusiasm, even as it dampened the Cubs' ardor. Not much later, with one out, Mickey Cochrane got to French for a single. Charlie Gehringer, the series' leading hitter, moved Mickey along with an infield out. This put the issue squarely up to Goose Goslin, a veteran of the baseball wars. He launched a line fly to right center. It fell to earth unchallenged, and in scampered Cochrane with the run that broke up the game and series.

Detroit had its first world championship in history. The Cubs had just written another chapter, the fifth, in their serial, So Near and Yet So Far, begun in 1910.

Throughout the long night of celebration and for weeks thereafter, Detroit found inspiration for conversation about the series, and the Tiger heroes, one and all. There was conversation galore in Chicago as well, but most of it was second guessing on Grimm's judgment in the ninth inning of the last game when Hack was on third with none out and the bottom of the batting order coming up.

Those willing to concede that Grimm did right in letting French bat for himself, because of the shape the Cub pitching staff was in, argued he should have used a pinch hitter for Jurges. When he didn't, and Jurges failed, it was argued that Grimm had no other alternative but use a pinch hitter for French, even if P. K. Wrigley himself had to work the rest of the game for the Cubs.

Nor did that argument abate with the years. When Grimm led his 1945 Cubs against a new set of Detroit Tigers, he was interviewed at length on that memento of his managerial past.

"If I had to do it all over again," he said, "I'd play it just as I did then."

This ought to close the incident, were it not for a more diverting touch given by Hack himself, a few years after the 1935 series. He had arrived at Detroit to take his part in the annual

All Star engagement in midsummer. When he arrived at Briggs Stadium, Hack went at once out on the field and took a quick look at third base, before going to the clubhouse to don his uniform.

"Just wanted to see if I was still standing out there waiting for somebody to drive me home," he explained.

⊗ XXVII ⊗

THE CUBS DISCOVER AMERICA

UNTIL NOW THIS STORY HAS CONCERNED ITSELF CHIEFLY WITH the Cubs in regular season. There is another phase of their existence which undoubtedly deserves more than the chapter which has been allotted to it. That would be the annual spring-training exhibition jaunt.

The tour of 1936 has been selected for the reason that in it the Cubs succeeded in surpassing all their previous efforts in wearing out a ball club before as much as a single ball had been pitched in the regular season.

It began when the first squad, composed of pitchers and catchers and a few others who couldn't wait, left Chicago February 18. They landed at Avalon three days later, to be joined by the infielders and outfielders on February 27.

For two weeks training was routine. There was a daily workout, generally after midday, since the dew had a way of clinging to Avalon's greensward for most of the morning's hours.

In their leisure, the big outdoor men of the Cubs went in for golf and for trips far back into the hills to open fire on the mountain goats scared there when Bill Killefer's Cubs took to the hills in 1922. The Cubs had a few golfers possessed of average skill. Manager Grimm had no objection to their playing the game. In fact he considered walking a golf course good conditioning for the legs. His lone golf restriction was that no one ask him to play. He was very firm about that. He had been cured.

Grimm had tried the Catalina course in the days when Cliff Heathcote was a Cub and Grimm's partner in song, in instrumental music, in fun and frolic. Heathcote, like Grimm, played his golf left-handed. He was about as well acquainted with the rules of the game and its finer touches as was Grimm. Both had wonderful hooks—save when a hook was indicated. Then each had perfectly amazing slices.

There is no need to give a stroke-by-stroke analysis of their match as they made their way from canyon to fig orchard; from fig orchard to dry gulch; from dry gulch to ravine; from ravine to tall grass, and from tall grass to some of Catalina's other pitfalls for the golfing unwise and unwary.

They came at last to the edge of the green at the third hole. As they arrived, Grimm's caddy was posted near a coil of hose which the greenkeeper was preparing to unwind for his late afternoon sprinkling of the putting surface and its approaches. Heathcote's caddy was on the other side of the green. Hard by was a gunny-sack roll in which the greenkeeper had piled up the grass lately clipped by his mower, preparatory to carrying it away.

"Your ball's in the sack of grass," said the caddy to Heathcote, "and you're away."

"I can drop out of there, can't I?" asked Heathcote. "This is a case of rub of the green if ever I saw one."

"Like hell you can drop out," said Grimm. "It will cost you the hole if you do. We're playing Missouri Valley rules. You play 'em as they lie."

"But I can't see the damn ball," protested Heathcote.

"Play the whole thing then," advised Grimm. "Use an explosion shot."

Which is exactly what Heathcote did, blasting gunny sack, grass, and from somewhere in the mess, his golf ball, amid the loud lamentations of the greenkeeper. No heed was paid him. All eyes were on Heathcote's ball which was bounding crazily among boulders in a dry creek several yards beyond the green. The last bounce, by some perverse freak, took it back towards the green; and the caddies, after a consultation, decided that Grimm's ball was now away, and it was his turn to shoot.

"Where's my ball?" he asked the caddy.

"Right there, sir," said the caddy, pointing to the very middle of the coil of hose.

"Remember the Missouri Valley code," said Heathcote. "Play it, sucker, play it."

He stood very close to Grimm, who was bent over, peering into the coil of hose. Thus it was that neither noticed the green-keeper had walked over to the near-by faucet or that he had turned the water on full force. They found that out when the nozzle began spurting, showering its liquid supply on Grimm and Heathcote alike.

You may have difficulty in getting Grimm to admit it; but that is why in all the years he has been with the Cubs since, he has remained as far away from the golf course as his duties permit.

Besides sharpening their sights on golf balls and baseballs and hunting rifles, the Cubs invariably give a lot of attention during spring training to the game of accumulative rummy introduced by sports writer Ed Burns many years ago. No Cub has yet become as proficient in the game as Professor Burns, the master.

Once the stay at Catalina Island is over, the Cubs go to Los Angeles to begin their series of exhibition games. Their opponents are the Chicago White Sox, such other major-league clubs as train in Southern California, and a few Pacific Coast League clubs.

In this spring of 1936 the Cubs spent just three days in Los Angeles, playing the White Sox. They caught a train then for San Antonio, where they played Pittsburgh. Next came Houston, where the Texas League club of that city was the opposition. From Houston they went to New Orleans to engage the Cleveland Indians.

After that only road secretary Bob Lewis seemed to know where they were due next, how they were to get there, when, and why. And long before the end of the tour even his generous supply of confidence in his town-finding ability was sapped. But the Cubs did manage to get in games with the New York Giants,

Detroit Tigers, Cincinnati Reds, New York Yankees, St. Louis Cardinals, Brooklyn Dodgers, Boston Red Sox, the Phillies, and the teams of Birmingham and Nashville.

A study of their operations reveals that one time or another (and sometimes twice) they were in Pensacola, Tallahassee, Lakeland, Tampa, St. Petersburg, Bradenton, Clearwater, Winter Haven, Sarasota, Selma, Dothan, Monticello, Montgomery, Gadsen, Thomasville, Attala, Birmingham, and Nashville.

They had left Los Angeles March 15. They reached Chicago April 10, having come by way of Arizona, New Mexico, Texas, Louisiana, Mississippi, Florida, Georgia, Tennessee, Kentucky, Indiana, and Illinois. They had traveled on the rails of twelve roads, and three bus lines were also impressed into this movement of baseball troops.

From the time they left Los Angeles until they reached Chicago they traveled in the same three Pullman cars. They slept in them nights, either parked on a convenient siding or rolling across the country. That such a trip would be productive of adventures goes without saying.

It was the custom of Lewis to secure rooms in each of the towns in which the Cubs were scheduled to play. There the players donned uniforms for the game. If there happened to be a spare room, it was reserved for the gentlemen of the press and for Lewis himself.

Early one morning they checked in at a hostelry in one of the southern towns, and Lewis found out that it had been used as a hospital during the Civil War. After a quick look at the "press" room it was decided to go back downstairs and see what breakfast might be like.

"Where's the dining room?" Lewis asked a man in the lobby, who looked as if he might have all the answers.

"Out the door and down the street a piece," was the reply. Lewis and his hungry friends followed directions. Quite a piece down the street they went before they came upon Joe's Place, or something similar. Too late, however. All the seats and most of the food were in charge of the ballplayers, who, for a change, had chosen to arise early that day.

In this town the Cubs played one of their exhibition games with the Giants, who were being trailed by almost as many sports writers as there were players on the squad. Ed Burns and a newspaper associate, having scouted the town, found a grocery store and laid in some supplies before going to the ball park, where there was more than normal crowding on the turns as both Chicago and New York authors strove to get action from the telegraph company. For that game there were three wires strung into the ball park. It was agreed that two should go to New York, one to be used for play-by-play description, the other for leads and features.

The Chicago men settled for the odd wire; and since Burns and his associates had graciously permitted Ralph Cannon to file the play by play, the first inning seemed as good a time as any to spread out the picnic lunch.

Burns saw to it that his old pal Cannon was fed, but any New Yorkers who wanted to partake, had to come and get it. All did, including the man whose job it was to send in the play by play for all New York papers interested. He left his wire in charge of the telegraph operator, and as the clatter of the key continued, thought no more about it for perhaps fifteen minutes.

Then with a Burns special sandwich in hand he returned to his post. He found the operator engaged in copying in longhand what seemed to be a very long message. Several sheets had been filled already. The New York author picked them up to find out who wanted what and why. To his amazement he found a beautiful play-by-play description of a game between the Yankees and another major-league club, which was being staged in the same area that afternoon. By some hocus-pocus, maybe sunspots, the man at the Yankee game was filing to the man at the Giants game, and whether the copy was traveling by way of New York, no one ever did find out. The operator, upon examination, said that his name was not Babe Herman, and the prosecution rested.

In another of the southern towns the Cubs and the Red Sox

arrived at practically the same time, which happened to be about 3:00 A.M. Lewis and his friends of the press had remained up in order to settle a bet, the press arguing that there couldn't be any such place as the one Lewis said was the next stop.

The press lost, but Lewis was prevailed upon to lead a march to the hotel, where perhaps he might be able to get a room or two so that a welcome change might be had from those Pullman berths. Lewis was able to negotiate the deal, and in one of the rooms, Cannon, paired with Jimmy Corcoran, decided to retire, while in an adjoining room Lewis and the rest of the press reached the conclusion that the Pullman berths weren't half bad after all.

Corcoran, an inquisitive soul, spent a while opening closet doors and inspecting antique pieces of furniture. He stood at last before a huge chest of drawers which towered over him, Corcoran not being a very tall man. He opened the drawers one by one, all save the topmost which resisted his efforts. With a final tug he succeeded in tipping over the entire set.

The crash must have sounded louder than the shot which was heard 'round the world. It roused Cannon, who looked sleepily down at Corcoran trying to struggle out from beneath the chest of drawers.

"Maybe that'll teach you to mind your own business," Cannon said—and resumed his sleeping.

It was at this same hotel that both Cub and Red Sox squads, almost to a man, reached the dining room for breakfast at the same time—and found one person, combination chef and waitress, in charge. That was the time the Cubs breakfasted on ham and cold eggs and liked it.

Somewhere along the line it was necessary for the Cubs to make a bus trip many miles to a near-by town to play the Red Sox. When departure time came it was raining heavily in the city where the Cubs had established a temporary base. Lewis phoned the promoter of the game to see if it were worth while making the trip. He was told to come right ahead, the weather was fine and had been all morning.

The Cubs took the bus ride. The farther they rode the more it rained. At their destination they found the Red Sox had been forced to answer the summons also.

Lewis was unable to find the promoter at once, but did accost a native, asking when it had started to rain there.

The native thought that over for a while.

"Seems so long ago I just forget when," he said.

"It's the lousiest day I've ever seen," said Lewis.

"Better'n no day 'tall," was all the satisfaction he got.

It would make a better story perhaps if the promoter made the two clubs play through the game in rain and mud. He actually did make them go as far as warming-up time before he relented and agreed that maybe it was a little too damp for comfortable baseball.

⊗ XXVIII ⊗

TIME OUT FOR REPAIRS

FOR ALL OF THEIR MILEAGE ON THE PLAYING FIELDS AND transportation lines in the spring of 1936, the Cubs were away to a good start in defense of their National League title. Before long it was felt that another starting pitcher of quality might come in handy. Much thought had been given to Curt Davis, who seemed able to pitch for the Phillies and win in spite of them, which constituted a latter-day miracle. It did not take the Cubs long to find out that Davis could be had—at a price, as could most anything else the Phillies used, save Baker Bowl, which nobody wanted anyhow.

The price for Davis was Chuck Klein. He had been away from Baker Bowl long enough, the Phillies felt. Baseball life hadn't been the same for them, or for him, since Chuck had gone away. The Cubs were not of a mind to protest too loudly at the return of Klein to the surroundings in which he had enjoyed his baseball life most.

There were a few minor details to be cleared away. The Phillies, while really wanting Klein, thought they should have some kind of a pitcher to replace Davis. As long as they felt that way about it, the Cubs suggested that they should have some kind of an outfielder to replace Klein. Finally pitcher Fabian Kowalik was designated to accompany Klein to Philadelphia. Ethan Allen, a sprightly athlete, became the traveling companion of Davis on the way to the Cubs.

Allen it was who made the Cubs motion-picture conscious. Much of the practice he had while with the Cubs, taking pictures of friend and foe, qualified him later for a place with the National League's promotional bureau.

He was highly intelligent, affable, and gifted with a fair share of baseball-playing talent, but he will be remembered by the Cubs chiefly for an incident he would just as soon have missed. In a game at Boston while sliding headlong into second base, he was badly spiked on the hand by one of President Ford Frick's umpires who had taken too literally the pep talk about being right on top of the play at all times.

Davis found a difference between pitching for the Phillies and for the Cubs. Klein had reached similar conclusions about the fine art of hitting. To continue the parallel, Davis, much of the time he was with the Cubs, was beset with aches and pains even as Klein had been.

The Cubs were very much in the 1936 race until late in August. Then the Giants came up with a rush that enabled them to take and hold the lead. The Cubs, gasping from the pace, had to settle with the Cardinals in a dead heat for second place.

Manager Grimm openly expressed his opinion that the duration of the spring exhibition tour had taken something out of his squad, and that they were not to be censured for having been asked to play what almost amounted to two seasons in one.

Bob Lewis, of the Baseball Writers' dinner team of Grimm and Lewis, had another version.

"It was those slot machines in Florida that got the boys down," he said. "They developed arm muscles they never knew they had, and couldn't use in baseball. Some of those guys are still trying to hit the jack pot instead of a ball."

As usual the Cub fans were very disappointed. They really should not have been, for the National League pennant winner was again confronted by another batch of those fearsome New York Yankees, once more in charge of all the baseball they surveyed.

Foremost in the Yankee cast was Joe DiMaggio. He had come up from San Francisco's North Beach to break in on the top floor of the American League. If the second guessing now rampant in Chicago over the Cubs ever communicated itself to the official family, there must have been some uncomfortable moments whenever P. K. Wrigley's eager-to-please helpers sat down to talk things over. For the Cubs had been given first search on DiMaggio by Charles Graham and Charles Strub of San Francisco and had passed him up. Perhaps this was not generally known, but it was a fact.

While playing for San Francisco, DiMaggio sustained an injury to his leg. Much was made of this. The question was raised whether it would affect his durability. His batting prowess and his fielding and throwing skill were such that major-league scouts by the dozen were on his trail, injured leg or no.

The San Francisco club, having dealt with the Cubs in the Augie Galan transaction to the satisfaction of all concerned, was anxious to continue business relations. Propositions concerning DiMaggio were discussed pro and con. The Cub representative expressed some misgivings about DiMaggio's leg. He was assured that it was (or would be) all right. Finally the San Francisco spokesman made his best offer.

"Take DiMaggio on trial," he suggested. "Give us so many players and so much cash. Keep DiMaggio until July and give him a thorough looking over. If you are not satisfied that he can make the grade, the deal's off."

The Cub representative turned the deal down! But the Yankees were not so fussy. They took DiMaggio, permitted him to round out another season in the Pacific Coast League, and then called him in to go to work. At last account New York fans, having contemplated DiMaggio in regular season and world series, were wondering if Tris Speaker or any other great center fielder could possibly have been as good as their boy Joe.

Joe, incidentally, was not the only one of the ball-playing DiMaggios the Cubs passed up. When Joe's small brother Dominic became a bit of a sensation with the San Francisco club, most of the major-league scouts looked him over. Among them was one from the Cubs. He made a careful study of Dominic and finally turned his gaze away, with no regrets.

160

"We couldn't use him," he said. "He just hits singles."

However, a deal was closed for another Coast League Dominic whose last name happened to be Dallessandro. The latter managed to retain a job with the Cubs, but there was never a time when he was as valuable an asset to them as the other Dominic was to the Boston Red Sox, who were willing to take a chance on Joe's little brother even if he did ĵust hit singles.

One of the Cubs' critics, in reviewing their experiences with the DiMaggios, was inclined to be charitable about it.

"It's just as well the Cubs didn't buy a DiMaggio," he said, "for like as not they'd have come up with the one who manages the restaurant at Fisherman's Wharf."

While the Cubs were not as active as they might have been in collecting the cream of the minor-league crop, they were rapidly getting to be artists in locating and dealing for major-league players who had established reputations elsewhere.

Such a player was Rip Collins, obtained from St. Louis before the 1937 season got under way. The Cubs must have wanted him badly, for part of the collateral in the deal was Lon Warneke, by long odds the pitcher most beloved by Cub fans since the time of Mordecai Brown.

Collins, a switch hitter, had several fine seasons with the Cardinals in which his batting average exceeded the .300 mark. He was not quite up to that with the Cubs, but while he lasted he was the life of the party at all times. His principal effect on the Cub plans of operation was to launch Phil Cavarretta on a merry-go-round ride which was still going on when spring training began for 1946. Cavarretta in all the years he has been with the Cubs, and they are many, has been kept grabbing for the brass ring— a regular place in the line-up in which to light and remain.

Cavarretta, who was to be named the National League's most valuable player in 1945, broke in as a first baseman of promise Thereafter he was destined to appear in various outfield positions and at one time was being groomed as a prospective pitcher. Wherever he landed he did more than a fair day's work for a fair day's pay. If the mind-changing Cub management had ever seen fit to station him at one place and keep him there, it is possible that his designation as the league's most valuable player might not have been so long delayed.

In preparation for the 1937 season, P. K. Wrigley and his artisans, who included the gifted Otis Shepard, the Rembrandt of the Wrigley Company with a dash of Dali, completed the first stage of the remodeling of Wrigley Field. Here was now the most beautiful of all the country's ball parks. It possessed a distinct type of bleacher, skirting the outfield. In dead center, high above the top row of the stands, was a mammoth scoreboard, perhaps the outstanding feature of the face-lifting job. Along the walls of the bleachers vines grew and flourished.

In this streamlined setting every wish of the patron for comfort was satisfied. Concession stands and rest rooms for the bleacherites were above what was considered standard in other ball parks for grandstand and box-seat patrons. There was a blending of colors within the field which enhanced the beauty of the place.

It had one loud and long complaint, which came not from the patrons, but from the Cub players themselves. They offered an objection to the seating of spectators in the center field portion of the bleachers, particularly during the summer months when the crowd afforded a solid wall of white shirts which made a background against which Cub hitters found it troublesome to follow the ball. (No explanation was ever made how the hitters on visiting clubs were able to follow the ball in the same setting.)

However, the Cub management, always eager to please its players, tried a system of blocking off portions of the bleachers, with Andy Frain ushers guarding the place lest a stray white shirt might get in the way of some Cub hitter who was having his troubles at the plate.

That didn't seem to improve hitting any, and after a time the spectators were permitted to return to the barred zone, wear white shirts if they cared to, or even strip to the waist as they enjoyed a sun bath, even if they didn't always enjoy the Cubs.

It was obvious that all these touches had required the expenditure of great sums of money. So, when the Cubs faltered in 1937 as they had in 1936, the prevalent wisecrack of the second guessers was:

"It certainly looks like money. Too bad Wrigley didn't spent some of it to get some ballplayers to appear in the park."

To that Wrigley had no reply—but in years thereafter, had he been so inclined, he might have indicated that he had proved his point, and that expenditures for a ball park beautiful were a sound investment. He was a firm believer in promotional advertising, and that when you advertise you must have something you can guarantee.

He realized that it was impossible to guarantee a player's performance for a game, a series, or a season, much less guarantee an entire team or a pennant. You could try to get the best players available, pay them satisfactory salaries, and hope for the best. But it was quite possible to prepare, advertise, and guarantee a pleasant place in which Cub baseball might be watched. And that was what Wrigley had in mind. It is Cub financial history that there was worth-while response to his sales talk along these lines.

The second phase of the remodeling of Wrigley Field was completed in 1938. The left field section of the grandstand was turned slightly. New concession stands were erected. More attention was given to sound equipment and the other details connected with the proper presentation of a ball game to the patron who paid or even to those who came in on passes.

The remodeling included attention to the chairs in the boxes and grandstand. The size of the chairs was increased, with a resultant drop in the park's seating capacity, but a tremendous increase in the comfort of patrons who had been jammed together on big days. Readjustment of the chair sizes brought Wrigley Field's capacity in box seats down to 14,097 while the grandstand capacity dropped to 19,343. About 5,000 represented normal capacity of the bleachers, though standees along the runways and eager fans in whom flagpole-sitting talents were latent invariably ran that bleacherite total far above the 5,000 figure.

With the exception of 1938, whose stirring events will be related anon, Wrigley Field, following its remodeling, was to come upon many seasons in which the baseball club was not much of a factor in the National League race. Some of the Cub hopefuls were so inept that their efforts were ludicrous at times. Yet in all those lean playing years the attendance was well above that which usually goes with a club that not only is not winning but is not coming close. Those were the years which proved beyond any reasonable doubt that P. K. Wrigley's plan of selling baseball amid pleasant surroundings was a happy thought and a profitable one.

The temper of the patrons changed during the time the Cubs' playing fortunes were at a low ebb. The most rabid fans stayed away from the park, though they kept on voicing their opinions. Those who did come out to see ball games did so because they did not care particularly whether the Cubs won or lost. Or if they did, refused to go into hysterics over it.

As the annual August-September jitters caught the Cubs, the Giants again came on to pass them and take the championship in 1937. Just for that the Giants had to play the Yankees once more in the world series. When it was over Joe McCarthy's club had added one more title to the Yankee string. Now it totaled a half dozen, or one more than Connie Mack had stored in his trophy room at Shibe Park, Philadelphia.

When the Yankees had done it again and convincingly, the thought came that maybe there might be something in their system which could be used to advantage in getting the Cubs on a winning beam and keeping them there. So the Cubs reached across the league borders and persuaded the Yankees to let them have Tony Lazzeri. This was not hard to do, for warming up on the New York side lines was Joe Gordon, a second baseman who was soon to make denizens of the Yankee Stadium forget there had ever been a Lazzeri—baseball fans being like that in the Bronx or in Medicine Hat.

Within three weeks of the close of the season Lazzeri came to Chicago and signed with the Cubs, a bit uncertain of his exact role, as were most others when news of the move became known. Surely the Cubs did not want him to play second base when they owned Billy Herman. There was no place for him at third with Stan Hack a fixture there. Bill Jurges was the league's flashiest shortstop, so Lazzeri was certainly not going to move him out. It did not seem logical that Tony was needed as a first baseman on a club which had Rip Collins with Phil Cavarretta handy on days when Rip was not in good voice.

Was he to be coach? Or was he to be the new manager? After all, Grimm had missed out on two pennants in a row, hadn't he? And after getting away to a fine start each time. Maybe Tony would take charge as soon as he had time to look the situation over.

No one knew for sure—and Lazzeri least of all. After his first session with Cub executives, A to Z, he seemed more bewildered than ever. He came out of the conference asking a friend who had known him in Milbrae, California, "What in hell were they all talking about?"

Throughout the long winter months there was ample time to discuss the Lazzeri deal, pro and con; and spring training was just about coming to a close when Cubs, Cub fans, and baseball generally had something else to discuss. This was the deal for Dizzy Dean, who had outlived his welcome with the remnants of the Gas House Gang of St. Louis and was up for sale.

In his time with the Cardinals Dean had been one of the truly great modern pitchers. He was anything but a shrinking violet, to be sure; but when his fast ball was at his beck and call, he could make any batsman roll over and play dead—and frequently did.

Unfortunately when the Cubs got around to him there was doubt raised as to the condition of the arm which had long terrified opposing hitters.

While on his spring tour of training camps, Clarence Rowland reached the conclusion that the Cubs might get a lot of service out of Dean, regardless of the condition of his pitching arm. The Cubs' chief scout and director of field operations was eminently correct. The Cubs did get a lot out of Dizzy Dean, and vice versa. The deal for Dean involved the largest confirmed sum of cash ever expended by the Cubs for a ballplayer. The over-all magnitude of the transaction may well make it the heftiest in baseball history. A check for $185,000 went to Sam Breadon, the St. Louis club owner, and along with it went three players. Two were pitchers, Curt Davis and Clyde Shoun, and the odd man was George Stainback, outfielder. It is pertinent to the argument about the size of this deal to point out that as late as the 1945 season, or seven years after Dean joined the Cubs, Davis, Shoun, and Stainback were still going concerns in the major leagues, though the Cardinals, as is their wont, had used them as media for barter and exchange with other clubs.

So the Cubs gave up much more than $185,000 for Dizzy Dean.

It did not take long to discover that the report of Dean's troubled arm was an understatement. There was reason at times to suspect that he had reached the Cubs with no right arm at all. The eager critics, much as they approved of Dean as an aid to spirited copy, any time, anywhere, anyhow, soon began to refer to Dizzy's "nothing" ball. His fast one was gone, never to return. But for a long time opposing hitters, having been fooled so many times before by Dean, were suspicious of him, lest he come through with a really fast one, when least expected. As a result many of them were continually off stride as they batted against his pitching movement rather than the ball which came towards the plate with all the fury of something blown out of a bubble pipe.

Dean always believed that his arm trouble was traceable to a too sudden return to the game after an injury sustained in the All Star game of 1937. In it Earl Averill of Cleveland had lined one back at Dizzy so hard it inflicted great damage to one of Dean's favorite toes. He took treatment for the injury, but was inclined to favor it when he resumed pitching.

He altered the smooth, sweeping movements that had made his every previous pitching effort sheer grace and artistry. This, he contended, put an unlooked for strain upon his arm. He was trying all the while to put as much on the ball as he had been doing before, and one day something gave in the arm.

In four of his seasons with the Cardinals Dean had won twenty games or more. In 1934 he boosted his victory total to thirty while losing but seven. Four years in a row he led the National League in strike-outs; and in 1933, as the Cubs had cause to remember, he had set down seventeen of them on strikes in one game. He was able to explain, whenever asked, that he could have fanned the other ten if he had been feeling just right that day.

This, of course, was the Dean who had been. It wasn't the Dean who came to the Cubs. The Dean the Cubs bought had all the mannerisms, all the conversation, all the beliefs that he was a law unto himself that the Dean of the Cardinals ever had—but the fast ball was gone, never to return.

However, Dean to the very end of his career, retained three of the requisites of a great pitcher, and no mishap on the playing field, no brush with the management, would deprive him of them. He had supreme confidence in himself. He had the pitching heart. He had the pitching head.

No deal in baseball ever had any more exploitation than this one. The baseball fans of Chicago could hardly wait to see Diz start his first game for the Cubs.

It became evident early that he was going to have to get by with the "nothing" ball. At times his arm seemed so weak even the "nothing" ball put a strain on it. This made no difference to the clamoring fans. They found Diz of interest whether he pitched or not. His antics provided an endless flow of words and phrases from the typewriters of all the baseball writers.

Dean was very outspoken at all times on the abilities or lack of them of his own teammates or opponents alike. One day with bases filled a Cub pitcher walked the next batsman forcing in a run.

"If I'm ever caught doing that," said Dean, "and Charlie

Grimm doesn't shoot me dead, I'll shoot myself right out there in front of forty thousand people."

Forty thousand was the popular conception of Wrigley Field's capacity. Far be it from Diz to concede that there would be any less than a park full whenever he was pitching. In his Cub era, whatever his artistic success, his estimate of his crowd-gathering powers was certainly right. Dizzy Dean really packed 'em in.

In all the uproar that followed in Dean's wake, it was but natural that Lazzeri, who had come from the Yankees, should be lost in the shuffle. Tony was the least communicative of all the Cubs. He was not the most colorful character in baseball either. So it was no wonder he was apt to be overlooked, day by day.

His playing activity was proportionately about the same as Dean's for that 1938 season. In one capacity or another Tony got into the line-up in fifty-four games. He drove in twenty-three runs and finished with a modest .267 average.

He may have shed some of the Yankee spirit to the Cubs by his presence. Or it may have been that another three years had elapsed since the Cubs had won their last pennant, and so they were destined to win another one. Whatever the causes, they did win in 1938, but not until they had undergone some of the most dramatic flourishes in their history.

⊛ XXIX ⊛

THAT MIDSTREAM SWAP AGAIN

THE ARM TROUBLES OF DIZZY DEAN ALONG WITH EVERYTHING else had furnished more fuel for the fires the second guessers were building under Charlie Grimm. His judgment in handling the ball club was being questioned. So was his supposed lack of firmness in taking disciplinary action against some of his errant athletes. Sports writers were sniping at him right along. Several of the members of his club were not above making remarks about the way things were going. Some of these players were hopeful that the managerial lightning would strike them. All they succeeded in doing for the time being was to add to the general confusion.

There was never a time then or thereafter that Wrigley lost faith in Grimm. He liked him personally, and he liked him as a manager. In an effort to brace Charlie and possibly make him feel more of a person in authority, Wrigley considered making a vice-president of the club out of his friend.

For all of his easygoing ways in public Grimm was given to a great deal of private fretting. As the days wore on and the outlook grew bleaker, he made up his mind to resign. There was no serious argument between him and the executive staff, and certainly none with Wrigley. If Charlie insisted on resigning, as he did, Wrigley was willing to accede to his wishes. On July 20, the twelfth Cub manager since Frank Chance, turned back the club to the owners and went his way.

Grimm's way was not very far, to be sure. Wrigley promptly rounded up for him a radio engagement. The baseball broadcasting act Grimm and Lew Fonseca put on for a season or so was often much more entertaining than the games they discussed. Their jobs called for them to broadcast all the home games of the Cubs and the White Sox. They did so, at times, with the voice of baseball experts, but more often than not they dropped in a few side issues which their listeners grew to appreciate even more than the standard mouthings of men at ball-park microphones.

It is the custom both at Wrigley Field and Comiskey Park for the announcement of the official attendance to be made on or about the seventh inning. It is relayed from the counting room to the press boxes and the radio booths. All other broadcasters were content to announce the figures and let it go at that. Grimm and Fonseca had a better idea; and, since it is improbable that either will again take up broadcasting for a living, there can be no harm now in exposing their technique.

Once in possession of the exact figures, unbeknown to their listeners, of course, Grimm and Fonseca would begin a daily argument over the size of the crowd. Each would make a guess, sometimes a few more over the exact figure, sometimes a few less. When they eventually decided to announce the exact figures, they marveled at each other's accuracy in estimating the size of a crowd. The listeners marveled, too; and many were the letters Grimm and Fonseca received complimenting them on their quality as crowd estimators.

One day Fonseca decided to hit the exact figure right on the head—and did. Having reached perfection, the boys decided to abandon that form of daily entertainment for their listeners, and so announced, Grimm explaining that there was no purpose in going any further since it was no longer a hard trick at all.

So perfect was the accord between Grimm and Wrigley, when the change in field management came up, it was Grimm who named his own successor. He asked for and obtained the job for Charles Leo (Gabby) Hartnett, the Cub with the longest service record of them all.

When Hartnett took charge, it did not seem that there was

going to be any repetition of 1932's history when the Cubs swapped managers in the midst of a pennant race and went on to win. Those six years before, Grimm himself had been the inspirational urge to a National League pennant.

The Cubs did not respond as quickly to Hartnett's driving tactics as they had to Grimm's soothing touch in 1932. There was about Hartnett some of the willingness to say what he meant when he meant it, and the easily ruffled Cubs did not all care for the sharp answer.

All through August and September it seemed improbable that the Cubs would overhaul the Pittsburgh Pirates. "Pie" Traynor's club had opened up a big lead, and the Pittsburgh management made elaborate preparations for the world series to come. (Press buttons prepared for that 1938 series in Pittsburgh, which didn't quite get there, are a collector's item to this day.)

Somehow the same faltering in the stretch which had been chronic with the Cubs, now caught up with the Pirates. Slowly at first, and then with alarming rapidity, the Pirates began to slide back, and game by game the Cubs drew nearer to them.

On September 27 the Pirates came to Wrigley Field for a series. They were then a game and a half in the lead. This then was a series in which every game counted. The Cubs could ill afford to lose one, since time was running out. The Pirates, now visibly affected by the pennant shakes for which even penicillin is no help, were just as fearful of dropping a single game in the series.

For the opening game Hartnett called upon Dizzy Dean, of the troubled arm and the fluid-drive conversation. Diz had not appeared in a game since September 18. Hartnett chose to gamble on him for two reasons. One, Diz had a way of coming through in the tough ones. Two, by pitching him Hartnett could give an extra day's rest to his superlative hurler, Bill Lee, whose tremendous effort, more than anything else, had brought the Cubs that close to a pennant.

In a spot such as this Dizzy Dean was perfectly at home. Here

171

was a park packed to capacity with popeyed fans. Here was a game on which an entire season might depend. If you had asked Dean—and many did—what he thought about being put on such a spot, Diz had but one answer: "Gabby's getting smarter every day. Who else would he pick to beat these jerks but Old Diz?"

Through eight excitement-charged innings Old Diz and his "nothing" ball befuddled the Pirates. In that time the Cubs had secured him two runs, or one more than he said he would need to win the game. In those eight innings no Pirate had managed to find his way around the bases, so it seemed that Old Diz was making good once more on one of his many boastful utterances.

The game went into the Pirates' half of the ninth, and Dean retired two men, though Woody Jensen succeeded in getting on base. Lee Handley timed one of Dean's bubble pitches and smashed it into the outfield for a double, Jensen being held at third, since it had to be two runs or nothing for the Pirates.

Hartnett's judgment in handling his pitchers was now up for close inspection. He might have gone through with Dean trusting his courage under fire would enable him to squirm out of the inning. But this was no time to press his luck. Hartnett removed the weary Dean and called upon Lee to finish up.

For one terrifying moment it seemed that Gabby had made a bad guess. Before he was completely loosened up Lee cut loose with a wild pitch, on which Jensen scored. With the game in the balance, Big Bill righted himself and struck out Al Todd. It was the Cubs' game, 2–1, and first place was now but a half game away.

Their victory had been costly in man power, however. In the second inning the luckless Augie Galan wrenched his knee and was carried from the field. This forced a realignment of the team for the rest of the game and series. It took Phil Cavarretta from first base to right field, while Frank Demaree moved from right to Galan's place in left. Rip Collins took up the job at first base.

The next day's game found almost all the Cub pitchers save Dean in action. It dragged on and on until the evening shadows began to creep over Wrigley Field. When the last half of the ninth

© *Chicago Daily News*

Dizzy Dean

Lou Novikoff

was reached, with the score tied at 5–5, and the first two Cubs went out, it seemed reasonable to suppose that the game would end that way. It was growing so dark that the start of another inning was out of the question.

Gabby Hartnett was the third batter for the Cubs in that memorable ninth inning. Mace Brown, pitching for the Pirates, promptly got two strikes on him. In ordinary circumstances a pitcher with two and nothing on the hitter might be wary about coming through with a good pitch on the next one. But Brown came to the conclusion that the thing to do was get the third strike over, on the general principle that Hartnett could not hit what he could not see. Brown, as well as all the other Pirates, was willing to settle for the tie. The thing to do was get the game over. So Mace wound up and fired the ball towards the plate, right down the groove where Hartnett was swinging.

Gabby landed squarely upon the pitch. That was the last seen of that ball—or of the Pirates' hope for a pennant that season.

Everyone within the confines of Wrigley Field or within the vocal range of frenzied broadcasters knew that was a home run. Brown knew it first. He did not even trouble to turn and peer through the darkness out toward left field in which direction the ball was moving when last seen. He started for the Pirates dugout almost as soon as the ponderous Hartnett left the plate on his way to first.

There have been many home runs slugged out of Wrigley Field since 1916, but none before nor since has created the stir within the place that followed Hartnett's wallop—not even Babe Ruth's so-called series shot against Charley Root. Wild-eyed fans broke out of the stands and on to the field. Even Andy Frain's well-drilled ushers were unable to stay the mad rush. Everybody wanted to get to Hartnett, the man who had put the Cubs on top in the race at last. Many of them did get to him soon after he had rounded second base. As they convoyed him toward third, with photographers' flash bulbs lighting the way, scores of other hilarious fans picked up the victory march.

Hartnett actually had to fight his way through the mob to find third base and touch it. His path to the plate was so congested it seemed for a time that he might never get there and make his pennant-winning homer official. When he did plant his foot on the plate, it was a long time before the aroused fans would permit him to retire to the comparative quiet of the clubhouse. It was even longer before the last exultant fan would permit himself to be shooed out of Wrigley Field.

Bill Lee, in action for the fourth day in a row, started the next game for the Cubs. As far as the Pirates were concerned, P. K. Wrigley himself could have pitched that one. The Pirates were done. They were licked. Hartnett's home run had removed the last vestige of fight from their systems. They were now a team merely going through the motions of baseball. They yielded to Lee and the Cubs, 10–1. The half-game lead had now grown to a game and a half. The pennant race, for all practical purposes, was over.

And now for some more of that repeating history.

The Cubs of 1932, who had changed managers in midyear and won a pennant, wound up meeting Joe McCarthy's Yankees in the world series. The Cubs of 1938, having made a similar managerial switch with like results, were also confronted with McCarthy's Yankees.

The Cubs of 1932 when called upon to vote on the split of their world series share, ignored Rogers Hornsby, who had managed them for much of the season. The Cubs of 1938 did likewise and forgot all about Charlie Grimm who had been manager of all, and friend of most, until his resignation just about two months before the Cubs had any immediate need for worrying about a world series share.

Such was the enthusiasm in Chicago over Hartnett's home run that even the mighty Yankees did not terrify the patrons of Wrigley Field. All the tall tales of the batting prowess of Joe DiMaggio, Bill Dickey, Lou Gehrig, Joe Gordon, and the rest did not disturb those Cub fans. Gabby's team would find a way.

Bill Lee was the logical choice to start the series for the Cubs. He pitched well, but "Red" Ruffing of the Yankees pitched better.

Stan Hack was the only Cub who found Ruffing any bargain. It was one of his three hits which scored Rip Collins in the third inning for the Cubs' lone run. By the time Collins tallied, the Yankees already had two, Bill Dickey driving in one, George Selkirk the other. This uprising—mild for the Yankees—took place in the second inning. On base in the seventh inning through his fourth hit of the game, Dickey was driven home by Gordon, and the game ended on that 3–1 note.

Lee had done two notable things in his pitching. He held DiMaggio hitless, and he kept the Yankees from making a home run. In those days McCarthy's club counted an afternoon lost in which one or more of its members were not clouting baseballs out of the lot.

From his place in the Cubs' dugout all through that opening engagement Dizzy Dean had talked a great game against the Yankees, so for the second time around Hartnett elected to let him pitch one. Old Diz and his "nothing" ball came closer to beating the Yankees than any other Cub hurler ever has. He held them to three hits through the seventh inning, and owned a 3–2 lead. He should have been leading 3–0, but for one of those fantastic happenings which seem to creep up on the Cubs whenever they are under the stress and strain of a world series. This bad break happened in the second inning while Old Diz was nursing a one-run lead which Joe Marty's timely hit had given him.

The Yankees moved against that in the second when DiMaggio led off with a single and Gehrig walked. But Old Diz was not concerned. He caused Dickey to pop out, and when Selkirk did likewise, the Cub fans breathed easier. Dean worked with great care on Gordon, and the count eventually reached three and two. The next ball was hit by Gordon, not too well, on the ground between Hack and Jurges. Either might have fielded it without trouble, but neither did. Worse than that, they collided and while they were rolling around on the well-kept Wrigley Field sod, the ball proceeded leisurely on its way to left field.

The two Yankees on base, running on the pitch, had no trouble scoring. Gordon went all the way to second base before the ball was recovered—and recovered by, of all persons, Dean himself, who had to run all the way into the outfield to get it, while the rest of his teammates were trying to get the names of witnesses to the Hack-Jurges traffic accident.

This mishap gave the Yankees a 2-1 lead, which they held until the third inning. Then Marty landed again on a suitable offering from his fellow Californian, Vernon Gomez, and home came two Cub runners. This established the 3-2 lead Dean protected until the game went into the eighth inning.

Myril Hoag batted for Gomez and got on base. All afternoon long Frank Crosetti had been swinging from his heels at the "nothing" ball with no results. This time he really hit one. His long fly dropped beyond the first row of the left field bleachers, and the game Old Diz had almost won was now lost beyond recall. To make it official, DiMaggio in the ninth came through with another Yankee two-run homer.

Joe McCarthy was now halfway toward his objective, that of turning back the Cubs for the second time in world series play without permitting them to win a single game.

The series moved on to New York after the havoc wrought in Wrigley Field. For game three the Cubs had to look at Monte Pearson, and Joe Marty alone of their number was satisfied with what he saw. Pearson allowed but five hits. Of these Marty made three. One was a home run, and another was a single which scored Stan Hack.

The Yankees picked up five runs off Clay Bryant, who started for the Cubs, and off Jack Russell and Larry French who drifted in and out as the game progressed. Bill Dickey and Joe Gordon furnished the homers to give the proper Yankee touch to the proceedings which had drawn 55,236 onlookers to the Stadium.

The Cubs had nothing left after this game, and the Yankees closed shop, 8-3 in the finale, doing about as they pleased from start to finish. Ruffing returned to action for the Yankees and had an easy time of it. He was given three runs in the second when the Yankees pounced on Bill Lee. Another tallied in the

176

sixth, but the big inning was reserved for the eighth, in which four Cub pitchers passed in review.

Vance Page was in at the start and presently gave way to Larry French. Then in came Tex Carleton, who pitched to just three men. Two of his pitches were as wild as any the Yankee Stadium had ever seen, and on each a run scored. It took Dizzy Dean to get the last man out, and four runs which the Yankees didn't need came swarming across the plate in that wild inning.

The Yankees were very much themselves throughout this closing number of the series. It was Frank Crosetti's day at the bat. His double and triple drove in four runs. The home-run production was handled by Tommy Henrich for the Yankees, though Ken O'Dea, who had replaced Hartnett as the Cubs' catcher for the game, hit a harmless homer for a lost cause.

This was the close of the Cubs' pennant-every-three-years program which had been going on since 1929, though no one realized it, just then. Neither did anyone realize that in this series Lou Gehrig's heroic figure was passing in review for the last time in any world series. This baseball immortal even then was in the grip of the malady which was to lead to his abandoning the game he loved and ultimately to his untimely death. In these four games Gehrig was not the power hitter he had been six years before when facing Cub pitching. His work at the bat was negligible, particularly in driving runs across the plate. In the 1932 series he was doing that nearly every time he came to bat—or so it seemed to the shaky Cub pitchers.

The money-loving Cubs, of which there were many, took a degree of satisfaction from the fact that each loser's individual share was $4,674.86—a new series record.

On the artistic side the games had left much to be desired by the critics of the Cubs. In reality they fared not much worse than any other world series opponents who were unlucky enough to draw the Yankees for the annual Fall showing.

The sting to the beatings however, was not so much in the fact that the Yankees overpowered, outpitched, and outfielded the Cubs. It was that in the most critical stages of the important games the Cubs looked very silly in defeat.

Again the Yankees had made better clubs perhaps than the 1938 Cubs look silly, but Chicago fans took scant consolation from that. They began to raise the "Something must be done" cry as soon as the last man had been retired in the Yankee Stadium and the Cubs themselves had nothing else on their minds but scattering to their respective homes. The fans had no such counterirritants to ease them through the late fall and longer winter.

☻ XXX ☻

"ERROR, BARTELL!"

O N THE "FUNERAL" TRAIN FROM NEW YORK TO CHICAGO, following the 1938 world series, Manager Hartnett in an ill-guarded moment declared he would be glad to get rid of everyone on his squad before another season started. Hartnett was very mad about it all, and while some made due allowance for his peeve, others were willing to concede that Gabby was as lacking in tact as Rogers Hornsby had been before him. Within two months of the close of the series, however, it really did appear that the club was to be subjected to a complete overhauling. There were enough players to start a new league moving in and out of Chicago.

A gigantic deal was arranged with the Giants, to start off the mass movement of players. For the time being the Cubs were abandoning their favorite marts at Philadelphia, St. Louis, and Pittsburgh. Three Giants for three Cubs was the size and shape of this deal. It never has been explained completely which one of the three Giants it was that Hartnett wanted most, though the finger of suspicion pointed to Hank Leiber. He was an easygoing, right-hand-hitting outfielder who might have been one of baseball's best batsmen if he ever had found time to get around to it. With Leiber came Dick Bartell, a peppery little shortstop, and Gus Mancuso, a mild-mannered and inoffensive catcher who had been in the National League a long time.

To get this trio the Cubs sent on their way the brilliant fielding shortstop, Bill Jurges, outfielder Frank Demaree, and catcher Ken O'Dea. The immediate effect of this deal was to disturb the fine friendship that existed on the Cubs among Jurges, Billy Herman, and Augie Galan. Leiber, a companionable sort, fitted into this organization within an organization, but everybody missed Jurges, on the field and off it.

Tony Lazzeri, who had finished out the season still wondering how and why he had ever become involved in it, departed from the pay roll with much less fanfare than had accompanied his arrival. Almost as quietly Tex Carleton and Rip Collins were eased out, leaving Dizzy Dean as the lone representative of the old Gas House Gang of St. Louis ready to do or die for the Cubs in 1939.

For all of the fact that it was the defending National League champion, this was a ball club that was a wee bit on the daffy side. It began to show signs before the spring-training stay at Catalina Island was over.

Bartell, a great conversationalist on and off the field, was exercising one day at the ball yard on the island when traveling secretary Bob Lewis and a Chicago newspaperman strolled by. Now Lewis carried considerable tonnage, and so did his companion. After a mild winter and plenty of well-cooked meals, both were inclined to be a few pounds, fifty or a hundred at a quick guess, overweight.

"When does the balloon go up?" cried Bartell, as Lewis and his companion went past. No one had ever told Bartell that while a stout man may refer jokingly to his own poundage, nobody else must, least of all a comparative stranger, as Bartell was to the Chicago newspaperman.

It is doubtful if Bartell even suspected the coals of critical wrath he had heaped upon his head with that ill-timed remark. If he had enjoyed a fine season with the Cubs in 1939, perhaps all might have been forgiven, for there is more than a little of the fan about any baseball writer. But Bartell didn't have a very good season. He specialized in fumbling balls hit at him. He executed many a throw to first base that had dugout denizens and even box-seat patrons scrambling to get out of the way.

The Wrigley Field press box is equipped with a public-address system over which the official scorer is accustomed to make his pronouncements on hits and errors and such. Over this, day after day, boomed a voice: "Error, Bartell!"

In time the public-address system wasn't needed. It grew to be a chorus whenever "Rowdy Richard" kicked another one, or let go with one of those scatter-arm throws. Everyone was chanting, "Error, Bartell!"

It is to be doubted if criticism of press or fans ever has troubled Bartell much. Certainly it has bothered him no more than hostile opposition pitches which have "dusted" him so frequently in his tempestuous career. So it is not being advanced here that the "balloon" episode in spring training was what made for Bartell's sorry year with the Cubs. But it helped.

In his first season with the Cubs Leiber did enough hitting in a leisurely way to lead the club with a .310 average.

Mancuso, who managed to get into eighty games as old playing age gradually caught up with Hartnett, is best remembered by the Cubs on two counts. He enrolled most of them in a whittling club for which he seemed to be a walking delegate, and he wore most of them, and especially Hartnett, out by constant reference to the way "we used to do it with the Giants." Of the three who came in the biggest shake-up the Cubs had undergone in years, Gus Mancuso created the least stir.

The Cubs were not done with dealing for 1939 even after the season had been well under way. A chance offered itself to bring Claude Passeau from the Phillies, and the Cubs didn't miss on that one. They paid what turned out to be a big price for Passeau, but it was a deal which the most exacting of the second guessers has been unable to take apart and finds flaws with.

To get Passeau the Cubs had to give the Phillies Joe Marty, their robust batting hero of the 1938 world series, and two pitchers, Ray Harrell and Walter Higbe.

Higbe had been in possession if not control of the Cubs since the spring of 1937. He had been scared up by scouts in Columbia of the South Atlantic League, and getting him to training camp at Catalina Island was probably the most trying job traveling secretary Bob Lewis had had, until he was confronted with the problem of transporting his squad to the island by air when the Cubs assembled for 1946 training.

Higbe reported in Chicago all right, and was seen at the railroad station the night the Cubs departed for camp. He was checked through the gate by Lewis, and double checked by Doc Lotshaw, who was doubling as a patrol judge. But when Lewis arose in the morning there was no Higbe on the train. Nor was there any trace of him for several days, when he finally reported that he had forgotten a toothbrush or something, and had gone back to Columbia, South Carolina, or thereabouts, to get it.

He showed possibilities as a pitcher, but he also showed possibilities as an eccentric; and as the Cubs were then featuring in the main ring the greatest eccentric of 'em all, Dizzy Dean, Higbe's side show didn't get the attention it deserved.

That may have had something to do with the fact that he was included in the Passeau deal. It was his pitching, however, which caused Brooklyn to become interested in Higbe less than two full seasons after he left the Cubs. The Brooklyn interest was so great that three players, one of them being catcher "Mickey" Livingston, and $100,000 went to the Phillies, that Higbe might become a member of the Brooklyn Dodgers, for whom he was designed by nature. It is definitely a part of this story to mention that Higbe's twenty-two victories were an adequate part of Brooklyn's successful drive to a pennant in 1941.

It might well be argued that this deal, if considered on the basis of Passeau for Higbe, was one of the very few in baseball which worked out to the complete satisfaction of all parties concerned.

Now functioning in the outfield was Dominic Dallessandro. He had led 1938's Pacific Coast League hitters with a large .368 average. In his 107 games with the Cubs in 1939, Dom's average was more commensurate with his size, and stocky Dallessandro is one of the major leagues' players who is built closest to the turf on which he treads. He batted .268 for the Cubs in this first season but was a popular figure with teammates, management, and fans alike.

Late in the season on the personal recommendation of Kiki Cuyler, the Cubs brought up another minor league outfielder in the person of Bill Nicholson. He had been terrifying pitchers in the Southern Association, and Cuyler insisted that Bill was the answer to all the Cubs' troubles.

This patchwork club with which the Cubs operated in 1939 managed to finish in fourth place. All things considered that was an accomplishment—even if the fans did not always think so.

Dizzy Dean's appearances as a pitcher were greatly limited in this season, though he continued active on all other fronts and managed to get more attention from press and public than all of the other Cub pitchers who were working steadily at the trade. Diz was in and out of nineteen games in all, pitched a matter of ninety-six innings, and showed a record of six won and four lost.

His extra curricular activities during 1939 and 1940 gained him great attention. As the Cubs were making their way back from spring-training camp, Diz became A.W.O.L. in one of the cities of the southwest, and Hartnett promptly suspended him. Suspending Diz was one thing, and getting rid of him was another. Dean, as usual, had what seemed to him a logical explanation of his departure from what Hartnett regarded as spring-training law and order, and loud and long Diz protested the wrong which had been done him. He announced finally that he was going to go directly to Chicago and take up the whole matter with Wrigley.

All the gentlemen of the press saw Diz to the train and cheered him on his way. Then they accompanied the Cubs to the next city on their spring exhibition stop, only to find that Diz had decided to visit there, too.

His most news-worthy moments with the Cubs, in his off-the-field activities, came in New York one evening. This was the incident of the telephone-table top. No one will ever know for certain just what happened, or when. There were almost as many versions as there were persons to give them. So, to take the incident apart chronologically, a start must be made on a Saturday evening in New York.

Dean and his wife, Pat, were out for the evening. They had invited Jim Kearns, a Chicago sports writer, to accompany them, but he pleaded a previous engagement.

The next afternoon the Cubs were in Brooklyn for a doubleheader. Dean was not with the team, but no one paid any attention, since he had not been scheduled to pitch, and there were enough other interesting characters in Brooklyn to tide over the afternoon.

However, a Brooklyn fan who felt that he wasn't getting his money's worth if there were no Dean yelled at Dick Bartell, asking where Diz was. Bartell replied that Dean didn't come out because he had cut his arm when he fell through a glass cigar counter at the hotel.

There was a rush of newspapermen for the New York hotel as soon as the two games were over. Then it was discovered that Dean and his wife had checked out, and further investigation disclosed that they had taken a train for Chicago.

Presently Hartnett arrived at the hotel, and all he cared to say was that he had ordered Dean home. This was not sufficient for the newspapermen and especially for Kearns.

"I know he didn't fall through any showcase in the lobby," Kearns told Hartnett. "I was in the lobby when Diz and Pat came in. It was about 11:10 last night. Diz bought the early editions of the Sunday papers and they went up in the elevator. You take it from there." But Manager Gabby continued to preserve a dignified silence.

Kearns kept on with his investigation. He learned from the hotel's records that a call had come from Dean's room for the house physician at about 11:25 p.m., so whatever had happened must have happended shortly after the Deans reached their room.

Eventually it became known that Manager Gabby and trainer Doc Lotshaw had both been out of the hotel at the time the house doctor was called. They were both out when the house cop also called, as a hotel routine which follows any late night summons for the house doctor.

While other reporters were scurrying around the hotel, Kearns reached the conclusion that the place to get the story was wherever Dean happened to be. Kearns, no mean student of timetables, figured that by taking a plane he could overhaul Dean before the latter reached Chicago. He was able to do so, and at Canton, Ohio, he caught up with the man of many mysteries.

"I don't know what Diz told Bartell," Kearns says. "Maybe he did say he had fallen through a cigar case. All I know is what he told me on the train leaving Canton. And I might add that he has never changed that story, as far as I know.

"I'm not exactly clear whether he said he was reaching for the phone to call his brother Paul, who was in New York at the same time, or whether he was reaching for it to answer a call Paul made him. In either event, Diz said he slipped and cut his left arm on the glass top of the phone table. I heard afterwards that there was absolutely no evidence in the room that this was the way the cut was made. I have also heard the John Hoffman, another baseball writer who was on the trip, practiced falls against glass phone-table tops for days, and was unable to cut himself on either arm. But that's what Diz told me did happen.

"He said the house doctor, after bandaging the arm, advised him to keep out of uniform for a few days. That was why he didn't go to Brooklyn the next afternoon. Dean's version was that leaving for Chicago was his own idea. Hartnett said he ordered him home because there was no use having him around.

"If you ask me, the whole incident was so screwy, nobody will ever know what happened."

These principal characters in the latest Dean sensation were taking up so much space that regrettably the most interesting interview of the entire episode got no attention at all. It was the one which was volunteered by Bob Lewis, the sorely tried road secretary. He had been summoned from his slumbers when the news of the accident to Dean first broke, and he was told that Diz had sustained a cut on his arm.

"It couldn't have been his right arm," said Lewis, "or he wouldn't be able to feel it."

What with the constant uproar created by Dean, and with another ill-starred trade having backfired, Hartnett's 1940 season as manager was an unhappy one. During the winter Bartell had been traded to Detroit even up for Bill Rogell, another veteran, who, if not as loud as Bartell, was just as funny trying to fill the space once occupied by such Cub shortstops as Bill Jurges and Joe Tinker. Gus Mancuso also closed his Cub career after this one season, being traded to Brooklyn along with pitcher Newel Kimball. In exchange the Cubs obtained title to Al Todd, who had been catching for various National League clubs for nine years.

Hartnett was given some relief in June when Dean was optioned to Tulsa, there to give his questionable arm the final test to see if the "nothing" ball was ever again going to turn into "something." It never did, but that didn't keep the Cubs from recalling Diz late in August, and once again the merry-go-round began to spin.

Dean's 1940 Cub record was one of fifty-four innings of work, spread through ten games, for which he was credited with three victories and charged with three defeats.

When he left the Cubs to take his place in St. Louis among the radio announcers, Diz left behind him very few pitching records at all comparable with those of the days of his greatness as a Cardinal. However, the vast sum expended for him was more than returned to the Cubs, and there have never been any regrets that he was one of them, even for such a comparatively short time. Whether pitching or not he provided copy and focused continual attention on a club that of its own efforts would have merited scant attention.

The deal for Dean is definitely not one which can ever be held against the Cubs as evidence of their hard luck or their lack of judgment. The Dean deal paid off, one way or another, far beyond its makers' fondest hopes.

Apart from its phases peculiar to Dizzy Dean, his coming to

the Cubs, his stay with them, and his eventual departure, did fit in with what was now a stock gag. So many of the players who had reached the Cubs after notable records elsewhere, immediately developed aches and pains, or brought them with them, that it was automatic for the critics to ask, as each new deal was made: "What's wrong with him?"

It was in Charlie Grimm's time, however, that this gag was given a switch by the young son of a sports writer, who had been taken down to the Cubs' dugout for a visit. Grimm reached into the ball bag and hauled out a glistening new baseball and presented it to the small boy with appropriate gestures.

The small boy held it in his hand, and inspected it closely.

"What's the matter with it?" he asked at last.

"It's a baseball, Bill," said Grimm. "It isn't one of my ballplayers."

⊖ XXXI ⊖

LET 'EM GO GALLAGHER!

WHEN THE CUBS LUMBERED INTO FIFTH PLACE AT THE END of the 1940 season as Cincinnati's Reds repeated their 1939 victory, there was ample evidence that a managerial change was in the making. Gabby Hartnett was definitely on his way out. Even as the season progressed, there had been speculation as to his successor. There had been some movement on the part of adherents of Billy Herman, and no doubt he had ambitions. He was one of the members of the senior class who had served through three managerial stages of the Cubs. He was his league's best second baseman and had been for many years. He might have made a fine manager, but the opportunity did not come his way.

P. K. Wrigley had reached the conclusion that the way to peace and quiet in his baseball property was not through the elevation of another player from the ranks. Though no ball-player himself, Wrigley knew when he had three strikes on him. The first was Rogers Hornsby. The second was Charlie Grimm. And the third was Gabby Hartnett. Great ballplayers all, but each seemingly lacking in that certain something which made for handling men and material in a fashion that would satisfy the exacting demands of the Chicago public which Wrigley aimed to please.

When he next came to bat, Wrigley intended to change his stance completely, but meanwhile he kept this entirely to himself and a few trusted confreres. A general overhauling of the Cubs' executive forces was in the making, and a change from

188

Hartnett to someone else was but a part of Wrigley's planning.

His chief executive, Boots Weber, was anxious to get back to his flower garden and his vegetable patch in California. Wrigley was willing to have him do so, but he first wanted to find a man to succeed him, and if possible one who would function along the lines Bill Veeck had operated on in one of the happier eras of the Cubs.

Wrigley was content to keep his plans to himself through the 1939 world series, and during the course of it he found the man apparently best qualified then to manage the Cubs.

As the Reds gained a world's championship that fall at the expense of the Detroit Tigers in a spirited engagement, the hero of heroes in Cincinnati was the veteran Jimmy Wilson. He had served as a catcher for a long time in the National League and had been manager of the Phillies for several years. He had come to the Reds as a coach and certainly had no idea of attempting to recapture his lost youth and again essay a daily stint as a catcher when the world series began. Yet that is exactly what he was asked to do, and what he was well able to do, when an emergency arose and Manager Bill McKechnie was left without an experienced catcher, following the action of the first game.

In it the slow-motion catcher, Ernie Lombardi, had been rendered null and void by an injury. After a hurried consultation with Manager Bill McKechnie, Wilson agreed to don the mask and chest protector once more and get into the series.

He had done very little active work for several seasons. He certainly was not in anything resembling playing condition. But he was ready and willing, and from his entry into the game until final victory perched on the Reds' banners, game and durable Jimmy Wilson proved that he was able.

He worked through six straight games of the series, batted .353, and in what was actually well beyond the twilight of his playing career, stole the only base that was pilfered in the entire series.

It was this all-round display of the thing called "guts" which brought Wilson to the attention of Wrigley and Weber. They were mindful, perhaps, that Wilson's long term as manager of the Phillies was additional proof of his ability to take it. These were the deciding factors in his appointment, though it suited the purpose of Cub critics later on to say that Wilson had clinched the Cub managerial job by stealing a base in the world series.

That put him one up on Hartnett, in whose time at least two other Cub players, Clay Bryant and George Stainback, had earned their keep most of the time by appearing as pinch runners for Gabby. Wilson ran for himself, around the Cincinnati bases and into the Cubs' job.

His actual acceptance of the post was deferred for a month or so. Before it became a matter of record, Wrigley had found himself the general manager he had been seeking all these years.

The long arm of coincidence, and again the parallel, came into the picture. For P. K. Wrigley reached into the sports department of the same newspaper his father had tapped many years before to secure the services of Bill Veeck.

James T. Gallagher, a small man with a big voice and positive opinions, was functioning as a sports writer and enjoying life immensely. Sometimes he traveled with the Cubs. Sometimes he traveled with the White Sox. He was an open advocate, long before others climbed on the band wagon, of the possibilities of professional football, properly staged.

He was an advocate of fresh air, even in the raw, cold days of early spring or late fall, when his activities took him into the press box at Wrigley Field. That comfortable abiding place of the baseball or football writers at work is equipped with windows which may be removed when the day is pleasant, or restored when the temperatures are low on the Fahrenheit scale. All of the other sports writers and the tappers of telegraph keys hollered for the windows to be put in at the first drop of the mercury. Not Gallagher. Windows might be restored on either side of him, but not in front of him. He loved fresh air, deep breathing, and chewing tobacco. He was a rugged individualist.

To him one day came Weber with an invitation to lunch. Gallagher accepted as a matter of course and promptly forgot about it. He was more concerned at the moment with the great possibilities of the T formation, the man in motion, George Halas, and his beloved Chicago Bears.

After a few days had elapsed Weber called up Gallagher to remind him of the luncheon date. This time Gallagher showed up and broke bread with P. K. Wrigley, among others. After lunch Wrigley, Weber, and Gallagher repaired to Wrigley's office where a general discussion of baseball took place. At the conclusion Gallagher was asked if he would care to take over the general management.

Being himself—which Gallagher is at all times—he told Wrigley very promptly that he didn't know whether he would or not.

"I'm doing pretty well where I am," he said.

"Well, think it over," said Wrigley, and left it at that point.

Subsequently Gallagher discussed this marked change in his life and work with his friend Halas, to whom he turned for advice. Halas told him very quickly that anybody would be nuts to walk away from a job such as that. Another close friend told him much the same thing and with even more emphasis. A third friend listened to the proposition and then said: "You better grab a cab and get back to Wrigley before he changes his mind."

So James T. Gallagher became the general manager of the Cubs, to the complete satisfaction of some of his Chicago sportswriting associates and to the chagrin of others. He brought into the Wrigley organization a personality such as the Cubs had never known before on their executive staff.

James T. Gallagher is a man with a tonal and a conversational change of pace. He can yell louder than the next man if it suits his purpose. He can outcuss the most profane ballplayer if occasion arises. He can be quiet and reserved and excellent company, cutting loose with nothing more emphatic than an occasional "Judas priest!" He can shy away from all contacts and talk to or with no one for long stretches of time. He can be most communicative, or he can make silent Cal Coolidge of happy memory seem like an entire public-address system turned on full blast.

The writer of these lines, who has worked beside James T. Gallagher and who has known him longer and perhaps more intimately than any of his contemporaries, can say truthfully that the Cubs general manager has never crossed a friend—nor often forgiven an enemy. Gallagher has many in both categories.

There is never a waking moment in which it is any problem at all to find out on which side of any given question Gallagher stands. If P. K. Wrigley ever deserved the rap of having surrounded himself with yes men, his final rounding up of James T. Gallagher more than atoned for that.

One of the first official questions put to him by Wrigley was his opinion of Jimmy Wilson as a manager.

"He ought to know baseball," said Gallagher. "He's been around long enough. He's a nice guy."

The Cubs were already committed to Wilson as their next field manager, and he may stand as Boots Weber's legacy to the club.

When Wilson checked in officially in November, he discussed with Gallagher the subject of coaches. Wilson said he wanted Dick Spalding, who had been associated with him during the time he managed the Phillies.

"Who else?" asked Gallagher.

Wilson said he didn't care but thought it might be an act of wisdom to hire some former Cub player who would be familiar to the fans.

"How about Charlie Grimm?" Gallagher wanted to know.

"The very man," agreed Wilson, "if we can get him. Maybe he wouldn't want to come back as a coach for the club he used to manage."

"I think he would," said Gallagher, "but before I talk to him there is something I think you should know about the situation here in Chicago. You know how fans are. If Grimm comes back, and things don't go too well for you, it will not be long before somebody starts yelling for Charlie to take over the club."

"Don't let that stop you," said the very blunt Wilson. "If things don't go too well for me, I'll expect to be fired. So what difference will it make whether I lose out to one of my coaches or to somebody else. I know darn well Charlie will never do any chiseling on me. Go get him if you possibly can."

Grimm, very happy about the whole thing, was duly restored to the Cubs in the capacity of coach, the first of many moves James T. Gallagher was to make as general manager. In the light of subsequent events it was an excellent start as an executive.

If you should happen into Gallagher's office at Wrigley Field one of these days and find the occupant in a mellow mood, he may reach into a desk drawer and come up with a multicolored folder on which is printed the vital statistics of the Cubs' reserve list as it shaped up in the spring of 1941. On it were listed the names of thirty-seven players.

"That," James T. Gallagher will tell you, if he is in the mood, "was what we had under control then. That's all we had. And a fine mess they were, come to think of it."

He might tell you, though in all probability he would not, that the Cubs were many thousand dollars in debt, and that before they were able to complete spring training a quick touch had to be made for more fresh money.

These statements are dropped in merely to show that James T. Gallagher did not start from scratch as general manager of the Cubs. He started from well behind it. It might be well to keep that in mind as the story of his regime unfolds.

His first operation designed to help the club was an attempt to secure an experienced shortstop. Bill Rogell had not been up to it, and the available quartet of minor-leaguers, Bobby Sturgeon, Len Merullo, Harvey Storey, and Lou Stringer were unknown quantities.

While Wilson was coaching at Cincinnati, Billy Myers was the Reds' regular shortstop. Wilson thought he might do for the Cubs in an emergency so Gallagher sanctioned the trade of outfielder Jim Gleeson and infielder Bobby Mattick to get him. But Myers turned out to be the third in the shortstop flop parade that had begun with Dick Bartell.

Wilson was an object of critical attention from the start. He had ideas which were radically different from any of those tried by previous Cub leaders. So, in his first spring-training session Wilson might have gained first place in the Attention Derby, all by himself, if it were not for the advent of the one, the only, the original Lou Novikoff, the scourge of the minor leagues, who came up for inspection by the Cubs that spring.

Novikoff was the idol of Los Angeles and the Pacific Coast League. He had been a sensation at Ponca City and Moline as well. Tulsa thought he was the last word in hitting power, and indeed he was, if you are discussing minor-league hitting. He was so much a riot in Los Angeles that when the Cubs appeared there for their regular spring exhibition stand every last one of the California baseball experts freely admitted the club's worries were over. With Novikoff they couldn't miss.

It didn't make any difference what kind of pitching was served him, they explained. He hit good pitching and he hit bad pitching. It wasn't even necessary for a pitcher to get the ball over the plate to him. He was likely to swing on a ball thrown behind him and cripple an infielder with the resultant drive.

There is no question but that the Cubs hoped and prayed that Novikoff would approximate even a modest part of the reputation which had preceded him. He was given every opportunity to make the grade, but there was something lacking once he donned a major-league uniform.

No one had ever made any claims that Novikoff was a fielding genius, and it was soon found out that inside baseball and signal systems were things with which he couldn't be annoyed at all. But Wilson and Grimm, and Gallagher in the background, were willing to forgive and forget Novikoff's clumsy defensive style if he would but hit the baseball the way he always had in every league save the National and American.

There were brief stretches in his Cub career when Novikoff did seem launched on a hitting streak something like those which had made Ponca City, Moline, Tulsa, and Los Angeles resound with his praises. But the Mad Russian couldn't keep it up. For every run he drove in he was as liable to let in one or more with his poor defensive work.

The vines which decorated the walls of Wrigley Field were a constant source of worry to him. Whenever a ball was hit over his head, the Mad Russian would back up so far, and no farther. More often than not, the ball recoiling from the wall bounded past him and in toward the infield with the Mad Russian in hot pursuit. It was in an attempt to rectify this that Grimm labored long and earnestly with Novikoff.

"I thought at first that he was susceptible to hay fever," Grimm explained, "so I got me some samples of golden rod and proved to Lou that the vines weren't that. He seemed relieved, but next time a guy hit a ball over his head he stayed farther away from the vines than ever.

"I talked this over with Wilson and Bob Lewis, and Bob said maybe Novikoff thought the stuff was poison ivy. So I took him out again, and this time, when I was sure Mr. Wrigley wasn't looking, I pulled a bunch of the vines off the wall and rubbed them all over my face and hands. I even chewed a couple of the leaves to prove they couldn't harm anyone. All Novikoff had to say was that he wondered what kind of a smoke they would make. But he wouldn't go near 'em to find out."

Novikoff was neither a thing of beauty in the outfield nor yet a joy forever in his first season with the Cubs. He lasted for sixty-two games in his first season before being dispatched to Milwaukee. In those sixty-two games he batted .241.

At Milwaukee he was himself again, the scourge of the minor leagues. In ninety games there he averaged .370, and for every hit he made there were at least one hundred words written by some anti-Gallagherite in Chicago, and at least five hundred by every Los Angeles advocate of the Mad Russian. They insisted that a great wrong had been done their Lou, and that the Cubs would never get any place if they didn't have sense enough to appreciate greatness when it was within their grasp.

However, Novikoff enjoyed life immensely at Milwaukee as did everyone else who paid any attention to baseball. The Milwaukee club which had been dubbing along for several years had recently become the property of young Bill Veeck, son of the former Cub president. Young Bill had grown up in Chicago. He made his way up from minor posts at Wrigley Field to a place of some consequence in the organization. Indeed, at the time James T. Gallagher was appointed general manager there were many who thought young Bill had such possibilities himself. They were definitely right about that. As owner and general manager, official greeter and master of ceremonies, young Bill did not take long to prove it at Milwaukee.

He retained a fine understanding with the Cubs from P. K. Wrigley on down the line, and he was not above reaching into the Cubs' reserves for help. His first grab was his most noteworthy. He came up with Charlie Grimm as field manager and part owner of the Milwaukee club. Grimm had lent a receptive ear to young Bill when the latter outlined the partnership at Milwaukee. There was no difficulty in Grimm's getting permission to abandon his job as coach of the Cubs, and thus began in Milwaukee a baseball combine which was going to turn the staid old American Association upside down.

No promotional idea was too fantastic for Veeck to attempt, and in Grimm he had one of baseball's most gifted entertainers on or off the field. If the Milwaukee script seemed to be prepared by Olsen and Johnson, the fact remained that the crowds turned out for the Veeck-Grimm productions as they never had before. While there was gaiety and laughter all along the line, the baseball was not bad. Milwaukee remained at the top of the heap right along.

Into this atmosphere came Novikoff after his first whirl with the Cubs. He was a natural for Milwaukee, and it is a wonder he didn't hit .570, so well did he fit into all the roles stage managers Veeck and Grimm had for him.

If Grimm was supremely happy in Milwaukee, not so were the Jimmys, Gallagher and Wilson, left to carry on in Chicago without too much of the materials of defensive or offensive baseball warfare.

⊗ XXXII ⊗

GALLAGHER MEETS MacPHAIL

AMONG THE TOURISTS WHO FOUND THEIR WAY TO SOUTHERN California in the spring of 1941 was Larry MacPhail of the Brooklyn Dodgers. All sorts of conjectures were made over the visit, especially when he dropped in to look the Cubs over in some of their spring exhibition games. The most popular guess was that MacPhail wanted Billy Herman for his Dodgers. They were assumed to be possessed of sufficient talent at all other positions to bring to Brooklyn the pennant that MacPhail had practically guaranteed his clients. MacPhail would not say that he was after Herman—just then. Nor would he say he was not after him.

He did say, more or less privately, and perhaps just to make conversation, that he would be willing to expend $100,000 or thereabouts for Lou Novikoff, and might even pay an agent's commission to anyone who might get him the Mad Russian at a price. Novikoff had yet to play a major-league game, but not even Babe Ruth, Bob Grove, Joe DiMaggio, Rube Marquard, or any other graduating minor-leaguers had ever reaped as much attention while ranging through the minor leagues. Novikoff had been the subject of words galore in the daily newspapers and in the slick paper magazines. He was the idol of the gentry who plied their sports reporting trade on the air lanes. He was, in brief, a natural for Brooklyn, and no one knew any better than MacPhail that the Cubs were not going to let him get away until every possible chance of fitting him into a regular job was exhausted.

For publication, at this time, MacPhail was content to say that he had made the trip all the way to southern California simply to satisfy himself that there really could be anyone like Novikoff. He went away without saying whether he was satisfied.

There could be a Novikoff, of course, and there was. In no time at all MacPhail was able to get a play-by-play account of that memorable June 2, 1940, when Novikoff had graciously accepted the *Sporting News'* trophy as the minor leagues' number one man.

It is well nigh an axiom of baseball that any player who has a "day," if he is a pitcher, invariably has his ears batted off immediately. If he is a batsman, he invariably fails to get a hit and often looks terrible at the plate. But this was Novikoff who was having a "day." This was different.

Two home runs and two singles were the Mad Russian's contribution on the afternoon he accepted the *Sporting News'* trophy. He threw out a man at the plate. He advanced boldly on the microphone of the public-address system and sang "My Wild Irish Rose." He followed that with an encore, "Down By The Old Mill Stream." Somehow he forgot to do a solo on the harmonica. Perhaps time did not permit.

All this with appropriate embellishments gave MacPhail—and should give you—a general idea of Novikoff, the scourge of the minor leagues.

MacPhail's visit to southern California was forgotten until early in May when the Cubs were on an eastern trip and James T. Gallagher traveled with them. He met MacPhail one evening and they sat down for a general discussion. Far into the night they talked of this and that. When the session broke up MacPhail was able to announce that Billy Herman belonged to Brooklyn. Gallagher was able to announce that he had obtained for the Cubs Charley Gilbert, an outfielder of promise, and an undisclosed amount of cash.

Gilbert promptly developed aches and pains as did so many other players coming to the Cubs in deals of major importance. He was of no immediate use at all, and great was the going over

Gallagher got from the Chicago press. All wanted to know how MacPhail's check was going to look batting second and playing second in the Cubs line-up.

Gallagher might have eased some of the blasting he was getting by setting forth then and there the platform on which he was operating. But among Gallagher's qualities is that of stubbornness. He said little if anything, preferring to let both hostile and friendly writers find out for themselves what he had in mind. It was not hard to do, if anyone had paused to reflect. Gallagher had simply reached the logical conclusion that his club as constituted was not going very far with what it had, so there could be no great harm in trying something else. He was definitely committed to the rebuilding of the Cubs with young players. His real problem was finding them.

Gallagher was working under a handicap at first, since he had very few developing grounds in the minor leagues. His long range program called for the location of farms in leagues of all classifications. The soundness of this system has been proven by the St. Louis Cardinals, the New York Yankees, and the Detroit Tigers.

Gilbert, the outfielder obtained in the Herman deal, was part of this rebuilding program. So was Novikoff, for that matter, but the Mad Russian, for one reason or another, seemed destined to grow and flourish only on minor-league soil, no matter what sort of natural and artificial stimulants were used upon him.

While Gallagher was preserving his dignified silence the whole National League chuckled over the deal MacPhail had put across.

"One of these days," said one of Gallagher's bitterest critics, "James Boy number one will sit down with MacPhail over a couple of raspberry phosphates, and Larry will trade him right out of Wrigley."

The departure of Herman had another effect on the Cubs which Gallagher had foreseen. It left Augie Galan very disconsolate. He had mourned the passing of Bill Jurges from the Cubs for three seasons. Now Herman, another one of his set, was gone. Little Augie tried to bear up bravely, but it was no use. Troubles simply dogged him. To his grief over the trading of Jurges and Herman was added the handicap of physical disability brought about by an apparently unending series of mishaps on the ball field. His style was so cramped by all of this that it was not long before his Cub number was up.

He was released outright to Los Angeles on the same August day on which Larry MacPhail took Larry French, the Cubs' left-hander, at the waiver price. Little Augie protested his return to the Pacific Coast League. He felt that he had some National League baseball left in him, especially if he landed at New York, where Jurges was, or at Brooklyn, where his pals Herman and French were. He was right in his conclusions. Inside of five days following his release by the Cubs, he was on his way to Brooklyn where a grand reunion of the Cub alumni was held as part of the general celebration as the Dodgers dingdonged their way to their first championship in twenty-one years.

The Cubs were going nowhere. As they sagged to sixth place in the final standings—lowest finish in sixteen years—and the Dodgers racked up the championship, critics of the Gallagher-Wilson regime were working overtime in Chicago. They were able to prove to their own satisfaction that Brooklyn was winning a pennant with material the Cubs had given away. In a sense that was correct for the Cub alumni chapter in Brooklyn was seven strong and each member was a vital part of Leo Durocher's championship machine.

Billy Herman, naturally, was the key man. Galan and French arriving somewhat belatedly had helped out. But Dolph Camilli, Walter Higbe, Hugh Casey, and Curt Davis, all important Dodger figures, had been Cubs, too.

Davis reached Brooklyn by way of St. Louis, where the Cubs had assigned him as part of the Dizzy Dean deal. He made the trip to Brooklyn in company with Joe Medwick during the 1940 season. In exchange the Cardinals accepted a batch of players they could not use for long, and the customary cash which they could always use.

Camilli had gone to Brooklyn from Philadelphia in 1938 for

Eddie Morgan and an estimated $45,000. He had reached Philadelphia from the Cubs in the trade for Don Hurst, most questionable of all deals the Cubs had ever made. Higbe's trip to Brooklyn by way of Philadelphia, bringing a heavy amount of cash to the Phillies and not to the Cubs, has been recounted already.

Casey, a Dodger regular pitcher, had been given a brief trial by the Cubs in 1935. He spent much of the time talking about hunting and bird dogs. He was left at Los Angeles and forgotten until he turned up in Brooklyn and began annoying National League hitters with a most effective curve ball.

Gallagher's critics had a gay time comparing what those seven ex-Cubs were doing for MacPhail and Durocher with what the material retained was doing for the Cubs.

This was second guessing par excellence. In going through with it the critics so exhausted themselves they had little left to say when the Cubs traded Hank Leiber back to the Giants for pitcher Bob Bowman. This deal removed from Wrigley Field the last trace of the memorable three-for-three deal that had been made with the Giants in 1938.

Gallagher refrained from issuing any statements, though in their fine frenzy the critics, or some of them, were now polling the National and American Leagues to show the number of former Cubs who were performing with varying degrees of success.

They neglected to point out, however, that with the single exception of Linus Frey, who had been sold to Cincinnati in 1938 after one season with the Cubs, none of the alumni save those making up the Brooklyn chapter had been able to do very much toward winning a pennant for anyone else. Frey, a second baseman by trade and most capable, had no chance whatever to break into the Cubs line-up as a regular, since he came along at a time when Billy Herman was with the club. It was a generous gesture on the part of the Cubs to let him go where he could play every day.

By its very nature, the 1941 season was one of noble experimentation for the Cubs. Not all of the experiments went well with the critics, and many were the barbed remarks passed on some of Manager Wilson's activities in this regard. He had one trait which at first amused the baseball writers, but afterwards irked them greatly. This was a bewildering series of daily line-up changes as he strove to get a combination which might click. All he succeeded in doing was to drive the baseball writers to distraction.

Prior to his dispatch to Milwaukee Novikoff was a principal figure in this uncertainty of operation. His in-again, out-again, in-again status presented some situations in which Wilson's critics really took off the wraps and started swinging. There was one school of thought which maintained that Gallagher was trying to run the club on the field as well as in the front office. As a matter of fact Gallagher had more than enough work to keep him busy without trying to plot paths for Manager Wilson. He was studying road maps, constantly seeking out cities in leagues from Class AA on down the alphabetical scale in which the Cubs might locate farms or establish working agreements. He made plans to augment greatly the squad of scouts, and was lining them up full time and part time. He was giving much attention to baseball schools at Wrigley Field for the close-up survey of the callow youth from whose ranks might emerge a few who could be started on the way to regular jobs with the Cubs.

So Gallagher probably didn't know whether Novikoff was going to be in the line-up on a given day or out of it, any more than did the baseball writers, even after Wilson had told them— for Wilson changed his mind often and without much notice.

The paying patrons who had been remaining away from Wrigley Field in alarming numbers responded a bit more in 1941 than they had in 1940, but Gallagher wisely refrained from attempting to make anything of a seasonal attendance gain from 536,443 to 545,159.

To the hodgepodge of young hopefuls, the Cubs had added in June an experienced first baseman, Babe Dahlgren. He was obtained directly from the Boston Braves but had been in the

American League for several seasons, being notable on three counts.

He was a brilliant defensive player. He hit home runs every once in a while. He had fallen heir to the first-base mantle of the great Lou Gehrig, after having held the distinction of holding baseball's softest job, that of understudy to a man who made a habit of playing every game.

Dahlgren was a distinct defensive improvement over Zeke Bonura, who had managed to pause with the Cubs for a while on his rounds of the major and minor leagues. But Babe wasn't one to get along too well with Manager Wilson, and his brief service record shows less than a year with the Cubs.

While Dahlgren was available, he lent his fielding skill to an infield that had at the opposite corner the easygoing Stanley Hack, and in between whichever pair of youngsters happened to hold Manager Wilson's fancy for any given game. Bobby Sturgeon, Lou Stringer, and Len Merullo in Wilson's time never did know whether they were shortstops or second basemen, and neither did anyone else.

By way of adding to the uproar this season, the Cubs held title to pitcher Vallie Eaves, who had methods of his own for breaking every rule of training and deportment ever devised by a baseball club. Even our friends of radioland who find greatness in all ballplayers found it difficult to rhapsodize on Eaves, who should have been a great pitcher, but just didn't get around to it. His comings and goings were so uncertain that one of the Cubs' most violent critics regarded him as a certain prospect to become manager of the club most any day, or at worst, another vice-president in charge of confusion.

Yet another critic who had been a steady follower of the Cubs for many years now gave up in despair, and while he remained interested, took his baseball by remote control.

"The way things are going," he explained, "I am afraid Wilson would have me in the line-up one of these days if he happened to see me standing around."

This recalled a caustic utterance by another and earlier critic of the Cubs in the Bill Killefer days. He refused to go to spring training to cover the story, lest he might make the team.

All of which serves as about as good an estimate as any of the way things were going with the Cubs in the season immediately preceding Pearl Harbor.

⊗ XXXIII ⊗

DURATION CUBS

BASEBALL'S FATE HUNG IN THE BALANCE FOR WEEKS AFTER the outbreak of World War II. The resultant marshaling of America's man power for the all-out effort indicated at first that there might not be very many able-bodied ballplayers left to go on with the game and that it would be questionable how their efforts would be received by the public if the game did continue.

It was debatable whether the 1942 season would begin, or having begun, whether it would complete its schedule.

Commissioner Kenesaw M. Landis and the major-league presidents, Will Harridge and Ford Frick, were quick to make their positions known. They asked no favors. The successful prosecution of the war came first. If it were possible for baseball to be played, even on a limited scale, that would be fine, if it were impossible for any baseball to be played, that would be all right, too.

In a memorable letter to Commissioner Landis, President Franklin D. Roosevelt gave his opinion that it would be good for baseball to continue. It would have to be subject to such restrictions as the demands of the war would make upon it. That included the drafting of men for various branches of the service. It also included a drastic curtailment of travel on the nation's transportation lines, not only in regular season but particularly in spring-training time.

On this basis baseball hung on. Each club was committed to the policy of doing as best it could with what it had while it had it. Baseball's fandom, its own ranks threatened with depletion by the demands of war, accepted these conditions and throughout the duration was reasonably tolerant of the efforts made by the stay-at-homes to approximate the playing standards of the hundreds of ballplayers who marched off to war.

The first marked change from prewar standards came when the clubs began spring training. Commissioner Landis had decreed that camps in the south and in the far west were out. The precious travel miles had to be saved.

In seeking a camp not too far removed from Chicago, the Cubs hit upon French Lick Springs, Indiana, a famous watering place where the genial Tom Taggart presided. The hotel was a roomy place, the food was excellent, and the surrounding acreage was much greater than had been at the disposal of the Cubs in their many spring sessions at Catalina Island. It was large enough for two clubs, and one morning when the Cubs looked up, there was a second club, the Chicago White Sox.

The White Sox, as was their wont when rising up to haunt the Cubs, were all in good voice, and their manager, Jimmy Dykes, particularly so. The two clubs being thrown together in this manner posed many a problem that the Cubs had not been asked to face while working out at their exclusive Avalon spring retreat.

All thought of long-range player development had to be abandoned in these war years. The many promising youngsters already enrolled by the Cubs were merely marking time until their respective draft boards sent them greetings. Thus it was with every other major-league club. As player after player, whether star or tyro went into the service, the clubs found themselves treasuring overage veterans, and such draftees as had been found unable to meet the rigid requirements of the armed forces.

There were very few enlistments from the ranks of the major-league players, and the Cubs were no exceptions. It was the accepted theory that each man was entitled to wait until his draft number was up, and that was the way the string was played out. Some of the Cubs were drafted early. Others lasted a season, or two or three, and at least one, such was the luck of the draw, was never called at all.

Cubs were to be found in nearly every branch of the service. Many of them entered the navy and became members of baseball clubs that were kept in competition much keener than was going on in either the National or American Leagues. Many of them, such as Ed Waitkus, a first baseman, became involved in some of the toughest fighting of the war; but all went to the places and did the things the service required of them.

Those who were permitted to retain a place in the line-ups were accepted as a ball club, playing on its merits. In no time at all, though many of the fans were now wearing uniforms of the services, it was discovered that their natures had not changed. The clubs which were able to win were wonderful. Those which were not able to win were just the same kind of bums as ever; and no one offered as an excuse that after all these were just players who were holding forth while the original owners were out of town for the duration.

The Cubs did no better in 1942 than they had in 1941. Nor was the 1943 season any improvement. The howling at Wilson grew in volume, but all the years he had spent managing the Phillies had given him defensive armor against the jibes of a disgruntled fandom. He went about his work unruffled.

He had few ballplayers who were up to prewar standards, and many of them were having difficulty keeping up with the parade that was now passing by, and not at a quickstep either.

Bill Nicholson, one of those the draft had passed by, led the National League in 1943 with 29 home runs, and his 128 runs driven in was also the best on record in the league that season.

Stan Hack retained his personal popularity. One of his many claims to baseball fame is that he is the only Cub of his time who didn't have fans or sports writers mad at him at one time or another. No one is ever mad at Hack, nor is Hack ever mad at anyone.

Claude Passeau, a great workman, continued to pitch excellently; and he too escaped the wrath of bleacherites and literary lights. But most of the other Cubs were targets of sarcasm or abuse right along.

Service demands in 1943 deprived the Cubs of practically all their catchers worthy of the name. A quick deal was made with the Phillies, Bill Lee, hero of yesteryear going away while Mickey Livingston came to the Cubs to do their catching. This was a satisfactory deal, but none of the critics of the Cub barter-and-exchange department has ever admitted as much.

Ed Stanky, an infielder with an impressive minor-league record, came up for the 1943 season and was stationed at second base. He remained for the season and part of the next before finding his way to Brooklyn, where he became adept at begging his way to first base on free passes.

Late in the season the Cubs brought up for survey Don Johnson, a veteran of the minor leagues. He more than measured up to specifications.

In that same 1943 season two new outfielders checked in from the Pacific Coast League. One was Harry Lowrey, who did not linger long before his draft board beckoned. The other, a late season arrival, was Andy Pafko. He gave immediate evidence that he might be around with the Cubs for a long, long time. He displayed robust hitting powers, a throwing arm the Cub outfield had not owned since Kiki Cuyler went away, and an ability to travel long stretches in successful pursuit of drives hit in his direction.

At odd moments during both 1942 and 1943 the Cubs in their desperation found employment for Jimmy Foxx, whose batting prowess was all behind him. Another veteran, Paul Derringer, was secured from Cincinnati for the 1943 season. He had some moments that were very, very good—and he had some others.

At the end of 1943 the Cubs were anchored in fifth place, and there was an insistent demand that Wilson be given his release and a new manager secured. The most persistent of the critics regarded this as a halfway measure. He wanted both Jimmys, Wilson and Gallagher, given the bum's rush.

As usual there was much speculation on managerial possibili-

James T. Gallagher

P. K. Wrigley

Ed Reulbach

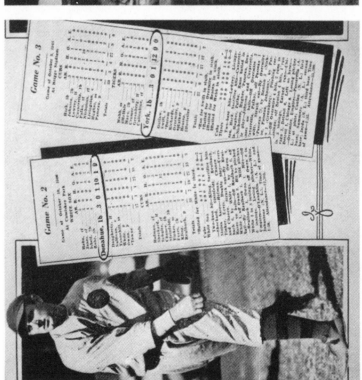

Claude Passeau

ties to succeed Wilson, when and if he were let go. The name of Bill Terry was discussed at great length, but Bill was having the time of his life at Memphis and displayed no great interest in the many rumors that he was to take charge of the Cubs. There were candidates from near and far, many of whom didn't know about it until they read some newspaper account. The Cub executives, Wrigley and Gallagher, held still and gave no indication that a change was in the making.

It is now possible to reveal that Gallagher had had the successor to Wilson in mind for a long time. Nor is it going too far afield to suggest that if Gallagher had become general manager of the Cubs a few months before his actual date of acceptance, there would have been no Wilson save Hack of the home-run prowess in the lengthy cast of Cub characters. For James T. Gallagher had a very high regard for Charlie Grimm as a friend and as a manager.

Oddly enough Gallagher had to sell Wrigley on the idea of bringing Grimm back as manager. This will seem strange, for Grimm is undoubtedly one of Wrigley's favorite persons in baseball, and he has always cherished the kindliest feelings toward him.

Grimm was doing more than all right with his share of the Milwaukee property with which he and young Bill Veeck were staging their baseball circus by day and by night. But there was in Grimm a strong yearning to return to the major leagues, and to the Cubs in particular, in a managerial capacity. He might have been a riot as a manager in the American Association, as indeed he was; but as an old trouper, the big league was the same to him as the Palace Theater on Broadway used to be to the vaudevillian who was laying 'em in the aisles on the Orpheum Circuit. It was nice, but it wasn't everything.

Wrigley's opposition was not based on any low estimate of Grimm's managerial worth. The Cubs' owner had always adhered to the opinion that if Joe McCarthy were not the best manager the Cubs had had after Frank Chance, then Grimm certainly must have been.

"It will look as if we are going backward instead of forward if we recall Grimm," was the way Wrigley put it.

As a student of Cub managerial form down through the years Gallagher might have pointed out that such a move would not be establishing a precedent. Johnny Evers had taken two separate shots at managing the Cubs. But being wise in the way of winning an argument, Gallagher advanced no such thought. He had been a talented baseball writer and therefore a coiner of the snappy phrase, so he was content to tell the Big Boss that if what the Cubs were doing now wasn't going backward, then he, James T. Gallagher, was going back to Notre Dame for a refresher course in such things as a sense of direction.

Wrigley was convinced. He was not so hard to sell on this project. Perhaps he had been using just the same psychological touch on Gallagher his father had used on Bill Veeck in the long ago when the matter of making a deal for Rogers Hornsby came up. You'll find the touch in any old-school copybook. It goes: "Be sure you're right, then go ahead."

If Gallagher were not sure he was right then and that he had to have Grimm, he was certainly convinced soon after the 1944 season began.

The Cubs opened that year against Cincinnati. With Henry Wyse pitching they defeated the Reds and Bucky Walters, 3–0. Three hits were all the Reds could make off Wyse. Every radio announcer in Chicago declared that it looked like a pennant sure. The Gallagher-Wilson program was paying off dividends at last —even though there were 153 games yet to go.

One of the radiomen, following this sensational start, began to twit the severest critic of the Gallagher-Wilson administration.

"I'll tell you what I'll do," offered the critic. "If you make the price right, I'll bet they don't win another game all season."

That was on April 20. It was not until May 11, or thirteen playing days later, spring weather being what it was, that the Cubs did win another game. Nine of those defeats at the very start of the season were too much even for the long-suffering Wilson. He resigned.

His resignation came so suddenly there wasn't time to get Grimm out of Milwaukee for the next game, even though a few raw cold days kept the Cubs idle. There were certain formalities connected with Grimm's part ownership of the Milwaukee club which had to be adjusted, and all this took time.

Someone had to manage the club until Grimm could report, so straws having been drawn, the unlucky man turned out to be Coach Roy Johnson. He established a record which stands alone in the National League. His team never won a game. To be sure he was on the job for but one playing day and then turned the team over to Grimm without even asking for a receipt. But his record stands just the same.

Those ten straight defeats had disorganized the Cubs to such an extent that Grimm himself, happy as everyone was to have him back, was unable to stop the slide immediately. Three more defeats, or thirteen in all, were registered before a halt was called.

It is fitting to call attention to the fact that Ed Hanyzewski was the pitcher of record when the lengthy losing streak began and when it ended. He triumphed over the Phillies, 5–3, after thirteen games in a row had been lost. At the time Hanyzewski appeared to be a most promising pitcher. He was to see little action with the club however, because of an arm ailment, though he was carried on the pay roll right along and was up for another inspection when spring training began in 1946, even though the date of his starting and finishing another complete game remained problematical.

Bob Lewis, the Cubs' secretary, had his own explanation for the long time between jobs for Hanyzewski.

"He's waiting to pitch a game when we're starting another thirteen-game losing streak," said Lewis, "so that he can then pitch another one to get us out of the slump. You know how it is with some of these pitchers—conditions have to be just so, or they don't do their best work."

The sudden, though not unlooked for, escape of Wilson from the club management gave the Cubs a variation in their managerial succession. It was the third time Grimm had been a party to these in-season readjustments. Allowing for Roy Johnson's inescapable one game term, it was the second time in their history the Cubs had needed three managers in one season. This tied the course record established by Bill Killefer, Rabbit Maranville, and George Gibson in 1928.

The Cubs' seasonal attendance in 1943, Wilson's last complete year as manager, was the lowest in more than twenty years. The paying patrons numbered 508,247. Many of the stanchest supporters of the club had gone into hiding. The average visitor to Wrigley Field in that season merely came out to see a ball game; and because he did not expect too much from the home team, he was usually satisfied.

The fans began to come out of their retreats very quickly once Grimm was installed as manager. His early appointment of the hustling Phil Cavarretta as field captain was a popular move. In good times and bad Cavarretta had been giving it all he had. Ed Burns once characterized Phil as a player who had made a career out of hustling—and he was eminently correct.

If you consider the fact that the Cubs had won but one game when Grimm took charge, and were imbedded in last place, even an advance as high as seventh would have been an accomplishment. But Grimm went beyond that. Before long the fans who began to storm the ball park were coming out for something beyond Grimm's personal popularity and his antics on the coaching line. He was being recognized now as a capable manager.

The players responded as well as their talents permitted. Some even played above their accepted standard. It became evident soon that this time around Grimm was a manager who knew what he was doing, and one who was going to make his own decisions. His experience in handling all those baseball curiosities at Milwaukee, and the time he had had to reflect on possible mistakes in his earlier major-league managerial career were now very helpful to him.

He picked up those scattered pieces of material which had been blown this way and that in the storms raging around Wilson. Gradually he put together a ball club, not of championship stature, even for the diminished values of duration baseball, but one which was visibly giving the very best it had at all times. Chicago fans appreciated this and showed it at the box office; for when the season's end arrived, the Cubs had played to 640,110 patrons on their home lot.

The artistic recovery of the Cubs under Grimm was one of the year's minor baseball miracles. The Cubs wound up in fourth place, and very nearly broke even in games won and lost. This after spotting the league thirteen games in the first month was quite a feat.

In its way it was as interesting as what Billy Southworth was doing at St. Louis with more material than he needed or what Luke Sewell was doing in the same city with material someone else had thrown away.

Whatever Grimm accomplished in righting the Cubs, he did without calling on Lou Novikoff, who presently was to be on his way back to Los Angeles, neither sadder nor wiser. The Cubs— and James T. Gallagher in particular—were willing to let someone else have a try at the Mad Russian, for better or for worse, until deals did them part.

Of all the 803 players, managers, and coaches who have found their way on to the pay roll of the Chicago National League club since 1876, and remained on it for at least one official game, Novikoff probably shares with Dizzy Dean the distinction of being the quaintest character of 'em all. This was quite an accomplishment, for players whose activities were not all reducible to box scores had a way of getting into Chicago uniforms sooner or later. The sad part of this was that most of the characters who did have playing talent when they found time for it reached Chicago too soon or too late.

Rube Waddell was a member of the cast at the turn of the century, but he did not linger long enough to be properly appreciated either as a great pitcher or as a character who gave his manager many a sleepless night. Buck Newsom was given a quick survey by the Cubs long before he became the greatest pitcher Buck Newsom has ever known.

Somehow the Cubs missed Art ("The Great") Shires, but when that doughty American Leaguer added fisticuffs to his many other off-field activities, Hack Wilson was all set to go four rounds with him in one of Chicago fight-promoter Jim Mullen's super-specials. And don't think that this one would not have drawn a capacity crowd. The fight was not held because Commissioner Landis advised the lads in a nice way that he would raise hell with them if they went through with the match.

Some of the more amazing characters did not get past the spring-training stage, and therefore are not listed in the 803. Yet they deserve some mention.

Grimm himself was responsible for one, a pitcher rounded up on the sand lots of St. Louis. This young man set an all time Cub record for eating. Every major-league club has one of these, but the Cubs like to think that their man who ate his way through one spring in California was the champion of 'em all. He would rise early and give the American-plan breakfasts at the St. Catherine Hotel at Avalon his complete attention. He played every entry across the board, straight, place, and show. On his way to the park to work out he would have a snack or two to tide him over. He stepped up in class at luncheon, and at dinner he was really a stake horse as he raced through the menu.

When the club was playing its spring exhibitions in various parts of California, the young man adhered to his schedule but also entered in a few other events whenever a ball park had concession stands. Whenever Grimm wanted him, which wasn't often, he always looked behind the nearest hot dog, and there was his man.

The baseball correspondents of 1946 at Catalina Island have been dwelling upon the Gargantuan appetite of Coach "Red" Smith. There is no doubt but that Red is a latter-day champion, but he just eats when he is hungry. Grimm's prodigy of yester-year just ate. Of all those whose dining-room checks have been picked up by Secretary Bob Lewis, Grimm's man is the only one who could drink a bottle of beer while he was chewing tobacco or gnaw on hot dogs with mustard and popcorn with butter at one and the same time.

At one time the Cubs held title to a college-bred, left-handed pitcher who was gifted with the art of beating Pittsburgh. He was constantly seeking information about pitching. No left-hander belonging to any other club was safe from him. From the great Carl Hubbell down the line the Cubs' pitcher cross-examined at great length all who came within vocal range. By the end of his career this left-hander must have had the greatest store of knowledge of the ways to pitch left-handed. Unfortunately what he knew and what he did were, as Doc Lotshaw often said, "the color of another horse."

Another left-hander, a tall, stringy, and very scared one, reported at Catalina one spring. It was learned later that he had been recommended to one of the Cub executives by a bartender in a northern California town. His first pitch was five feet over the head of the catcher sent out to warm him up. He got better before he went back to the bartender. By the time the Cubs let him go he was missing the catcher by not more than two feet at a pitch.

In the 1946 cast of the Cubs there is a pitcher, Paul Erickson by name, who showed signs of belonging to the character club on the very day he reported. He turned up for observation one morning at the school the Cubs maintain at Wrigley Field for young hopefuls. He was taken to the clubhouse by Secretary Bob Lewis and given a uniform. Lewis then returned to his own office and about a half hour later left the park to go across the street to an emporium which served food and drink. There at the bar, decked out in his Cub uniform, was the young pitcher, sandwich in one hand, beer glass in the other.

"The ball park is across the street," said Lewis, who is accustomed to players who get lost now and then.

"I know," said the pitcher. "I was so excited about getting a trial I almost forgot I hadn't any lunch. I got to have my strength before I let them look me over. This is serious."

The young man still has his strength. At camp in the spring of 1946 one baseball expert wrote that perhaps the young man was going to be another Dizzy Dean. After that start who knows?

The Cubs owned a catcher at one stage who worried more in reality about slurs to the South than Fred Allen's radio character does in the spirit of fun. Several of the Cub regulars became aware of this and "needled" the catcher continuously.

One day at Pittsburgh, just before game time, the catcher resented one of the remarks and a fight broke out. It was stopped then, but resumed later in the day. And what was it all about? Simply that the catcher had been told he really belonged on the South Side of Chicago—which is the habitat of the White Sox. Well, in Chicago, when you liken a Cub to a White Sox, you'd best say it with a smile.

None of these characters ever gained the yardage in the press that was accorded Dean and Novikoff, but in their own way they contributed toward keeping Chicago baseball writers working on a twenty-four-hour schedule.

☻ XXXIV ☻

HISTORY REPEATS

IT HAS BEEN DEEMED FIT AND PROPER TO CALL FREQUENT AT-
tention to history's repetition in the life and time of the Cubs.
So here we go again. . . .

When World War I was drawing to a successful close for
America and her allies in 1918, the Cubs won a National League
pennant. When World War II reached the same sort of conclusion in 1945, the Cubs won another pennant.

In the opinion of many the Cubs' 1945 victory represented a
complete scrambling of baseball dope. The St. Louis Cardinals,
surcharged with material despite the demands of the service, had
been a general selection to win the pennant off by themselves as
they had done in 1944.

The only dissenting voice raised in the early spring of 1945
was that of James T. Gallagher. He allowed that he would not
be surprised if the Cubs won the pennant. He was promptly told
that he was nuts. Since he had been told that before, he refrained
from further comment. This was not hard to do, for the sports
writers of Chicago were then divided into two general classes:
(a) those who were not speaking to Gallagher, and (b) those
to whom Gallagher was not speaking.

Much of this break in diplomatic relations was traceable to an
incident in spring training, when the Cincinnati Reds suddenly
made up their minds to join the Cubs at French Lick Springs.
The correspondents in camp with the Cubs found this out from
Manager Bill McKechnie of the Reds, and some of them made
an issue of the Cubs' keeping this news item a secret.

On another occasion Gallagher made a trip to French Lick and later watched part of a double-header at Louisville between Cubs and Reds. He spoke to no baseball writer and no baseball writer spoke to him. On his return to Chicago a stay-at-home sports writer called him to ask if there had been any significance to the visit.

"Yes," said Gallagher. "I went down to see Grimm. I saw him. Period."

What a man in those days of acute white paper shortage! It's too bad the baseball writers didn't appreciate James T. Gallagher more.

Once free from the refining influences of French Lick and launched on their first full season under Grimm, the Cubs, young and old, began to show possibilities. They were not able to do much in interclub games with the Cardinals from start to finish, but the Cardinals found other pitfalls. They were forever taking a tumble against some of the lesser clubs when a tumble would hurt most. The Cubs, meanwhile, were making a career out of beating Cincinnati; and with reasonable success against all others save the Cardinals, it was not long before Grimm's club was being accepted by the entire National League as a real menace. The Cubs simply refused to be shaken off by the Cardinals.

The Cubs were now making a race with a club that was made up for the most part of their own farm products. Roy Hughes, a veteran who took over shortstop when Len Merullo grew too erratic, Claude Passeau, and Paul Derringer were the regulars who had been successful elsewhere before the Cubs obtained them. Ray Prim in his younger days had been in the major leagues, and a few of the utility players had appeared in other major-league uniforms. But the entire outfield, made up of Bill Nicholson, Andy Pafko, and Harry Lowrey, now back from the service, had not played major-league baseball for anyone but the Cubs. In the infield Phil Cavarretta, Don Johnson, and Stanley Hack had similar records. So too had the catchers, until Mickey Livingston came back from his war duty.

Henry Wyse was a regular starting pitcher of quality and kept

218

pace with Passeau and Prim. The balance of the staff was a curious mixture of youth and age. It was not a foolproof staff; for Paul Derringer, on his way out of the major leagues, was having a very listless season.

Gallagher and Grimm had sensed this pitching weakness at the start of the year and were on the watch for a deal that might prove useful. Gallagher had turned a deaf ear to the suggestion from St. Louis that the Cubs might be able to use Morton Cooper. When Cooper eventually passed to the Boston Braves and arrived with a sore arm, Gallagher breathed a sigh of relief. In his time, and before it, the Cubs had dealt for enough players who were unable to get into regular action. There were two other pitchers considered; and after giving much thought to both, Gallagher passed them up. Again he had guessed right, for both had 1945 seasons which were among their worst.

In midseason when a break in the schedule afforded the Cubs a day off, Gallagher and Grimm went on a fishing trip. Shortly before that Gallagher had been looking casually over a waiver list sent out by the New York Yankees as part of baseball routine. There was a pitcher on it that Gallagher thought of claiming, but before he made a move he consulted with a friend who kept closer track of things in the American League.

"Three times in the last six months," he said, "I had just about made up my mind to deal for a pitcher. Each time I passed it up. Each time the fellow I had in mind turned out to be a bit of a bust. Now I'm thinking of refusing to waive on So-and-so of the Yankees. Could he help us?"

"No," said Gallagher's adviser and proceeded to tell why. His reasons were sufficient, and Gallagher went off on his fishing trip still wondering where he might get Grimm another winning pitcher.

It was very late when Gallagher returned to his domicile. He was told that New York had been calling all through the afternoon and evening. A bit tired, Gallagher was about to retire and forget about fish, pitchers, and phone calls from New York. He still shudders whenever he recalls what might have happened if he had adhered to that plan.

He put the phone call through and it was Larry MacPhail on the other end.

"What will you give us for Borowy?" MacPhail wanted to know. Gallagher wasn't sure that he had heard that right. In his judgment Borowy was one of the best pitchers the Yankees owned. He asked MacPhail to repeat the question.

It was Borowy, all right, B-o-r-o-w-y.

"How the hell can you ever get waivers on him?" Gallagher demanded.

"I've got the waivers," said MacPhail. "Do you want him, or don't you?"

There was much more to the conversation. A price of $100,000 or so and a parcel of ballplayers was what MacPhail wanted, and that's what he got.

There were no "angles" to the deal and no skullduggery as many charged. It was the age-old exemplification of the utter silliness of the waiver rule.

Periodically each major-league club asks waivers on ballplayers on its reserve list, possibly to establish whether there is any demand for them, possibly just to keep in practice. Most clubs have become committed to the theory that it is useless to refuse to waive on any player who is known to have two arms and two legs, since most of the time the waivers will be withdrawn anyhow. So clubs are apt to be careless in perusing the waiver lists, and even more careless in making an immediate note of someone who must be claimed at once.

In the instance of Borowy such American League clubs as said (afterwards) that they could have used Borowy, quite forgot to make a claim for him until it was too late. His name escaped the entire American League, and MacPhail was within his rights in selling him to the best market he knew—the Chicago Cubs.

But that didn't stop the howling of rival American League club owners for a time. They quieted down when President Will

Harridge announced that the proceedings had been entirely in order.

Stripped of all its mystery that is how Hank Borowy happened to come to the Cubs on July 27, 1945, after he had already won ten while losing five for the Yankees.

That is how James T. Gallagher was able to tie the score in the competition with Larry MacPhail which had begun when Billy Herman left the Cubs to go to Brooklyn four years before. Brooklyn was then haunted by MacPhail.

When Gallagher let Herman go, it was reasonable to suppose that he had immediate need for the cash which was part of the deal. It was just as reasonable that MacPhail had need for ready money when he sold Borowy. But everyone wanted to find some other, less simple explanation.

Borowy was startled at first with the rapidity with which he had been transferred from one league to another, since he had reason to believe that he had been giving the Yankees service. He joined the Cubs, however, with the fires of determination burning.

New York comment, some of it attributed to MacPhail, had nettled him. The reason the Yankees had let him go, one version read, was that he was unable to finish ball games he started.

The Cubs did not find any such weakness in him. In what was left of the National League race he finished most of what he started. He was defeated but once, and literally pitched the Cubs into a pennant, winding up with an earned run average of 2.14, the league's best performance.

He was the pitcher of record on September 28 when the Cubs clinched the pennant with a 4–3 victory over Pittsburgh.

It was Paul Erickson, one of the lesser pitching lights, however, who put the finishing touch to the Pirates, who had some ideas of doing unto the Cubs as the Cubs had done unto them in the season of 1938.

Borowy went through this decisive game until the last half of the ninth, holding a 4–3 lead. When he encountered some trouble then, Grimm replaced him with Bob Chipman, a left-hander, who served his purpose. Erickson came in to pitch against pinch hitter Tommy O'Brien, while the tying run was on third base.

Erickson, a very fast right-hander, is given to wildness, and poise in the pitching box is something he had not yet acquired. On his first pitch Erickson's cap started to fall off. He went through with it. If he had paused, he would have committed a balk, permitting the run to score. The pitch was a blazing strike.

That gave Erickson all the confidence he needed. He made up his mind to show that O'Brien a pitch that was really fast. He did, too. It was the fastest pitch Erickson had ever thrown, and very nearly the wildest. It went much closer to O'Brien than to the plate, and in his rush to get out of the way, O'Brien's bat flew up and ticked the ball. What should have been a run-scoring wild pitch thus became the second strike.

The Cubs were plenty jittery now, but there was nothing any of them could do but watch and pray. Erickson was the least disturbed man on the field. He had decided now that he would be a smart pitcher. He would use his curve in this spot and get the game over.

No one on the Pirates' squad and O'Brien least of all ever suspected that Erickson had a curve or that in a spot such as this he would attempt to throw it. It is possible that Erickson's catcher was a little surprised, himself. But there was nothing he could do about it. So a curve is what Erickson threw. A very fine curve at that. One which bent briskly and cut through the very heart of the plate for a called third strike which gave the Cubs a pennant.

They were champions at last, and the Gallagher regime was paying off its first dividend.

Literally and figuratively it was doing just that. For in the course of the season before and after the Borowy deal, fans had been packing Wrigley Field in numbers unreported since 1931. The final count revealed that 1,036,386 had paid their way into the park in the 1945 season.

The critics, for a welcome change, were strangely silent, or else their voices were drowned out in the general acclaim that came the way of Borowy, of Claude Passeau, of Andy Pafko, Phil Cavarretta, the league's most valuable player, Stan Hack, Grimm, and all the other heroes—even Bill Nicholson who had chosen this pennant-winning year of 1945 to have the worst season since he had joined the Cubs.

Perhaps Nicholson was entitled to an off year. He had led the league in home runs and in runs driven in during the 1943 and 1944 seasons. This put him in very fancy company, for a two-year leadership in these important functions had never been recorded before in the National League and but twice in the American League, where the long-distance hitters seemed to swarm.

Babe Ruth (1920–21) and Jimmy Foxx (1932–33) were the two illustrious personages Nicholson joined in his two-year effort. So, many thought, Bill was entitled to sit this one out. But since he was a Cub, and as such a natural target for second guessers, he came in for many a catty remark. He found to his sorrow that the man who first said that in baseball you're a hero today, and tomorrow a bum, spoke naught but a simple truth.

☻ XXXV ☻

THOSE CUB DEALS

BEFORE MOVING ON TO THE 1945 WORLD SERIES, ON WHICH note this story of the Cubs comes to an end, it would seem that a discussion of Cub player deals, and one or two other items is in order. These things have been dealt with in their proper order as they were made, but there are some circumstances which have been passed by until now.

In the modern (1900–1945) era of the Cubs, nothing they have accomplished has caused as much commotion as their player deals. It would seem from some comments, that whenever they went into the market, they were played for suckers by everyone with whom they dealt. That is not true.

They have made four major deals.

The first was for Rogers Hornsby. A championship came with it. And so did a dividend for the stockholders.

The second major deal was for Chuck Klein. He was not nearly the ballplayer for the Cubs he had been for the Phillies; yet he did help to a championship. And more dividends for the stockholders.

The third big deal was for Dizzy Dean. A championship came quickly when Old Dizz was around. Great as was the amount of money and player talent expended for him, he was worth all that and more to the Cubs, not only for what he did on the field but for the interest he commanded. Winning or losing, the Cubs created more stir when he was with the club than they have ever done without him. There were stockholders' dividends in Dean's time.

The fourth major deal was for Hank Borowy. It is not necessary to repeat his artistic and financial triumphs for the Cubs. It was doubly interesting in that, for the first time, the other party to the deal was getting all the savage criticism for having made it. It was a welcome change for the Cubs and may even have quieted for all time that familiar question, "What's the matter with him?" that has been raised every time the Cubs dealt for a new player.

These four major transactions more than balance the deals which blew up in the Cubs' faces.

Included in these backfiring deals might be the one which brought Lou Novikoff to the Cubs. A great sum of money for a minor-league ballplayer was paid the Los Angeles club for him. But as a sort of poor man's Dizzy Dean he certainly entertained enough patrons to justify whatever the Cubs paid for him and whatever salary was his. If there were no stockholders' dividends in Novikoff's time, it was no fault of the Mad Russian.

The one indefensible deal the Cubs have made was the trade of Dolph Camilli for Don Hurst.

All their other transactions, whether good, bad, or indifferent, and whether they involved seasoned major-leaguers or well-advertised minor-leaguers, were not to be distinguished from deals other clubs were making right along as they tried to satisfy the demands of their patrons.

The wholesale swap of 1938 with the Giants did not mean a great deal artistically to either club. Bill Jurges, Frank Demaree and Ken O'Dea were proportionately of no more service to the Giants than were Hank Leiber, Gus Mancuso, and Dick Bartell to the Cubs. In neither case was either club weakened or strengthened by the deal enough to make an issue of it.

Another constant source of criticism of the Cubs has been their managerial changes. In calling the roll it would seem that it is more or less automatic to score the Cubs' history play Anson to Chance to Grimm. Yet it is surprising how many of the oldsters in Chicago resent the inclusion of Chance, the Peerless Leader, among the great managers of the game.

This was intensified during 1945. The Baseball Writers Association, in failing to hit upon any new tenants for the Hall of Fame at Cooperstown, did wind up with Chance's name leading the list for the second successive time, though the requisite number of votes to confirm a Hall of Fame reservation for him were lacking.

Chicago sports writers in commenting upon this were surprised at the number of communications from the "I knew him when" folks who professed surprise that Chance should be considered at all for the Hall of Fame. One letter writer pointed out that Chance was a bum fielder, not much of a hitter, and seldom played more than half of his club's games in a given season. Then the writer got around to Chance's leadership values.

"Why don't you fellows do something about putting Frank Selee into the Hall of Fame, and forget about Chance?" he wrote. "Selee was a great manager at Boston. He was the one who assembled the Cubs that made Chance look good. Anybody could manage that club."

Well, in Chicago one never knows, does one?

It was a Chicagoan, and a rival American League manager, who once characterized Joe McCarthy of the Yankees as a push-button manager—and who pointed out that with the constant supply of material coming to him, all McCarthy had to do was press a button and up jumped a twenty-game winning pitcher, a great double-play combination, or a .350 hitter.

All this is parenthetical. It is introduced merely for the purpose of indicating that while baseball's opinion changes are much the same all over, there seem to be more of them in Chicago, and they seem more violent.

In concluding this interlude it might be well to take up another favorite criticism of the Cubs, that of front-office interference with the manager. Many of the facts in each of these instances have been chronicled already, but there is another side to the story which has been reserved until now. Best qualified to discuss it is owner P. K. Wrigley himself.

"I had my first experience with this," he says, "when Bill

Veeck decided to change from Rogers Hornsby to Charlie Grimm. That happened while the Cubs were in the east and Veeck was with them. I was in Chicago. Calls cut through to me, and I was asked all sorts of questions. I tried as best I could to establish that Veeck was in charge of the club's affairs. To my surprise this merely gave rise to a general expression that I was not interested in baseball and cared nothing about it.

"Thereafter when I would attempt to show I was interested by answering all questions put to me, the charge of front-office interference was raised. If there was any happy medium it seemed very difficult to find it for a long while."

Veeck's utter frankness in his discussions of baseball business and his availability to interviewers made his office a happy hunting ground for item seekers in the years that followed Bill Veeck's death and up to the installation of James T. Gallagher as general manager.

In all fairness to the many interviewers it was a fact that coming and going, some of the executives below Wrigley were an unpredictable lot. Most of them were willing at all times to give opinions, though not always qualified to do so. This precipitated a wave of contradictory statements and irked the sports writers no little.

There was in existence a minority group which did not care to say that Wrigley Field was at Clark and Addison Streets without first getting a clearance from P. K. on the statement. It is a question whether they caused the interviewers or Wrigley himself the more annoyance.

Basically both Wrigleys have never deviated from the theory that the successful operation of a baseball property calls for a certain number of persons at the key positions and the rest is so much window dressing. If P. K. Wrigley prefers to have his windows nattier than some of his rival magnates do, that is his business.

The key men are owner, general manager, field manager, and traveling secretary. For all evidence to the contrary the last is one of the most important factors of all. For while it has been true that the Cubs, since 1927, have not always known where they were going, it is equally true that Bob Lewis has always managed to get them there and get them back.

In the present setup the Cubs have the most workmanlike front office they have possessed at any time since Bill Veeck's death. In Charlie Grimm they have the most popular manager, on and off the field, Chicago has ever known. In Bob Lewis they have an able road secretary who always finds time to double as a pantomime artist with Grimm in an unending series of fun and frolic which has lightened the tension many a time while pennant pressure is on.

Lewis has had a suppressed desire for many years to be an umpire. He gets an outlet only at the Catalina camp games where he teams with Doc Lotshaw. He gave up all thought of pursuing a professional umpire's career when he became unable to decide whether to model his career on that of Bill Klem or "Beans" Reardon. He can give excellent imitations of each. Lewis came to the Cubs as a box-office man, having been a theatrical treasurer at an earlier age.

One of his cronies, Al Eckardt, now with the Cubs part time, combined with Lewis when both were younger to make life miserable for motormen and conductors at one of Chicago's busiest transfer points. Night after night, at the height of the rush hour, Bob and Al would attempt to get on a car while carrying a folding cot. At long last, the cot finally got on but they did not; the effort, however, qualified both for life with the Cubs later on.

Before he went into the theatrical profession Lewis vaguely hoped to be an undertaker. He gave that up, he says, when they started calling themselves morticians.

Not the least of the characters who have been with the Cubs and of them is Bob Lewis.

⚾ XXXVI ⚾

WORLD'S WORST SERIES

BASEBALL WRITERS FROM ALL OVER THE COUNTRY WERE AS-sembled at Detroit when the Cubs arrived to begin the 1945 world series. An Associated Press reporter made his rounds asking each individual writer which club he thought would win. When he approached a writer from Chicago, expecting to get the customary "Cubs" reply—such is civic pride—he was startled to be told:

"I don't think either one of them can win it."

That came close to being the best forecast made of that or any other world series.

It went the full seven games before the Tigers took the odd contest and became world's champions. Long before that point was reached even the players themselves had given up trying to figure out what might happen next. Fly balls were dropping beside fielders who made no effort to catch them. Players were tumbling going around the bases. The baseball was as far removed from previous major-league standards as was possible without its perpetrators having themselves arrested for obtaining money under false pretenses.

That, of course, was the supercritical reflection of trained baseball experts. No matter how goofy was the series, and it yielded to no other for incredibly inept incidents, America's baseball fans in Briggs Stadium, in Wrigley Field, or listening to play-by-play accounts around the world, seemed able to generate and sustain lively interest from start to finish.

The paid attendance was 333,457, largest ever. The gross revenue, $1,492,454 for tickets and $100,000 for radio rights, was also a new high.

Somebody must have liked it, even if the experts did not.

The oddities began to trickle into print before the first ball was pitched at Briggs Stadium. The Cubs reached Detroit without their owner, P. K. Wrigley. He had remained in Chicago to do what he could about the usual turmoil over world series tickets. This was nothing new for Chicago, but when the disappointed ticket seekers made so many charges that the speculators were in charge, Wrigley felt it was due the public to make a statement. It appeared as a paid ad in the Chicago papers. It is worth repeating here:

WE'RE BURNED UP, TOO,

CUB FANS, ABOUT SCALPING
OF WORLD SERIES TICKETS.

The Cubs went to a lot of trouble and extra expense to engage outside office space and a large force of bank tellers and clerks to try and do an extra good job of distributing evenly and fairly the comparatively limited supply of World Series tickets, the sale of which, because the proceeds go into a special account of the Commissioner of Baseball, have to balance out to the penny; to say nothing of settling up with Uncle Sam for the exact tax on the printed price of each ticket.

However, once the tickets are in the hands of the public, there is nothing to prevent individuals from selling their seats at a neat profit through scalpers.

Unfortunately, there are always a few people who prefer a quick profit to anything else. We all know this to be true, but as we said to start with—we still do not like it.

CHICAGO NATIONAL LEAGUE BALL CLUB

It is doubtful if the preparation of that bit of writing soothed any of the injured feelings of those who had sought tickets in vain, but it did have the effect of keeping Wrigley from seeing his club in some of its greatest moments. These they had at Briggs Stadium more than at Wrigley Field as the series stumbled on its course.

The Tigers led by Manager Steve O'Neill had emerged victorious in an American League race which was in doubt until almost its closing innings when Hank Greenberg's homer boosted the Tigers home in front.

The series marked the Cubs' eighth attempt to recapture a title which had eluded them since Frank Chance's team had downed Hughey Jennings' Tigers in 1908. This time the Cubs were reasonably confident they would make it. They did not hold the 1945 Tigers in the same awe as they had Yankees, Athletics, or even previous Tigers they had encountered in world series play.

They granted that Detroit had three great pitchers in Hal Newhouser, Dizzy Trout, and Virgil Trucks, who had emerged from the navy a few days before the series began. But the Cubs were very proud of their own pitchers, Hank Borowy, Claude Passeau, Henry Wyse, and the venerable Ray Prim, who had enjoyed a most successful season.

Borowy, who had specialized in beating Detroit when he was with the Yankees, was a natural to open the series. The weather was very cold and continued that way through the second game, causing Manager Grimm to switch from his original one-two plans, Borowy and Passeau, and start Wyse in the second game.

Borowy drew Hal Newhouser as his opposition and the Cubs promptly went to work on Hal, who was not helped much by the slovenly defense of his teammates.

In that first game the Cubs looked and acted like champions. As a team it was the only time in the series that either side even approximated prewar skill in demonstrating before all those people that this was the major league and not an annual Elks' picnic game between the married men and the single men with a barrel of beer on third base.

Though Newhouser was the American League's best, the Cubs —and his own defense—treated him as if he were Joe Smith hastily summoned from the bleachers because the regular pitcher had not shown up. Seven runs and eight hits were made off him in the two and two-thirds innings he pitched. When the Cubs cantered to a 9–0 victory, small wonder if their rejoicing followers felt that the long-sought world's championship was no longer too far away.

Newhouser's troubles began in the first inning. Don Johnson scratched a hit with one out and stole second. Phil Cavarretta also made a fluke hit, and a passed ball permitted Johnson to score. Newhouser was ordered to pass Andy Pafko and take his chances with the slumping Nicholson. Bill was able to slam a long fly out towards the right field stands. There was room enough for Roy Cullenbine to back up and catch it but he failed to do so. The fly went for a triple and two runs scored. Mickey Livingston then came through with the inning's only legitimate hit and the Cubs were four runs to the good.

They were docile enough in the second, but in the third Johnson started things again with a double. He scored on Cavarretta's hit. Pafko followed with a double scoring Cavarretta, and when Livingston also batted safely to score Pafko, Newhouser was replaced with Al Benton. Benton and Jim Tobin, who succeeded him, kept the Cubs quiet until the seventh, when Cavarretta hit a homer, and hits by Pafko and Nicholson accounted for one more run.

Borowy was inclined to be unsteady for six innings but the Cub defense was spectacularly efficient. In the third inning Cavarretta made a diving stop to keep "Skeeter" Webb from a certain double. In the fifth Pafko's great throw to third caught Eddie Mayo and broke up a Tiger rally.

After the sixth inning Borowy was on his own. He retired the Tigers as rapidly as they came to bat and walked off with his 9–0 victory.

Wyse, starting the second game, was opposed by Trucks. It was Hank Greenberg rather than either pitcher, who was responsible for the turn in this game. Greenberg, described as a throwback to the days when there were ballplayers in the major leagues, was the big difference.

The Cubs got Wyse a run in the fourth on hits by Cavarretta and Nicholson. The Tigers were shut out until two were out in the fifth. Then Webb singled, and Wyse, becoming overcautious, walked Mayo. Roger Cramer came through with a score-tying single.

Now Wyse was in trouble, and he showed it. Hank Greenberg was advancing to the bat, and for him the Cubs had a wholesome respect—as well they might.

The count went to one and one, and for the next pitch Wyse essayed a curve. A very good curve it was, too. But it was a very fast ball when it left Greenberg's bat and sailed away to lodge in the left-field stands, bringing in three more Tiger runs and the ball game, for that 4–1 was the final score.

Passeau had his chance in game number three and he made the most of it. He conquered the Tigers, 3–0. He allowed but one hit, Rudy York's single in the second, and issued but one pass, Bill Swift getting it in the sixth. His was the best pitching performance in any world series since the games had been inaugurated, and it couldn't have happened to a better man.

Stubby Overmire, a pudgy left-hander, had the ill luck to be thrown against Passeau. He stayed even for three innings, but in the fourth the Cubs made a pair of runs on Harry Lowrey's double and hits by Nicholson and Roy Hughes. Passeau helped himself to a run in the seventh with a long fly off Al Benton while Livingston was on third base, waiting to score.

Dizzy Trout made his first appearance in the series when the fourth game began, and the scene was shifted to Wrigley Field. Ray Prim was on display for the Cubs. Prim did well for a time. He retired the first ten men to face him, and then the Tigers climbed all over him, just when the press-box hundreds were wondering if he were going to exceed Passeau's best effort of the day before.

Eddie Mayo drew a pass with one out in the fourth. Greenberg and Cramer singled, one run scoring. Cullenbine kept the rally going with a double. One more run came in and Prim went out of the ball game.

His relief man, Paul Derringer, was ordered to pass Rudy York, who was forced by Jimmy Outlaw as Greenberg scored. Richards then came through with the inning's fourth hit, and Cullenbine scored its fourth run.

That was all the scoring the Tigers did, and more than they

needed, for the Cubs would not have scored at all off Trout but for some of the fielding madness which characterized the series from start to finish.

Don Johnson led off the seventh with a triple. Lowrey tapped to Outlaw and Johnson was trapped between third and the plate, being nearer the latter than the former. Outlaw chose to let him run and made the play at first base for Lowrey. Instead of continuing on to score, Johnson reversed himself and broke back for third, with Outlaw in hot pursuit, just in case York had ideas of flinging the ball that way. Rudy had those ideas, but Outlaw might as well have remained where he had been. Rudy's toss sailed high and far away into the Cubs' dugout and Johnson was able to score on his second try with something to spare.

With the series tied at two games each, the opening game's pitchers, Newhouser and Borowy, were at it again. There was no rapid start for the Cubs against Newhouser this time, and Borowy needed some spectacular fielding plays by Pafko on long drives to keep the game on a 1–1 basis through the first five innings. Borowy had started his own run with a double, scoring when Stan Hack singled to center and Roger Cramer failed to make a play at the plate.

The sixth inning found the Tigers launching another of their familiar four-run innings. Cramer singled and went on to second when Pafko fumbled. Greenberg hit safely to score Cramer, but heroic Hank added to the gaiety of the occasion by sprawling going around first base. However, no damage was done, and hits by Cullenbine and York got Hank home eventually.

They also got Borowy out of there. He was replaced by Hy Vandenberg who presently distinguished himself by passing the pitcher, Newhouser, with the bases filled, forcing home a run.

In the seventh while Paul Derringer was pitching, there was another outbreak of strange fielding. Lowrey and the erratic Len Merullo couldn't decide which should catch Greenberg's fly, and it fell safe for a hit. Then Derringer fielded a bunt to third base too late to get Greenberg, who scored in a few minutes on a long fly. The Tigers now led 6–1, and the Cubs were getting nowhere against Newhouser. They did get a pair of runs in the seventh, Lowrey scoring on an infield out and Livingston doubling to score Pafko.

The only effect this had on the Tigers was to start them rallying again, this time at the expense of Paul Erickson. Cramer was hit by a pitched ball. Greenberg doubled. Then Cullenbine's drive was lost in the vines of the outfield wall. While Pafko and a Cub posse put on a frantic search there was time for Cullenbine to have circled the bases twice. However, a ground-rule double anchored him at second base, but the Tigers had two more runs.

Another weird fielding display helped the Cubs to their final run. This time it was a fly ball by Cavarretta which fell between Cramer and Cullenbine, neither attempting to make the catch. Cavarretta reached second and scored on a hit by Nicholson.

The final score was 8–4, and the Tigers needed but one more victory to be world's champions.

They had to wait a bit for it. The next game, the sixth, perhaps the daffiest ever played in a world series, went to the Cubs, 8–7, in twelve innings. The struggle, and it was no less than that for players and fans alike, lasted three hours and twenty-eight minutes. Each side impressed into service nineteen men to make the compilation of the box score something the official scorers will always remember.

Manager Grimm had no choice but Passeau for this game, and Virgil Trucks came out for the Tigers. Passeau's wildness cost him a run in the second, a pass to Richards with the bases filled getting a run across.

The Cubs drove out Trucks in the fifth when they scored four runs on robust hitting combined with some poor defensive play on the part of the Tigers.

Another run was secured off Tommy Bridges in the sixth. In this inning the Tigers failed to score, but Jimmy Outlaw's drive paved the way for Passeau's retirement. He tried to stop the ball with his pitching hand and injured it so badly that much of his efficiency was gone. He insisted on staying with the job, and Grimm agreed.

In the seventh the Tigers ganged on Passeau, and he was taken out. The Tigers scored enough to make it 5–3, which was too close for Cub comfort. So out went the home guard in its half, to round up two more runs, which made the score 7–3 as the eighth inning was reached.

Bill Swift began it quietly with a walk and went to third on pinch hitter Hub Walker's double. Hack misplayed Joe Hoover's roller, and Swift scored. Mayo lined a single to center scoring Walker, but Mayo still didn't believe that Pafko had a throwing arm and kept on for second, being tossed out handily.

A switch was made at this point from Wyse to Prim, because left-hand hitters were coming up. One of them, Cramer, sent a fly to left field. On it Lowrey made a sensational diving catch but he was unable to keep Hoover from scoring.

At this stage Greenberg came through with a crashing home run to tie the score.

It remained thus through the ninth inning, by which time Hank Borowy was back in for the Cubs and Dizzy Trout was trying to hold things for the Tigers.

The end came in the twelfth with one out. Frank Secory delivered a single off Trout, and Bill Schuster was sent in to run for him. Stan Hack, who had made three hits already, lined one to left field. Greenberg came in to block it, but the ball took a bounce over his shoulder and on to the fence. Schuster raced all the way around to score the winning run.

That should have been all there was to it, but this being the kind of a series it was, the official scorers first charged Greenberg with an error. Since Hank had not touched the ball, this seemed an injustice, and after thinking about it for a few hours, the scorers cancelled the error. Nothing like that had ever happened in a world series before.

Since this victory of the Cubs made necessary the playing of a seventh game, a day off was in order to permit the distribution of the tickets. It really didn't need an entire day for there wasn't a ticket available by noon the next day.

The advantage was all with the Tigers now, for Manager

O'Neill had pitching strength, and all of Grimm's seasoned hurlers were exhausted from their earlier efforts.

Borowy was selected to start the final game, once more being opposed by Newhouser. Hank lasted long enough to pitch to three men all of whom hit safely, one run scoring. The game but obviously weary Borowy was taken out. His successor, Paul Derringer, was no improvement. He succeeded in walking a man with the bases filled, forcing in a run, and then was hit for a base-clearing double by Paul Richards.

These five runs were more than Newhouser needed, but Derringer's generosity helped them to more in the second. When two were out, Cramer singled, and then no less than three Tigers in a row walked, forcing a run across and Derringer out of the game and the Cubs' life forever.

The Cubs made a run in the first when Cavarretta drove Johnson home and got another in the fourth when Cramer forgot to catch Pafko's long fly, permitting Cavarretta to score.

The Tigers were not yet done. Richards picked on Erickson for a double in the seventh, to score Cullenbine, and in the eighth, while Passeau was trying to pitch, injured hand or no, Webb and Mayo found their way around.

In the last half of the seventh the Cubs managed to get Harry Lowrey around for their final run, and on this 9–3 basis ended the most weirdly wonderful of all the world series.

The Cubs were able to point with pride to the individually pleasing performances of Hack, Cavarretta, Livingston, and Pafko, who fielded brilliantly and hit well. There was a lot to say about the earlier pitching moments Borowy and Passeau enjoyed, but neither the Cubs nor their clients were able to escape the fact that they had failed for the seventh successive time in a quest for a world's championship.

They'll be back for more, however. They always have come back. They always will, for, as was set forth 'way back yonder, if National League baseball can't always get along with the Cubs, neither can it get along for long without them.

☉ XXXVII ☉

HEROES AND SUCH

ANY ATTEMPT TO RANK THE 803 PERSONAGES WHO HAVE drawn Chicago National League baseball pay checks at one time or another, obviously must lead to argument. Well, why not? The Cubs themselves have never been above arguing. So why should their historian be shy?

Before entering into a general discussion of the men who have passed in playing review from A. G. Spalding to C. J. Grimm, it has to be explained that in the author's opinion several of the truly great ballplayers who found their way on to a Cub roster, attained their greatness elsewhere. Some of them reached the Cubs in the twilight of their careers. Others made a getaway just after dawn.

If the Baseball Hall of Fame at Cooperstown, New York, is any criterion, the Cubs and their predecessors have done quite well. The collection of plaques, which is growing steadily with the years, includes those of Spalding, Adrian Anson, Hugh Duffy, Clark Griffith, Frank Chance, Johnny Evers, Joe Tinker, Rube Waddell, Rogers Hornsby, and Grover Cleveland Alexander.

Of these, Duffy and Waddell left Chicago before they became players whose fame endures. Hornsby and Alexander, while competent enough in their stretches with the Cubs, had their most memorable years elsewhere. Griffth, while a notable pitcher of the Anson era, is best remembered perhaps for his activities in the American League, as player, as manager, as magnate, and as a leading figure in the organization's rise and expansion.

To make a start at cutting down this squad of 803 to a more

wieldy figure, not too much consideration has been given the changing conditions under which baseball has been played since 1876. It is assumed that it is as idle to worry about whether Pop Anson could hit 1946 pitching as it is to remain awake o' nights wondering if Claude Passeau, forced to use the same rules as Larry Corcoran and John Clarkson did in the eighties, would have been able to stop the hitters of that era. Or, for that matter, if Kiki Cuyler had to run his bases while equipped with a flowing mustache and a uniform whose shirt laced down the front instead of zippered, would he have been the darling of Ladies' Day—or if handsome, dashing, debonair Bill Lange, perhaps the greatest of all Chicago's outfielders, would have captivated the crowds of the thirties, doing the same things that endeared him to the patrons of the horse and buggy days?

So let us to the assembling of the all time list of Cubs, with such explanatory phrases as seem indicated.

OWNERS AND PRESIDENTS

William A. Hulbert and A. G. Spalding. These two started it all, you know.

William Wrigley Jr. and William Veeck. These two recognized the rights of the patron as well as those of the player.

Phillip K. Wrigley and James T. Gallagher. These two have a record for distinguished service above and beyond the call of "Play ball!"

There were other owners and presidents in between, but let's talk about something else, such as:

MANAGERS

Adrian C. Anson, Frank Chance, Charlie Grimm. Neither explanation nor defense is needed for any of these three.

In the string of fifteen other managers who have held sway, there is no denying the place in baseball of either Frank Selee or Joe McCarthy. However, Selee did his most effective work as a manager at Boston before being summoned to Chicago, and McCarthy's ranking among the all time greatest of managers will be made on what he accomplished with the New York Yankees, after he left the Cubs. When McCarthy resigned his Yankee job in the second month of the 1946 season, he left behind an amazing managerial record. In his stay with the Yankees he guided the team to eight American League pennants and seven world's championships, four of them (1936-1939) in succession. Those marks may well stand for a long, long time.

Catchers: Mike Kelly, John Kling, Jimmy Archer, Gabby Hartnett.

First Basemen: Adrian Anson, Frank Chance, Charlie Grimm, Phil Cavarretta.

Second basemen: Johnny Evers, Billy Herman, Rogers Hornsby.

Third basemen: Harry Steinfeldt, Stanley Hack, Heinie Zimmerman.

Shortstops: Joe Tinker, Bill Jurges.

Outfielders: Bill Lange, Frank Schulte, Riggs Stephenson, Hack Wilson, Kiki Cuyler.

Pitchers: Larry Corcoran, John Clarkson, Clark Griffith, Ed Reulbach, Mordecai Brown, Jim Vaughn, Grover Cleveland Alexander, Charley Root, Lon Warneke, Claude Passeau.

That's it, folks—the All Time Chicago National League Baseball Squad.

Now all you have to do is arrange your own starting line-up and give it to the field announcer.

STATISTICAL ADDENDA

The Chicago National League Club, managed by Albert G. Spalding, won the championship in 1876, the year the League was founded. Under the management of Adrian C. (Pop) Anson, Chicago won championships in 1880, 1881, 1882, 1885, and 1886.

Since 1900 the club's record, with managers, is as follows:

YEAR	MANAGERS	W.	L.	PCT.	FINISH
1900	Tom Loftus	65	75	.464	Fifth
1901	Tom Loftus	53	86	.381	Sixth
1902	Frank Selee	68	69	.496	Fifth
1903	Frank Selee	82	56	.594	Third
1904	Frank Selee	93	60	.608	Second
1905	Frank Selee	92	61	.601	Third
1906	Frank Chance	116	36	.763	First
1907	Frank Chance	107	45	.704	First
1908	Frank Chance	99	55	.643	First
1909	Frank Chance	104	49	.680	Second
1910	Frank Chance	104	50	.675	First
1911	Frank Chance	92	62	.597	Second
1912	Frank Chance	91	59	.607	Third
1913	John Evers	88	65	.575	Third
1914	Hank O'Day	78	76	.506	Fourth
1915	Roger Bresnahan	73	80	.477	Fourth
1916	Joe Tinker	67	86	.438	Fifth
1917	Fred Mitchell	74	80	.481	Fifth
1918	Fred Mitchell	84	45	.651	First
1919	Fred Mitchell	75	65	.536	Third
1920	Fred Mitchell	74	79	.487	Fifth
1921	John Evers				
	Bill Killefer	64	89	.418	Seventh
1922	Bill Killefer	80	74	.519	Fifth
1923	Bill Killefer	83	71	.539	Fourth
1924	Bill Killefer	81	72	.529	Fifth

Year	Managers	W.	L.	Pct.	Finish
1925	Bill Killefer				
	Rabbit Maranville				
	George Gibson	68	86	.442	Eighth
1926	Joe McCarthy	82	72	.532	Fourth
1927	Joe McCarthy	85	68	.556	Fourth
1928	Joe McCarthy	91	63	.591	Third
1929	Joe McCarthy	98	54	.645	First
1930	Joe McCarthy				
	Rogers Hornsby	90	64	.584	Second
1931	Rogers Hornsby	84	70	.545	Third
1932	Rogers Hornsby				
	Charlie Grimm	90	64	.584	First
1933	Charlie Grimm	86	68	.558	Third
1934	Charlie Grimm	86	65	.570	Third
1935	Charlie Grimm	100	54	.649	First
1936	Charlie Grimm	87	67	.565	Second
1937	Charlie Grimm	93	61	.604	Second
1938	Charlie Grimm				
	Gabby Hartnett	89	63	.586	First
1939	Gabby Hartnett	84	70	.545	Fourth
1940	Gabby Hartnett	75	79	.487	Fifth
1941	Jimmy Wilson	70	84	.455	Sixth
1942	Jimmy Wilson	68	86	.442	Sixth
1943	Jimmy Wilson	74	79	.484	Fifth
1944	Jimmy Wilson				
	Roy Johnson				
	Charlie Grimm	75	79	.487	Fourth
1945	Charlie Grimm	98	56	.636	First

(In the 1876–99 era, Bob Ferguson managed the Chicago club in 1879 for part of the season before Adrian Anson took charge. Tom Burns was manager in 1898 and 1899.)

CLUB BATTING LEADERS

Year	Batter	Avg.	Year	Batter	Avg.
1876	*Barnes	.403	1912	*Zimmerman	.372
1877	Anson	.335	1913	Zimmerman	.313
1878	Start	.345	1914	Zimmerman	.296
1879	*Anson	.407	1915	Fisher	.287
1880	*Gore	.365	1916	Williams	.279
1881	*Anson	.399	1917	Mann	.273
1882	Anson	.362	1918	Hollocher	.316
1883	Gore	.334	1919	Flack	.294
1886	*Kelly	.338	1920	Flack	.302
1887	*Anson	.421	1921	Grimes	.321
1888	*Anson	.343	1922	Grimes	.354
1889	Anson	.341	1923	Statz	.319
1890	Anson	.311	1924	Grantham	.316
1891	Anson	.294	1925	Grimm	.306
1892	Dahlen	294	1926	Wilson	.321
1893	Anson	.322	1927	Stephenson	.344
1894	Anson	.394	1928	Stephenson	.324
1895	Lange	.388	1929	Hornsby	.380
1896	Dahlen	.361	1930	Stephenson	.324
1897	Lange	.352	1931	Grimm	.331
1898	Lange	.332	1932	Stephenson	.324
1899	Lange	.324	1933	Stephenson	.329
1900	Green	.299	1934	Cuyler	.338
1901	Hartsell	.339	1935	Hartnett	.344
1902	Slagle	.313	1936	Demaree	.350
1903	Chance	.327	1937	Hartnett	.354
1904	Chance	.310	1938	Hack	.320
1905	Chance	.316	1939	Leiber	.310
1906	Steinfeldt	.327	1940	Hack	.317
1907	Chance	.293	1941	Hack	.317
1908	Evers	.300	1942	Hack	.301
1909	Hofman	.285	1943	Nicholson	.310
1910	Hofman	.325	1944	Cavarretta	.319
1911	Zimmerman	.307	1945	*Cavarretta	.355

* Led National League.

(1884–85 records of entire club not available. Anson batted .337 and .310 in those seasons.)

CLUB HOME-RUN LEADERS

Year	Batter	H.R.	Year	Batter	H.R.
1884	Williamson	27		Grimes	6
1900	Mertes	7	1922	Grimes	14
1901	Hartsell	7	1923	Miller	20
1902	Tinker	2	1924	Hartnett	16
1903	Chance	2	1925	Hartnett	24
	Tinker	2	1926	*Wilson	21
1904	Chance	6	1927	*Wilson	30
1905	Chance	2	1928	*Wilson	30
	Tinker	2	1929	Hornsby	40
	Maloney	2	1930	**Wilson	56
1906	Schulte	7	1931	Hornsby	16
1907	Howard	4	1932	Moore	13
1908	Tinker	6	1933	Herman	16
1909	Schulte	4		Hartnett	16
	Tinker	4	1934	Hartnett	22
1910	*Schulte	10	1935	Klein	21
1911	*Schulte	21	1936	Demaree	16
1912	Zimmerman	14	1937	Galan	18
1913	Saier	18	1938	Collins	13
1914	Saier	18	1939	Leiber	24
1915	Williams	13	1940	Nicholson	25
1916	*Williams	12	1941	Nicholson	26
1917	Doyle	6	1942	Nicholson	21
1918	Flack	4	1943	*Nicholson	29
1919	Flack	6	1944	*Nicholson	33
1920	Robertson	10	1945	Nicholson	13
1921	Flack	6			

* Led National League.

** National League Record.

CLUB LEADING PITCHERS

YEAR	PITCHER	W.	L.	PCT.
1876	*Spalding	47	13	.783
1880	*Corcoran			.798
1881	*Corcoran			.667
1882	*Goldsmith			.655
1885	*Clarkson			.790
1887	Clarkson	38	20	.655
1888	Crock	25	14	.641
1889	Dwyer	16	14	.533
1890	King	33	20	.623
1891	*Hutchinson	43	19	.696
1892	Gumbert	23	18	.561
1893	McGill	17	17	.500
1894	*Griffith	20	11	.645
1895	*Griffith	25	11	.694
1896	Griffith	23	11	.676
1897	Callahan	12	8	.600
1898	Griffith	25	12	.676
1899	Callahan	21	12	.636
1900	Menefee	9	5	.643
1901	Waddell	14	16	.466
1902	Taylor	22	10	.688
1903	Wicker	20	9	.689
1904	Lundgren	17	9	.654
1905	Lundgren	13	5	.722
1906	*Reulbach	19	4	.826
1907	*Reulbach	17	4	.810
1908	*Reulbach	24	7	.774
1909	Brown	27	9	.750
1910	Cole	20	4	.833
1911	Cole	18	4	.720
1912	Cheney	26	10	.722
1913	*Humphries	16	4	.800
1914	Vaughn	21	13	.618
1915	Vaughn	20	12	.625
1916	Packard	10	6	.625
1917	Vaughn	23	13	.639
1918	*Hendrix	20	7	.741

245

Year	Pitcher	W.	L.	Pct.
1919	Alexander	16	11	.593
1920	Alexander	27	14	.659
1921	Alexander	15	13	.536
1922	Alexander	16	13	.552
1923	Alexander	22	12	.647
1924	Alexander	12	5	.706
1925	Alexander	15	11	.577
1926	Jones	12	7	.632
1927	Root	26	15	.634
1928	Nehf	13	7	.650
1929	*Root	19	6	.760
1930	Malone	22	8	.690
1931	Bush	16	8	.667
1932	*Warneke	22	6	.786
1933	*Tinning	13	6	.684
1934	Warneke	22	10	.688
1935	*Lee	20	6	.769
1936	French	18	9	.667
1937	Carleton	16	8	.667
1938	*Lee	22	9	.710
1939	French	15	8	.652
1940	Passeau	20	13	.606
1941	Olsen	10	8	.556
1942	Passeau	19	14	.576
1943	Passeau	15	12	.556
1944	Passeau	15	9	.625
1945	*Borowy	11	2	.846

* Led National League.

CUBS WORLD SERIES RECORD

1906—Frank Chance, manager, lost to Chicago White Sox, 4 games
      to 2.

1907—Frank Chance, manager, won from Detroit Tigers, 4 games to 0,
      one game ending in a tie.

1908—Frank Chance, manager, won from Detroit Tigers, 4 games to 1.

1910—Frank Chance, manager, lost to Philadelphia Athletics, 4 games
      to 1.

1918—Fred Mitchell, manager, lost to Boston Red Sox, 4 games to 2.

1929—Joe McCarthy, manager, lost to Philadelphia Athletics, 4 games
      to 1.

1932—Charlie Grimm, manager, lost to New York Yankees, 4 games
      to 0.

1935—Charlie Grimm, manager, lost to Detroit Tigers, 4 games to 2.

1938—Gabby Hartnett, manager, lost to New York Yankees, 4 games
      to 0.

1945—Charlie Grimm, manager, lost to Detroit Tigers, 4 games to 3.
      The Cubs have won 19 games, lost 33, and tied 1 in world
series play.

CUBS VS. WHITE SOX

The city series between Cubs and White Sox, began in 1903 and was continued more or less regularly until 1943 when it was abandoned. The record:

1903—Tied. Each club won 7 games.
1905—Cubs, 4 games to 1.
*1906—White Sox, 4 games to 2.
1909—Cubs, 4 games to 1.
1911—White Sox, 4 games to 0.
1912—White Sox, 4 games to 3, 2 tied games.
1913—White Sox, 4 games to 2.
1914—White Sox, 4 games to 3.
1915—White Sox, 4 games to 1.
1916—White Sox, 4 games to 0.
1921—White Sox, 5 games to 0.
1922—Cubs, 4 games to 3.
1923—White Sox, 4 games to 2.
1924—White Sox, 4 games to 2.
1925—Cubs, 4 games to 2.
1926—White Sox, 4 games to 3.
1928—Cubs, 4 games to 3.
1930—Cubs, 4 games to 2.
1931—White Sox, 4 games to 3.
1933—White Sox, 4 games to 0.
1936—White Sox, 4 games to 0.
1937—White Sox, 4 games to 3.
1939—White Sox, 4 games to 3.
1940—White Sox, 4 games to 2.
1941—White Sox, 4 games to 0.
1942—White Sox, 4 games to 2.

* World series.

The White Sox have won 19 series, the Cubs 6, with 1 tied series. The White Sox have won 96 games, the Cubs 62, with 2 tied games.

INDEX

Joseph P. Murphy Jr. of the Bibliography Committee, Society for American Baseball Research, prepared this index. The text contains numerous misspellings of proper names. The correct spellings are used in the index.

253